I0816257

'This book started as a scientific survey of the sport of mountain/ultra/trail running and evolved into three years of prodigious work by a very dedicated author – there is absolutely nothing else like it. This is the definitive description of a sport loved by millions. I highly recommend *Dirtbag dreams* – everyone will learn things they didn't know.'

Buzz Burrell, co-founder of Fastest Known Times

'A fascinating history of our great sport.'

Damian Hall, author of *In It for the Long Run*

'A fascinating book, filled with brilliantly selected stories, that makes an important contribution to our understanding of the development of mountain, ultra and trail running.'

Michael Crawley, author of *To the Limit*

'Carl Morris provides an illuminating and greatly needed genealogy of the mountain-ultra-trail sporting phenomenon. *Dirtbag dreams* is full of vivid storytelling of key races, told with the precision of an academic and the warmth of someone who clearly loves the sport. Highly recommend!'

Sabrina B. Little, author of *The Examined Run*

'*Dirtbag dreams* is as ambitious as running 100 miles. Carl Morris surveys the quirky historical strands of pedestrianism, alpine running and fell running that underpin today's mountain, ultra and trail running scene. For anyone serious about the sport, this book will help you understand where we've been and where we're headed. Read it and every run will feel just a bit richer.'

Doug Mayer, author of *The Race That Changed Running*

Dirtbag dreams

Manchester University Press

Dirtbag dreams

A history of mountain, ultra and trail running

Carl Morris

Manchester University Press

Published by Manchester University Press
Oxford Road, Manchester, M13 9PL

www.manchesteruniversitypress.co.uk

British Library Cataloguing-in-Publication Data
A catalogue record for this book is available from the British Library

ISBN 978 1 5261 9018 5 hardback

First published 2025

EU authorised representative for GPSR:
Easy Access System Europe, Mustamäe tee 50, 10621 Tallinn, Estonia
gpsr.requests@easproject.com

Typeset
by New Best-set Typesetters Ltd
Printed in Great Britain
by Bell & Bain Ltd, Glasgow

Contents

Introduction

The making of a modern sport

It is a little after midday, on a Saturday, in the sleepy Swiss village of Trient. Nestled in the heart of the Alps, the snow-tipped Mont Blanc massif looms overhead, framed by blue skies and September sunshine. Trient is a typically pristine Alpine village. A handful of guesthouses, gabled chalets with painted shutters, and a raspberry-hued baroque chapel – all standing watch over the high mountain pass of Col de la Forclaz. For centuries this was a pilgrimage destination. More recently, the village has witnessed travellers of a different sort – hikers and tourists – who every summer can be found traversing the surrounding woods and steep-sided gorges. It is a place of contemplation, solitude and quiet movement.

Today is a little different. American ultrarunner Courtney Dauwalter is climbing with leaden legs up the narrow trail to the waiting village. The buildings are not yet in sight, but she can already hear the roaring of the crowd, clapping and hooting, whistles and horns, and the clanking of cowbells. After running for 90 miles in often-exposed mountain terrain – for 18 hours by this point – she is exhausted and emotionally fragile. Turning the corner, Dauwalter is engulfed in an overwhelming tunnel of people, noise and spectacle. Red smoke billows from burning flares, handmade placards are held high, hundreds of cameras record every moment. A mass of hands reach out to brush against her – devotees grasping for that fleeting and electric touch of benediction. Hundreds of thousands are watching live over the Internet. Millions will view these remarkable images over the coming weeks. This is UTMB Mont-Blanc – the most prestigious trail and ultra running event in the world – and, in September 2023, American ultrarunning history is being made.

From humble beginnings in 2003, Ultra-Trail du Mont-Blanc (UTMB) has become the most established trail running events brand in the world, with a series of competitive and massively oversubscribed races, of varying distances, held at the end of August, every year, in Chamonix. The crown jewel is a 106 mile race – UTMB Mont-Blanc – which involves 2,500 athletes circumnavigating the Mont Blanc massif. Over the course of two decades, it has become the most important space for the concentration of international and competitive talent. In the words of elite American athlete Tim Tollefson, himself a podium finisher: 'This is the *de facto* world championship every year.'[1] Other races have been added over time, such as the 100 km CCC and 55 km OCC (each also fiercely competitive), with more than 10,000 athletes competing every August in a week-long festival of trail running. Most of the participants are recreational athletes, admitted through a complicated ballot entry system, but the event also attracts many of the very best professional trail and ultra runners from around the world. It is an undeniable sporting, media, and commercial phenomenon.

The 2023 race was perhaps always destined to be historic. American women have often found success here. The list of past winners is long: Krissy Moehl, Nikki Kimball, Rory Bosio, Courtney Dauwalter and Katie Schide. However, this year, Dauwalter is aiming to become the first person to complete the 'triple crown': victories in the same year at the three most high-profile 100 mile trail races in the world – Western States, Hardrock and UTMB Mont-Blanc. Only weeks apart from one another – and with each arduous race taking a debilitating toll on the body – there is widespread doubt that such a feat is possible. UTMB Mont-Blanc is the final race in this unofficial series – Dauwalter has already secured victories at the first two (both were course records) – so hopes are high for a boundary-breaking performance by this phenomenal athlete.

American men have never secured a victory at UTMB Mont-Blanc. They have been close – Topher Gaylord and Brandon Sybrowsky finished joint second in 2003, and there have been multiple third place finishes – but the ultimate prize has remained elusive. Understandably, given the depth of American ultrarunning talent, the anguished speculation is intense. Perhaps American men simply want it too much, racing aggressively only to crash and burn; perhaps they are overtired after a busy racing season at home; or perhaps the Alpine landscape requires a different type of training and physical conditioning. More than just a feat of endurance, ultrarunning is an intellectual puzzle. At an elite level it requires the perfect alignment of every shifting and multifaceted piece.

In 2023, Jim Walmsley is back for his fifth attempt at UTMB Mont-Blanc. While utterly dominant on the American racing scene, he has only actually finished twice – and has twice dropped out during the race (a 'DNF' – did not finish) – but fans are hoping that this time he might make it work. Walmsley has spent a year living in the Alps, training with multi-time winner François D'Haene, and he has no athletic goal other than this all-consuming race. But he is not the only American man chasing history. Zach Miller – another UTMB veteran, renowned for his daring, full-throttle racing style – is back after prolonged injury. They are joined by a deep field of around a dozen elite American men – each dreaming of a career-defining podium finish and the inevitable sponsorship deal that will follow.

The race begins at 5 p.m. on Friday evening, beneath a cream-coloured Benedictine church, grand hotels and bustling restaurants in Chamonix town centre. Elite athletes are corralled into a dedicated space just behind an enormous, logo-studded blue arch. A little further back, over 2,000 recreational runners, from more than 100 different countries, are jostling to find a place in the throng. There are more than 50,000 spectators here for the weekend. Most of these are crammed into the surrounding streets, or hanging from balconies and balustrades in search of a better view. After various announcements and pre-race suspense building over the loudspeaker – with only minutes to go – the crowd falls silent as the UTMB opening song begins to play: 'Conquest of Paradise' by Vangelis. With a deep, rising percussion – and basso chanting in pseudo-Latin – this stirring piece was written for a film that portrayed the expedition of

Columbus to the New World. Today, in ironic reversal, it is Europe that faces journeying Americans in search of conquest.

Three, two, one – the song reaches a crescendo – and the runners are off. The elite pack races ahead in an unsustainable charge alongside the valley river, roughly five miles, to the nearby village of Les Houches, and then up the first climb of Col De Voza. The leading men will run much of the first half of the race in a tight group, only seconds or minutes apart, anxiously watching one another. Who can hang on? Who will begin to fade first? Meanwhile, Dauwalter takes an early lead over the other female competitors, one that will only continue to grow. She is racing against herself. Despite a deep field of exceptional athletes, the tiredness from Western States and Hardrock will be the only competition that Dauwalter faces today. She will either finish and win, or drop out from injury and exhaustion.

After the bedlam of the start, the sun sinks, and the runners head up into the night: first, towards the mist-obscured heights of the Col de la Seigne, followed by a traverse around the technical section of the Pyramides Calcaires, and then down into Italy. Reaching the halfway point of the Courmayeur Sports Centre – at around the 50 mile mark – the lead runners are clocking in somewhere between eight and nine hours. Their support crews are waiting in the wide-beamed hall, with fresh clothing and nutrition arrayed on tables and benches, while dozens of journalists and volunteers hover behind barriers.

Walmsley arrives first, greeted by the methodical organisation of his partner, Jess, a one-woman NASCAR pit stop. There is no time to waste. He changes shirt while eating rice pudding and potato chips and swigging liquid nutrition. Jess replenishes his race pack. Running in the mountains at night creates a mysterious racing dynamic. How far behind is second place – minutes or seconds? Not far, it seems: Miller arrives only two minutes later. With hardly a glance, a cool and collected Walmsley gathers and adjusts his pack, before loping back out into the night. With his quarry in sight, Miller hardly stops. Grabbing a handful of food, he follows, now only 30 seconds behind. More leading men arrive, followed by

Dauwalter, 50 minutes behind Walmsley, but with a 20-minute lead over the other elite women. Dauwalter's characteristic smile looks a little forced. Lines of tiredness are already criss-crossing her face, as her partner, Kevin, provides well-oiled crew support and words of encouragement. As Dauwalter herself likes to say, ultrarunning is a team sport.[2]

A little more than 10 miles down the valley, at the next aid station in Arnouvaz, there is palpable shock as Miller arrives first, having overtaken Walmsley somewhere in the early morning gloom. He is out within two minutes, seconds before a tense-looking Walmsley arrives. With dawn light now touching the tops of the Mont Blanc massif, they face a steep climb to Grand Col Ferret, the highest point in the race, at 2,500 metres, and down towards the small Swiss village of La Fouly. Across Europe, viewers are waking to watch the UTMB livestream – total viewership will clock up to 2.4 million over the course of the race. On the English-language channel, the commentators – Corrine Malcolm (American) and Keith Byrne (British) – are busy speculating about the unfolding race. The runners are in a crucial phase – around 70 miles – where victories are made or broken. Miller arrives first at the tented aid station in La Fouly. Incredibly, in the space of only two hours, he has extended his lead to 10 minutes. Walmsley finally arrives – to find that Miller is long gone – and the drama elevates another notch as it becomes apparent that third-place runner Germain Grangier (France) is now only three minutes back.

It is a fast and relatively flat eight miles along the valley floor to the lakeside village of Champex Lac. Miller's lead extends to 12 minutes – Walmsley and Grangier arrive together. 'This is a huge mental boost [for Miller]', remarks an excited Scott Jurek, himself a legendary American ultrarunner, now sitting in the livestream commentary booth alongside Malcolm and Byrne. With typical Tiggerish-energy, Miller is out within minutes, the tantalising lure of ultrarunning history pulling him onwards. The runners climb out of the valley on rising, wooded trails, heading westward and closing the loop back around towards France. It is here where tragedy appears to strike Walmsley. On an innocuous-looking climb – in an echo of 2022, where he dropped from first to third (eventually finishing fourth) – viewers around the world watch as Grangier slowly overtakes him. The past is repeating itself – a slow-motion drive-by – as Grangier moves past, with the tip-tap of running poles, before pushing hard in an effort to break a seemingly deflated Walmsley.

Away from the competitive drama, Dauwalter is still leading comfortably – over an hour ahead of second place – but the final podium spots are in fierce contention between Blandine L'Hirondel (France), Fuzhao Xiang (China) and Katharina Hartmuth (Germany). They arrive in that order, with only minutes between them. Dauwalter is locked into first place, but uncharacteristically grim-faced – a mental battle taking place deep within.

Reflecting afterwards on his duel with Grangier – and the comparison with his disappointing race the previous year – Walmsley will say: 'He passed me, and he looked a little rough. And I was like, I know I look the same, but internally, I actually felt better than that. So, I was like, well, I've got to stay with him.'[3] Stay with him he does, dogging Grangier's every step down into the next valley. Running together, the pair are drawing energy from each other – a curious kind of mental drafting – and they arrive at the next aid station together, having reduced Miller's lead to nine minutes.

Spotting an opportunity, a revived Walmsley dashes out first. He quickens as they begin the long climb up the Bovine trail, which swings upwards and around before a fast charge down towards Trient. Miller and Walmsley are both running hard now, battling for first, but with Miller's lead gradually beginning to slip. As they push up Col de la Forclaz towards the waiting crowds in Trient, there has been an unexpected reversal of fortunes: Walmsley is back in front, although leading by mere seconds. For two decades, American men have been unable to secure victory at UTMB – and yet here, today, Miller and Walmsley are locked in contention for this coveted prize.

There remain more than 15 miles to go – plenty of time for the battle to continue – but it seems that Walmsley has discovered a hidden reserve of energy and determination. There is a short, steep climb around Mount Carraye, on the northward spur of the massif, and then down over the French border into Vallorcine. Miller continues to drop back. He is still running hard, just not hard enough: at every timing point, Walmsley's lead increases – 5 minutes, 9 minutes, 14 minutes. Walmsley arrives at the final aid station, La Flégère, a ski resort overlooking the Chamonix valley. Spectators line the trail, clapping and cheering as he climbs slowly but firmly up to the large cable car building, and then down for the final descent. It is a little over four miles to the finish. Barring mishap, his lead is now insurmountable – a solid 22 minutes.

The trail spills out onto the outskirts of Chamonix, up and over a footbridge, and then along a cordoned route through the town streets. The crowds thicken with every step, thousands cheering, as Walmsley relishes every moment, floating through the final kilometre past apartment blocks and neat-looking chalets. Zigzagging through the town centre – which is shut down for the race – he moves through a tunnel of high fives, grinning in delight. Operatic music booms through the loudspeakers, as his victory is announced with dramatic flair. He jogs up the finishing runway, slowing down to walk beneath the blue arch, hands raised in triumph. Surrounded by cameras, he hugs Jess and proud-looking family members. The emotion is too much – he begins to cry, covering his face and wiping away the tears, before being ushered to the finish line interview. He is asked what it feels like to be the first American winner. Looking a little surprised, he gently corrects the questioner: 'No, it just feels like I'm adding my name to join the strong U.S. women contingent. You can't take it away from them, they've done it again and again here, and I'm just happy to stand on their shoulders.' Graciousness aside, Walmsley is not just the first American *male* victor at UTMB; he has also set a new course record: 19:36:19. It is a tremendous culmination of personal and national obsession.

The interview finishes and the focus switches to Miller. Despite victory having slipped out of sight, he has continued to push, chasing every second on the clock. Racing towards the finish line, he sprints – arms pumping, baseball cap cocked backward, in brightly-tinted reflective shades – to cross the line for second place. It is the fourth fastest finish of all time: 19:55:30. Walmsley walks out to embrace him. They smile together, sharing a private joke and a moment of intimacy before the crowds and the cameras. Fifteen minutes later, Grangier arrives, in another stunningly fast time. In most years, this third-place finish would have been enough to clinch victory. They are followed in quick succession by the other leading men. The sport is getting faster, the breadth of competition deeper.

It is now all about Dauwalter. Roughly 11 miles back, in Vallorcine, she has a comfortable lead of an hour, moving at a reasonable pace, but with pain and exhaustion radiating out from every single step. Dauwalter likes to talk about the 'pain cave' – a metaphorical inner place that endurance athletes inhabit during moments when it seems physically impossible to continue: 'That's when your mind takes over', she explains, 'and you dig in with your brain to help your body keep going.'[4] Famous for her carefree and smiling exuberance, right now she is contained entirely within herself. For the hundreds of thousands watching over the livestream, it is a relatively brief three hours until Chamonix. Yet for Dauwalter, every grinding step no doubt seems like a lifetime. Finally, she arrives, surrounded by a moving mob of fans and spectators, her grimace breaking into a roar of triumph as she crosses the line in 23:29:15. History has been made again today as Dauwalter accomplishes the impossible – the triple crown of victories at Western States, Hardrock and UTMB Mont-Blanc. With renewed energy, she runs alongside the cheering crowds, showing her gratitude, high-fiving and shaking hands, before standing alone, gazing upward, in a circle of disbelieving triumph. It is an achievement that will likely never be matched by any athlete ever again.

The fierce battle for second and third plays out – clinched by Hartmuth and L'Hirondel – followed over the next few hours by the last of the top ten women. The elite race is now effectively over, but spread out across the Mont Blanc massif, more than 2,000 recreational runners are still engrossed in their own personal journey. In total, they have 46 hours and 30 minutes to traverse the full loop. Many will not make it – the completion rate in 2023 is a little over 65 per cent – and the average finish time will be around 40 hours. Finally, the last few exhausted runners cross the line; the media and corporate circus begins to pack itself away and the biggest spectacle in trail and ultra running is over for another year.

UTMB Mont-Blanc is the competitive pinnacle of a sport – mountain, ultra and trail (MUT) running – that has changed considerably over the course of 200 years. It is a long and eventful history, over the course of which athletes and adventure seekers have combined foot-based endurance and mountain craft in ways that have often been creative and pioneering. The sport has enabled escape from the hustle and bustle of everyday life, for life-affirming journeying in the silence of the mountains, but it has also sometimes been the focus for media and commercial spectacle relating to daring tales of competition and mental toughness.

Starting at the end of the eighteenth century – and with a focus on North America and Britain – I will chart this history through to the present day.

I want to understand why people have subjected themselves to feats of endurance that are so challenging and often gruellingly painful. I want to explore how the values and practices of the sport have changed – or not changed – over several centuries. I want to comprehend how the sport has been shaped by moments of social upheaval – such as suburbanisation in the 1950s, or the rise of digital media in the 2000s – and what it can tell us about who we are and the world that we live in. Perhaps most importantly, I want to understand the waxing and waning of the sport – and why participation has grown at very specific historical moments, including dramatic growth and associated commercialisation over the last decade or two.

As I will argue, the sport has developed a complicated set of identities that are rooted in the existential lure of nature-based challenge and spiritual clarity, while also being built on the civilisational wealth and opportunities of the modern world. The idea of being or becoming a 'dirtbag' – someone dedicated to the purity of outdoor adventure at the expense of a comfortable consumer lifestyle – is an animating fantasy for many. It is a 'fantasy' precisely because our ability to escape from everyday life is itself a form of privilege and temporary reprieve. The old frontiers are gone – the systems and structures of the modern world are stifling – and yet in the silent chambers of nature it is possible to cultivate our mental and physical capacities, and to search for new purpose and meaning. These tensions and complexities can often be found running in different guises throughout the history of the sport, from the earliest days of Victorian tourism and spectator athletics to the present day.

It is helpful at this point to now properly define 'the sport' – although this is more complicated than it might sound. The idea of mountain, ultra and trail running as a clearly defined sport is essentially a recent invention. A large part of the problem is that the sport is inherently diverse. Skimming the pages of a specialist running magazine, one might read accounts that vary from tightly regulated elite competitions, on an internationally certified track, through to multi-month solo adventures on the Appalachian Trail. In some respects, it is remarkable that these different practices are bracketed together as belonging to the same sport or recreational pursuit. One of the outcomes of this book is to consider how MUT running has been *created* as a sport.

In the late 1990s, a gathering of American runners, event organisers and industry representatives came together to make sense of diverse running disciplines, many of which had their own heritage and history. These disciplines varied in technique and style – a slow-burn 24-hour track event, for example, is very different to a blood-pumping ski slope race – but there was an understanding that they were attracting many of the same athletes. Nancy Hobbs, the head of the American Trail Running Association (ATRA) – which had been established in 1996 – recalls their lengthy discussion:

> Somebody suggested that we call it 'extreme running', but those of us that participated didn't really feel that it was that extreme, even though it looked extreme to people that thought 'this is crazy'. So, we settled on Mountain Ultra Trail – MUT. We were the MUT group.[5]

This focus on naming might seem a distraction from the simplicity of running, but advocates of the sport were searching for political and financial leverage within wider sporting institutions. To name something is to make it real. The term therefore combined three different but interrelated disciplines of running and gave substance to a running culture/community that had been coming together for decades:

- Mountain running: a foot race or running activity on a course involving significant elevation change in a mountainous landscape.
- Ultrarunning: a foot race or running activity that extends in distance or time/difficulty beyond the standard marathon (i.e., an ultramarathon). Such activities can take place on paved surfaces, track, or in a natural setting (i.e., off-road).
- Trail running: a foot race or running activity in an off-road and natural environment, such as deserts, forests, mountains, arid plains, coastal paths etc.

Hobbs introduced the MUT terminology at a USA Track and Field (USATF) conference, in 1998, and subsequently established an MUT subcommittee that has given the sport a voice within American athletics. Similar debates were taking place among fell and mountain runners in Britain during the early 1990s around their relationship to the British Athletics Federation (BAF). And yet there is no universal agreement about terminology or disciplinary boundaries – the sport remains something of a loose federation of different cultures and running styles.

Americans conceived and popularised the term 'ultrarunning'– a term that now has global cachet – in the 1960s, but despite widespread use in Britain, there are those who prefer the 'more British' designation of 'long-distance running'. In northern England, 'fell running' has deep and enduring roots, dating back to the nineteenth century, tied to place, people and to the rugged 'fells' (mountains/hills) and communities of Cumbria, Yorkshire and Lancashire, while it is 'trail running' (another American term) that is more closely linked to the rumpled plains and coastal paths of southern England. Others choose to locate themselves within the 'sky running' circuit – an Alpine-origin series of mountain races that combine steep climbing, often at altitude, with rough, jaw-dropping scrambling over technical terrain. Meanwhile, 'fast packers' and 'fastest known time' (FKT) aspirants often look to traverse vast distances – sometimes thousands of miles – in a supported or self-supported push that can involve carrying sleeping gear and survival equipment, with a rate of progress that blurs the distinction between running and hiking.

Individuals will gravitate towards a disciplinary description that makes sense for them, such as 'trail runner' or 'ultrarunner' or 'fell runner'. These identities are often contextual. Damian Hall, an elite British athlete, illustrates these shifting identities. Despite running regularly on the fells in Britain – and notwithstanding his undoubted fame within fell running circles – Hall conceptualises fell running as a community that is strongly associated with the north of England, within which he feels (in his words) 'an imposter':

> I've been on American podcasts and they will say 'you're a fell runner, aren't you?'. And actually, I've never really felt that way. It sounds absurd because I've done the Dragon's Back and I've actually had the record for a couple of fell running rounds... but I'm just not from part of the country where people say 'fell running' very much.[6]

Similarly, there are those, such as American 'Speedgoat' Karl Meltzer – famous for more 100 mile victories than any other athlete – who embrace the technicality of mountain landscapes and resist the often-ubiquitous use of 'trail running' in American running circles: 'I'm a mountain runner. A mountain runner is someone who's not afraid to run the hills, not afraid of technical terrain, not afraid to go up high. A trail runner can be anybody who's on a cement path down by the beach.'[7]

Those involved in the sport identify themselves in diverse ways. These categorisations matter; they reference variations in style and technique, aesthetics and values, culture and belonging. Rather than considering MUT running a single community – or a cohesive sport with clear boundaries and distinctions – it might instead be better conceived as a series of intersecting communities and sporting disciplines with a 'family resemblance'. To borrow the language of the philosopher Ludwig Wittgenstein, while we might not see *one thing* that all hold in common, we can see 'similarities, relationships, and a whole series of them at that'[8]. But whether we recognise

MUT running as a singular 'sport' or not, it certainly has a complex genealogy, with all the inherent idiosyncrasies, rivalries and affections contained within any extended family group.

I want to consider the place where these traditions intersect. An entire book could be written about road ultramarathoning – or fell running – or international mountain running – or sub-ultra trail running. At times I will discuss the origin and influence of each of these running disciplines. But the central thread running through this book is my focus on ultra-distance endurance in the mountains and other wild places of the world. As I will argue, this is the beating heart of MUT running, and it is around such endeavours that this particular sporting culture has developed.

The contemporary sport remains mostly recreational and participative – it is something that people do for fun and personal enrichment. At an elite level there are a growing number of sponsored/professional athletes – which is important as a commercial driver for the shoe and apparel industry – but in raw numbers these athletes are a small part of the sport. Despite the media attention given to races like UTMB Mont-Blanc, most events are small and grassroots, managed by independent race organisers and staffed by volunteers. In 2023, there were approximately 2,500 ultra-distance events in the United States and 500 in Britain. Most were off-road/trail events. A clear majority had fewer than 100 entrants – very few climbed much higher than this – and they often attract participants from surrounding geographic localities.

At this grassroots level it is still a local and regional sport, but a small number of competitive races will attract participants from farther afield – sometimes with a starting field that registers in the thousands. International travel to 'destination races' is becoming increasingly common. Race finishers might return to the same event in subsequent years, or to similar events, and they are often able to develop sustained friendships with other participants. While tens of thousands participate in ultra-distance running – almost half a million globally – the sport has clusters of engagement that give it a strong sense of community. This is strengthened by the shared social and cultural background of participants. Like many outdoor pursuit activities, it is a sport that attracts those from more privileged economic, educational and ethnic backgrounds – that is to say, the sport is predominantly white and middle class. This is slowly changing, following energetic advocacy from groups like Black Trail Runners, but this lack of diversity is engrained in complex social and cultural inequalities that are historically rooted.

While the ultra-distance side of the sport is seemingly small – with 74,000 active ultrarunners in the US and 26,000 in the UK – the sport has a wider cultural impact. There is particular growth in the sub-ultra trail running market – and, indeed, British fell running has always been characterised by shorter distance racing. Casual and occasional runners – of whom there are millions in the United States and Britain – are moving away somewhat from road running to trail events in local parks and natural spaces. It is therefore becoming an aspirational sport that can be accessible for athletes at every level. There is further evidence to suggest that ultrarunning has become the 'new marathon' – that is, a 'bucket list' challenge for casual runners – and there has been substantial growth in 50 km events for first-time ultrarunners. This can bring with it high rates of churn. Casual runners might complete their first ultra but then have little engagement with the sport beyond this.

There has been a connected evolution in everyday fashion aesthetics that highlight outdoor identities – so-called 'Gorpcore' and 'Trail Chic' – with running leggings, T-shirts and trail shoes becoming a staple in everyday clothing. This consumer market helps to explain the rapid growth of outdoor apparel companies. Ultrarunning and outdoor adventure have furthermore been integrated into other modern fitness cultures. For example, the motivational speaker, author and ex-Navy SEAL David Goggins – who has a following of millions – is noted for his 'warrior mentality' and macho encouragement to 'get hard and stay hard'. The sport can also attract those who develop a celebrity profile through public feats of endurance despite having no competitive or 'authentic' place within the wider sporting culture, such as British runner Russ Cook ('Hardest Geezer'), whose celebrated run across Africa followed other media spectacles, including being buried alive for seven days and running a marathon while towing a car.

MUT running is therefore complicated. It is both an organised sport – with a committed community of participants and a sporting heritage – but also a looser cultural phenomenon connected to wider fitness, media and consumer trends.

Writing more than a decade ago, the ultrarunning athlete and media commentator Andy Jones-Wilkins outlined a divide between those that he called 'purists' and 'pragmatists':

> the purists argue that the introduction of prize money to ultramarathon running would only serve to corrupt our otherwise clean sport and could lead to such unsavoury things as cheating, performance enhancing drug use, and corporate greed ... On the other end of the spectrum are the pragmatists who suggest that the addition of prize money would increase competition, bring increased attention to the sport, and add an air of professionalism to a sport that has been rather loosely organized and administered for over 30 years.[9]

He was reflecting on the issue of prize money – which remains a rarity in MUT running – but these arguments were rooted in wider advocacy for foundational sporting values. Central to this ethos is the notion that MUT running is a 'soul sport' – or a lifestyle sport – whereby involvement is motivated by a love for running in wild and remote places, rather than external validation or reward.[10] Lifestyle sports are typically understood as a countercultural challenge to traditional rule-bound, competitive and masculine sporting practices. Equally, sports such as skateboarding and surfing have often been vulnerable to co-optation by forces of consumer capitalism. Similar tensions can be found within MUT running.

A rare glimpse was recently provided into the growth of the commercial sporting market. In 2024, Amer Sports, a conglomerate with a portfolio that includes Salomon and Arc'teryx, was valued for a public offering on the New York Stock Exchange. Corporate balance sheets documented sales that had risen from $2.4 billion in 2020 to $3.5 billion by 2022[11] – a level of growth that would be the envy of any company. In relation to the wider industry, estimates have suggested that trail shoes now comprise 40 per cent of the running shoe market, and that this market will double in size between 2021 and 2031.[12] The sport is increasingly big business.

Even the most casual of observers can witness this everyday commercialisation. There are an increasing number of recreational athletes joining the sport, most of whom inevitably kit themselves out with everything they need (or think they need): from running packs and shoes, to GPS watches, poles, and a continuing supply of gels, drink mixes, shakes and power bars. Fired up with enthusiasm, many quickly become avid media consumers: magazine subscriptions, films, podcasts, books. Inspired by stories of competition and community, organised events and races become a regular occurrence, incurring entry fees, race insurance, travel costs and possibly overnight accommodation. As the competitive juices bubble away, coaching might make sense: whether personalised coaching with an elite athlete/coach, via video call, or a lower-cost training app.[13]

The MUT running industry is built upon these four financial pillars: apparel/equipment, media, events and coaching – along with a new generation of professionals who provide or promote these products and services (sponsored athletes, media creators, coaches, event directors etc).

Professional athletes are the visible face of this growing commercial industry – and yet only a handful earn six-figure salaries. Lower-level tiers of sponsorship are more common. This might include a complicated arrangement of free shoes/apparel, travel expenses and entry fees, cash honorariums, financial incentives for social media engagement, contractual bonuses for race victories, and (perhaps) a small salary. Most professional athletes live modestly and juggle their athletic ambitions with another line of work (both inside and outside the sport). Dylan Bowman, a professional athlete and founder of Freetrail – an influential media company in the sport – captures the nature of this struggle by suggesting that 'being a pro-athlete is just fucking brutal ... it's a very hard way to make a living'.[14] There is a glamorous side to the professional sport, but this conceals a hidden world of dedication, exhaustion, constant pressure and short-term contracts – all alongside the need for most 'professional' athletes to hold down paying work elsewhere.

These financial pressures are significant when we consider that there is little institutional funding or support, even for prestigious international competition. In 2023, USATF offered Team USA athletes a small $600 stipend to compete at the IAU (International Association of Ultrarunners) 24-Hour World Championships in Taipei.[15] This was not sufficient even to cover travel and accommodation expenses, let alone a supplementary income for lost earnings. British athletes faced a similar dilemma: Team GB received minimal funding from UK Athletics and were required to launch a crowdfunding appeal to ensure that Britain was represented at this championship international event.

Commercial sponsorship is therefore often necessary for elite athletes to compete at this high level, but sponsorship carries with it an obligation to build a public and media profile. Buzz Burrell, a mountain athlete with decades as a business leader in the outdoor industry, suggests that being a professional 'doesn't necessarily mean being a good runner – it means bringing eyeballs to your sponsor'.[16] In a sport that celebrates values of authenticity and modesty, this is not always a comfortable experience. Elite athletes express private unease at the need to constantly project themselves and the demanding role of social media – but they also recognise that this is what it means to be a professional athlete.

The sport is also rooted in deep countercultural and environmentalist values, so this rising tide of consumerism can pose a dilemma for professional athletes. We need shoes, clothing and equipment to safely explore the mountains – so some level of commodification is necessary – but many professional athletes feel a responsibility to promote sustainable and modest consumption. Anton Krupicka, a poster boy for minimalism and simplicity, but also one of America's first professional ultrarunners, has long wrestled with his role as a sponsored athlete. He has a professional responsibility to his sponsor but does not want to become (in his words) just another 'corporate schill'.[17] It can be a delicate balance. Damian Hall, a co-founder of the environmental campaign group The Green Runners (TGR), works with his sponsor to develop more sustainable products and a repair/recycle scheme. Meanwhile, another TGR co-founder, Jasmin Paris, the only woman to complete the notorious Barkley Marathons and subsequently receive an MBE in 2024 for her contribution to sport, took the decision to leave her sponsor: 'If I'm gonna be talked about on social media', she remarks, 'then let it be for something that I think is really worthwhile.'[18] Paris, who has a career outside of running, is keen to stress that she does not need a sponsor to support her running ambitions, while others are required by circumstance to make different and no less valid choices.

The growth of the professional sport is exciting, but it is also complicated. This new generation of elite athletes face a challenge: to navigate the pressures of a commercial sport, while also looking to adhere to the values that define the ethos of that very same sport.

The vast majority of athletes are recreational runners with little incentive for involvement beyond personal growth and enjoyment. The sport requires an enormous investment of time and energy – 40 per cent of amateur ultrarunning participants combine daily, or near-daily, running with additional strength and conditioning work[19] – and race outcomes are difficult and uncertain. Runners might train hard for months, only to drop out of their target race due to injury or exhaustion. There are far easier ways to keep fit and experience nature.

Even seeming 'success' during a race involves pain and misery. As runners stumble towards the finish line, exhausted and grim-faced, it is commonplace to vow 'never again' – only then to enthusiastically sign up for another race within days of finishing. Short memories have become something of a persistent joke within the sport. There is evidence that 'selective amnesia' can be at work here – the mind able to dampen memories of pain, while enhancing those of joy[20] – but this does not explain why participants are drawn to these arduous feats of endurance. The psychological profile of ultrarunners has been of understandable academic interest. Studies repeatedly find that ultra-distance runners have higher levels of affiliation (i.e., positive social interaction), psychodiversity (i.e., mental adaptability), self-esteem, and a more task-oriented approach to adversity.[21] These findings clarify resilience and motivation *during* endurance attempts, but they do little to explain why participants choose *this* sport, specifically, rather than some other challenge.

It has been argued that off-road and endurance running is particularly satisfying because it enables a reprieve from the 'taskscape' of daily life: work, bills, family, civic responsibility and so on.[22] Our lives are complex, structured and relentless. Endurance running in the natural world provides a way to subvert and escape from these mental and physical frameworks. As Michael Atkinson argues, running in nature allows us 'to focus the mind on the present, and the body on the culturally uncooked nature of the space'.[23] Running can therefore be a form of 'moving meditation' or mindfulness – a spiritual and transformative act – while for others it is a more grounded and material process of emotional and mental decompression. Outdoor enthusiasts of all types report similar experiences – from hikers and climbers to skiers and canoers – so it is unsurprising that off-road endurance runners are often also multisport athletes and recreationalists.[24]

However, running in nature is arguably the purest and most primal form of human movement there is. It confronts us with only the simplest and most urgent of priorities: movement, navigation, nutrition, safety – everything else in life becomes background noise. The sport is replete with this urge to somehow 'escape' from the pressures of modern life.

This sentiment, the idea of escaping to nature, is connected to a fascination that participants have with the seeming limits of the human body. We continue to grapple, as a species, with a knotty philosophical divide between anthropocentric and biocentric approaches to the natural world.[25] Our bodies are both transcendent – seemingly *beyond nature* and capable of rationalised enhancement – but also immanent – that is, *within nature*, and therefore subject to the same frailties and limitations. The sport possesses both of these attitudes: a desire to challenge and overcome nature – through training, mental discipline and technology – tempered against the unknowability of our experience within an unforgiving landscape. Off-road endurance runners are located at this point of tension. For some, their efforts are self-actualising and spiritual – finding 'flow' and becoming one with the landscape. For others, it is a methodical process of training and strategy – a struggle to 'conquer' the natural world or overcome our own physical and mental limitations. There is more often a mixture of these sentiments: finding a connection to nature but also using the landscape as a whetstone against which we can be sharpened.

Ideas of human enhancement have found new importance within the growth of contemporary fitness and wellness culture. Wellness has roots in the alternative medicine industry, but Carl Cederström and Andre Spicer rightly suggest that it references a deeper sentiment relating to individual improvement – the compelling idea that 'we all have a hidden potential within'.[26] Similarly, anxieties around fitness and health are not new – the idealisation of physical vigour and fit bodies can be found throughout human history – but such concerns have recent connotations that relate to individual 'self-mastery'. Writing about the 1970s running boom and 1980s gym/studio culture, historian Shelly McKenzie argues that 'the fit body had become a new form of physical capital'[27] – that is, it enabled individuals to distinguish themselves as superior to others (including their past selves). This twentieth-century fitness culture has continued to develop and find new impetus within twenty-first-century digital subcultures.[28]

Ultrarunning can at times intersect with this cultural drive towards personal enhancement and self-mastery. While there remains a stable core of committed outdoor enthusiasts at the heart of the sport, circling the wagons can be found a new generation of online fitness influencers and wellbeing gurus (such as David Goggins and Russell Cook). Many of these digital actors promote 'finishing an ultra' as a utilitarian goal within a larger quest for self-improvement. Their exhortations to fitness and health can also intersect with other social anxieties: for example, Goggins has a performative machismo that reflects changing gender roles and the supposed 'crisis of masculinity'. Rather than necessarily having a commitment to the sport, or the sporting community itself, for those within the ambit of fitness and wellbeing culture, ultrarunning becomes just another personal growth box to be ticked.

These diverse sentiments might often seem paradoxical, but they reflect the different motivations and values that can be found churning within the sport. The task remains to examine how they are connected and what they can tell us about the recent growth and popularity of the sport.

If there is a central argument that I develop over the course of this book, it is that MUT running is a profoundly *modern* sport – both because it embraces the contemporary world, but also because it pushes back against it.

Even from its earliest decades – with Victorian pedestrians running loops around indoor tracks, or mountain runners climbing rocky slopes – the sport has embraced new technologies and forms of media performance, while simultaneously yearning for the raw physicality of human experience and the silent majesty of the natural world.

This ambivalence stems from a deeply modern condition that has long been an area of interest for sociologists and historians. As societies become more developed – richer, yet also more complex and interlinked – there is an understandable anxiety that perhaps we are losing something: that we lack a sense of purpose, that our bodies are growing soft, that our capacity for self-reliance is diminished, that we suffer from a lack of 'new frontiers'. Such concerns are widespread and have emerged time and again, from the early nineteenth century through to the present day, in a way that often links health and fitness together with a desire for heroism and challenge. This concerns not just our physical and mental capacities, but also our sense of meaning and purpose. Anthropologists argue that work is increasingly cognitive and distributed among complex social and economic systems.[29] This can be alienating. While we are often more objectively productive, our individual contributions might seem less visible and tangible, with our efforts disappearing into a corporate or bureaucratic ether. Where then do we seek purpose and achievement?

The irony is that we often deploy the tools of modernity in pursuit of reclaiming or reconnecting with this lost humanity, whether that be advances in rationalised health care and technology to improve the body; adventure tourism to experience the challenges of the natural world; or spending vast amounts of money on commodified artisanal recreation (from cheesemaking kits to carpentry courses), or cultural genres that emphasise individual autonomy and personal jeopardy (such as westerns and post-apocalyptic fiction). Of course, we don't *really* want hardship or inconvenience – modern Western lifestyles are tremendously beneficial – but neither do we want to abandon the cultivation of mental and physical attributes that relate to self-reliance.

MUT running is an expression of this deeper cultural ambivalence. It is an activity that allows participants to explore personal boundaries and experience moments of real challenge. In a complex world where outcome and our societal contributions can be elusive, it is an activity that combines simplicity with difficulty: move – keep moving – finish. It enables a connection to our internal lifeworld – emotionally and physically – and to the natural world. Yet it is also structured, rationalised and relatively safe. Runners embark on mammoth feats of endurance, but usually within the confines of an organised event, or with a pre-arranged support crew. Training and expertise are honed through engagement with extensive systems of knowledge and coaching. Commercial companies produce ever more sophisticated outdoor clothing and equipment. Sponsored athletes promote consumer lifestyles that celebrate rugged self-sufficiency and adventure. Digital and print publications mediate a vast interlinked sporting culture and draw our imagination towards the wild places of the world.

These themes will animate my discussions in this book, with a long history that begins in the late eighteenth century and then charts a course through to the present day. In the first section, I consider various proto-versions of the sport – such as pedestrianism and early mountain running – but also the formative role played by wider traditions of sport and recreation (such as hiking, athletics and mountaineering). In the second section, I examine the rise of MUT running disciplines in the post-war decades – everything from ultramarathoning and amateur fell running, to long-distance 'challenge hikes' – and through to the commercialisation and professionalisation of the elite side of the sport.

Through consideration of this complex history, I intend to show that MUT running is not an isolated sporting phenomenon, but that it is connected to deeper currents of social and cultural change – and, perhaps, to also suggest that this incredible sport might shed some light on the human condition and our place in the modern world.

Part I

Fragmented origins

Chapter 1

An age of spectacle

An April morning in 2021. Sixteen British and international athletes are running loops around the maroon-red track at Julie Rose Stadium, in Ashford, Kent. A grassy lawn slopes down from the sidings towards an idyllic lakeside setting, the rolling expanse of the North Downs just visible in the distance. The stadium stalls are empty – there are few spectators here for this rather idiosyncratic athletic competition – but a line of open-sided pavilion tents and food-laden trestle tables have been erected trackside. From sunrise to after sunset, the runners continue. Digital timers record their progress with each monotonous and grinding loop: click, click, click. This is the Centurion Track 100 race, organised by race director James Elson, the founder of Centurion Running. Elson has put together a carefully invited roster of elite competitors. Most are here with the hope of setting a personal best in the 100 mile running format; a small number have their eyes on something more ambitious. Sure enough, the athletic world is left stunned as Lithuanian Aleksandr Sorokin maintains a relentless pace to complete 100 miles in a world record time of 11 hours, 14 minutes and 56 seconds. Running on the same track, Samantha Amend sets a new British female 100 mile record, in 14 hours, 34 minutes and 3 seconds.

This is not the first time that Ashford has hosted endurance running record attempts. In the same month, almost two centuries prior, in 1824, Edward Rayner – the 'Kentish Pedestrian' – set a 100 mile world record of 17 hours and 52 minutes.[1] It was a record that would not be bested until 1878. Rayner was one of many endurance athletes pioneering a proto-version of athletics – known as pedestrianism – which swept across Britain and North America during the nineteenth century.

The 'father of pedestrianism' was Foster Powell (1734–1793), a law clerk living in London, though originally from the small village of Horsforth, midway between the booming textile economy of Leeds and the pastoral edge of the Yorkshire Dales.[2] Small and slight, he was described as 'a quiet inoffensive lad, shy, and somewhat unsocial, with nothing in the faintest degree remarkable in him'.[3] Continuing a pastime that had been developed during his youth – and no doubt keen to escape the grime and bustle of London – Powell would take long, solitary walks into the countryside surrounding the city. Provoked by a bet with colleagues in 1764 – to much jeering and disbelief – Powell demonstrated his prowess by racing against two fellow clerks on a 50 mile route to Windsor and back. His competitors had dropped out by the twentieth mile, but Powell made it to the finish. Celebrating his achievement, colleagues began to spread word among London's legal and professional class.[4] Spurred by this ripple of local fame, Powell made another pedestrian attempt later that year by 'walking' (more accurately, jog-trotting), in heavy leather breeches and a great coat, along the rutted coach road from London towards Bath, making it 50 miles along the route in around seven hours.[5] More than a decade later, in 1786, he would repeat this journey, before returning to London on foot, thereby reaching the numerically and historically significant mark of 100 miles in a little over 23 hours.[6]

Powell made many long-distance walking attempts during a career that would span decades, mostly in Britain, although also to great fanfare in France and Switzerland. He reached a pinnacle of fame, in November 1773, with a 400 mile London to York 'out and back'.[7] In an earlier time, or another place, this feat would perhaps have been overlooked and forgotten, but London was the centre of the first large-scale newspaper industry, driven by the innovation and affordability of the printing press in Britain's hectic trading capital.[8] Powell's achievement was chronicled for a mass audience, making him an overnight national celebrity, as with this account in the *Leicester Journal*:

> Mr. Powell undertook to walk from London to York and back again in six-days, for which purpose he set off from Hick's stall on Monday the 29th of November, at nineteen minutes past twelve o'clock, and arrived at Stamford that night. He reached Doncaster the next night, and at half past two o'clock arrived at York, where he delivered a letter to Mr. Clark, watchmaker. He stayed at York one hour and a half, and returned to Ferry-bridge that night. The next night he slept, or rather sat himself down, at Grantham, for he rested here but two hours, having strained himself, and being behind his time. He came to Baldcock on Friday evening, and at the above time, to the joy, surprise, and astonishment of all his friends, returned to London. It is imagined, there were three thousand people on foot, horseback, and in different carriages, attended him from Highgate, accompanied with French horns, and near an hundred links.[9]

With thousands of spectators lining the streets of both York and London – and with Powell fuelled by toast, tea, water and beer – he achieved his goal of completing the attempt within six days (the seventh day was an expected day of rest in Christian Britain).[10] One can imagine Powell on his triumphant return to London: in darkness, during the early hours of the sixth day, accompanied by crowds and lit by the bobbing, ruddy glow of torch-bearing 'linkboys'[11]. A new racing format was created: the six-day race.

Powell died in 1793, relatively poor and still working as a legal clerk in London. Reporting on his death and burial, the *Leeds Intelligencer* honoured the modesty of their homegrown hero:

> His pedestrian feats … by which he might with proper management have profited to much, never produced him enough to keep him above the reach of indigence. Poverty, which he ought always to have kept a day's march behind him, was a constant companion in his travels through life, even to the hour of his death.[12]

Accompanied by a walking procession of twenty black-robed attendants and three mourning coaches, he was laid to rest beneath the only tree in the burial ground at St Paul's Cathedral.

Following Powell there were other pedestrian record attempts in Britain during the late eighteenth century: for example, Thomas

Savager, a labourer, who, in 1790, managed to better Powell's six-day record with a 404 mile walk between Hereford and Ludlow.[13] Raising two guineas to bet on himself, at 10/1 odds, Savager battled through snow and sleet to earn a modest prize of twenty guineas.[14] These attempts were partly driven by a desire to break records and push the boundaries of human achievement and heroism[15] – to see *what was possible* – but more importantly (and perhaps unlike Powell), these prospective athletes were motivated by the lure of prestige and financial reward. Early pedestrian attempts therefore drew in a motley collection of fortune seekers, from soldiers and clerks to footmen and farmers.

At the turn of the Victorian era, pedestrianism was not yet a rationalised or organised sport, but it was certainly becoming a feature of British cultural life. Diverse sporting traditions already existed at the end of the eighteenth century – including an eclectic range of genteel and aristocratic pursuits[16] – but for the working poor, sport tended to be irregular, based on custom and ritualised festivity, and predominantly rooted in small town and village life.[17] This was changing with the accelerating impact of industrialisation and urbanisation. As Samantha-Jayne Oldfield suggests, the development of working-class leisure was becoming linked to a new industrial landscape. Sport was evolving from 'an ad-hoc, seasonal-driven activity associated with rural festivals' into an 'organised and structured urban entertainment scheduled to coincide with the working week'.[18] New and diverse leisure activities were an outcome of this change – an astonishing surge described as the 'Victorian leisure revolution'[19] – with pedestrianism among the most significant.

Pedestrianism reached a zenith of public interest in Britain during a ten-year period, 1808–1818, with an event known as the 'Barclay Match'. This craze was initially sparked by a rivalry between Captain Robert Barclay (1779–1854), a wealthy Scottish aristocrat and military officer, and George Wilson (1766–1839), an itinerant peddler, originally from Newcastle. In September 1808, Barclay – who had been developing and promoting his reputation as a pedestrian since the late 1790s – announced his intention to walk 1,000 miles in 1,000 hours (around 41 days).[20] Believing he could better this, the unknown Wilson declared that he would cover that same distance in only 20 days. Both would go on over the years to complete impressive feats of endurance.

Barclay was the first to actually traverse the 1,000 mile distance – in 1,000 hours, between 1 June and 12 July 1809, on a half-mile loop near the town of Newmarket – winning a prize of 100,000 guineas (equivalent to around £6 million today). His performance was captivating. It received rapturous coverage in both Britain and the United States, with Barclay's fame no doubt magnified due to his social standing and privileged class background. He was portrayed through sketches as a dashing figure, in fashionable long coat and top hat, the epitome of Victorian martial gentility. An account of his 1,000 mile achievement was published by Walter Thom, in 1813, with a breathtakingly detailed log of hourly mileage, time and weather conditions. There was an intriguing section in the book, entitled 'An Essay on Training', which provided a scientific breakdown of Barclay's athletic preparations – it was an undoubted precursor to the yet-unrealised discipline of endurance sports coaching.[21]

Wilson proved to be an almost perfect working-class foil to the aristocratic Barclay. With a precarious background in pawnbroking, shoemaking and second-hand trading, it is likely that he saw pedestrianism as an opportunity for prestige and riches. He had several failed attempts at the 1,000 mile distance, although these failures served to highlight the notoriety of the spectating culture that was beginning to develop around the event. In 1815, Wilson was arrested, after covering more than 700 miles, in 16 days, in a loop around Blackheath Common.[22] Sponsored with lodging and food by the local Hare and Billet pub, his attempt attracted a riotous 7,000-strong crowd by the tenth day. Things soon deteriorated. Men with bayonets were required to clear his path, the sale of alcohol was banned by watchful authorities, and fist fights broke out between those betting on his progress. On the sixteenth day, he was stopped and placed under house arrest for the crime of 'disturbing the peace' with 'a very tumultuous assemblage of people' (this included circus acts, drunkenness and prostitution).[23] He came back the following year to finally complete the distance, in Hull, taking less than 18 days and thereby setting a new record. In 1817, another attempt by Wilson, this time in Liverpool, was abandoned once again due to an overly rowdy and disruptive crowd. Much like a travelling show, Wilson was moving from one part of Britain to another, seeking out new crowds and untapped markets, with sideshows that included musicians, an elephant and a pop-up theatre.

Both Barclay and Wilson were incredible athletes. They achieved national fame, but their endurance attempts were overshadowed by this slightly mad, carnivalesque culture. During Barclay's 1809 attempt, an extensive betting economy ensured that vast amounts of money were changing hands, leading inevitably to skulduggery and interference. After being shot at several times, Barclay carried pistols tucked into his belt and was accompanied by a retired pugilist to ward off violence from those betting against him. Wilson was at one point physically attacked and was also to claim that stomach issues were the result of poisoning by supposed supporters.[24]

The success of pedestrianism in Britain at the time was linked to several key factors. Barclay and Wilson's efforts were travelling performances – much like the big top circus shows that criss-crossed Britain[25] – and similarly they were unashamedly commercial, tapping into a new Victorian leisure and gambling economy. Their attempts were also promoted by a thriving newspaper and journal industry, which sought out spectacle and bravado for an eager readership. Cashing in on this receptive audience, Wilson published an autobiography in 1815, *A Sketch of the Life of George Wilson, the Blackheath Pedestrian: Who Undertook to Walk One Thousand Miles in Twenty Days!*, which revelled in the notoriety of his pedestrian performance. As pedestrianism flourished, spectator sport and Britain's new industrial landscape were becoming linked in two important ways. First, sport acted as a 'pressure valve' for urban discontent, allowing working-class reprieve from the inequalities of industrial capitalism. Second, industrialisation was driving a general rise in living standards – and thereby creating a new economic market for leisure activities – which in turn enabled sharp-eyed entrepreneurs to encourage the commercialisation and subsequent growth of spectator sport.

At the turn of the Victorian era, public houses, inns and taverns were already the beating heart of working-class leisure in Britain, but they received new impetus and growth following the liberalising Beerhouse Act of 1830.[26] As these rowdy and thriving venues became more socially and legally permissive, sporting activities and exhibitionism – pedestrianism, pugilism, wrestling, billiards and so on – were staged as part of a competitive drive to attract prospective customers.[27] Publicans were quick to recognise the potential for ticketing and other money-making schemes, including singing saloons, concert halls, dancing and acrobats.[28] With growing urban density and improved transport links, the economic basis for spectator sport was flourishing to the extent that publicans were able to construct enclosed grounds and grandstand seating, first in London, from the 1850s, and then in other large cities. The White Swan tavern, for example, constructed a 543-yard circular track, enclosed by a 1,000-seat grandstand, with standing capacity for an additional 50,000 spectators.[29] These new venues were multi-purpose and could be used to stage a variety of different sports. Unwittingly, they were also formalising commercial and organised sporting activity in a way that would be replicated by team-based sport towards the end of the century.[30]

The commercialisation of sport brought with it another decisive change: professionalism. Gambling had been a vital component of this new sporting culture from the outset. Often managed by publicans themselves – or franchised out to dedicated bookies – spectator sport in the nineteenth century was dominated by this thriving gambling economy. This served to create a new professional sporting class: the athletes themselves, many of whom would receive payment through appearance fees, sponsorship and prize winnings,[31] but also promoters, who would seek out and sponsor prospective sporting talent.[32] Entire systems of professional activity were being erected around this emergent sports economy.

It was a male-dominated activity, but away from the spotlight of the promoters and the racing grounds, hundreds of women would also successfully attempt pedestrian performances over the course of the nineteenth century.[33] Unsurprisingly, they often encountered hostility and acts of interference from unruly crowds. Emma Sharp (1832–1920), in Bradford, was shot at, tripped and attacked with burning embers and chloroform, before eventually receiving a police escort and carrying a pistol for protection.[34] Despite this misogynistic aggression, in 1864 Sharp became the first woman to replicate Barclay's 1,000 mile feat. She used the winnings from her attempt to establish a rug making business.[35] Reporting on her success, newspaper accounts were quick to sneer at Sharp's temerity in transgressing gender norms:

> Mrs. Emma Sharp, the wife of a mechanic residing at Bowling, has undertaken to perform the arduous pedestrian feat of walking a thousand miles and in a thousand successive hours … The fair pedestrian is a woman of about thirty years of age, of middle height, and of light but active frame. She was dressed in male attire – red and checked coat and inexpressibles [leggings/tight trousers], white waistcoat, laced boots, turndown collar, and scarf – almost the only indication of her sex being in her large drooping straw hat, which was ornamented with a white feather and other feminine adornments.[36]

Female pedestrians received little newspaper acclaim. When they did, as with Sharp – 'the wife of …' – it was frequently accompanied by condescension and descriptions that highlighted their 'unfeminine' physical stature and apparel.[37]

Pedestrianism was an intoxicating and rambunctious sporting culture – but one that would not last. It had become widely seen as a corrupt and untrusted sport, with accusations of cheating, match fixing and impersonation, which brought it into disrepute from as early as the late 1840s.[38] The rapid rise of working-class commercial and professional sport also began to provoke a critical response from the hallowed halls of upper-class privilege. In the second half of the nineteenth century, this new ideology of sport – amateurism – would flourish within university and private school associations.[39] The proponents of amateurism argued that professional sport undermined the spirit of true sporting excellence. This was accompanied by a puritanical distaste for gambling, prostitution and drunkenness, which were so obviously associated with the culture and appeal of professional sport. Amateur sports clubs were formed from the 1850s, leading eventually to the establishment of amateur governing bodies in the 1880s. New values were appended to sporting culture, such as fair play, moral character, the purity of sporting achievement, along with a widespread injunction in amateur circles against the financial renumeration of participants. Amateur sports rose to dominance and in doing so they smothered the energy and economic basis of working-class professional sport. As Steven Pope argues:

> This emergent group of amateurists articulated a class-biased critique of professionalism in terms of the ways it corrupted 'true' sport through the exploits of working-class athletes, who were unschooled in the virtues of the amateur ethos. Sport, they argued, should be a recreation, not a business. With privileged social, economic and political connections, this rising generation of amateur spokesmen effectively institutionalized their biases into resilient athletic structures, and thus defeated a more popular but yet unorganized group of professional sport promoters.[40]

Amateurism signalled the death knell of pedestrianism and professional sport (see Chapter 3). Interest began to decline precipitously from the 1880s, as the economic basis for the sport diminished and other amateur sporting cultures became ascendent. In time, the golden era of pedestrianism was to become largely forgotten by a public that would look elsewhere for sporting exhibitionism.[41]

Given the strong cultural links between Britain and the United States, it was perhaps to be expected that pedestrianism would eventually travel across the Atlantic. While long-distance walk/run attempts had already been completed in the United States, during the eighteenth and early nineteenth centuries it was the 'Barclay Match' 1,000 mile craze that helped to give rise to competitive and professional pedestrianism in the United States. Joshua Newman, visiting from England in 1830, accepted a wager to perform the 1,000 mile attempt in Philadelphia, in part to demonstrate to his American brethren the possibility of covering 1,000 miles in 20 days. He was successful – in less than 18 days – despite attempts to block his path by spectators (many of whom were presumably betting against him).[42] For the next two decades, pedestrianism developed in a muted way across the United States, largely as freakish and singular acts of endurance, little more than absurd spectacles for public entertainment. The performance of walking along a plank, popularised in the 1850s by William Hughes, from California, became a particularly appealing attraction at saloons and bars in various parts of the United States.[43] As in Britain, it was less of a sport, and more performative exhibitionism for a drunken crowd of revellers and gamblers.

This changed in the 1860s with the rise to national fame of Edward Payson Weston (1839–1929). Before the Civil War, there had been little in the way of a spectator or competitive sporting culture in the United States. Blood sports could be found on the margins of society, including bare knuckle boxing and cockfighting, all of which revolved around an illicit gambling economy. Baseball was played by a small set of privileged American men on the East Coast – the first recorded game took place in New Jersey, in 1846 – but did not become more widely popular until the 1860s, when soldiers during the war enthusiastically started to participate.[44] By and large, though, competitive spectator sport had yet to make a mark on the national consciousness of America.

Weston was an itinerant writer, originally from Providence, Rhode Island, who spent time during his youth travelling with the Hutchinson Family Singers, the most famous musical act of antebellum America, noted for lyrics that promoted abolitionism and workers' rights. He was a natural performer and no doubt this colourful upbringing played a significant role in his athletic career. Living in Boston, in 1860, Weston struck a wager with a friend that Abraham Lincoln would lose the presidential election. The loser of the wager would be required to walk from Boston to Washington so as to witness the inauguration of the new president, which was due to be held on 4 March 1861. Lincoln did win the election, so, true to his word, Weston walked the 478 mile route, in a time of 10 days and 4 hours. Over the course of the journey Weston's fame spread. There was widespread newspaper coverage. Telegraph operators transmitted word of his progress, and crowds gathered to meet him as he passed through their locale. He just missed the ceremony itself, but was rewarded with a handshake from Lincoln at the inauguration ball that evening.[45]

With some interruption due to the Civil War – during which time Weston served as a Union army messenger – his fame grew by means of carefully nurtured self-promotion, including a self-authored book in 1862 which detailed his Boston to Washington journey. In 1866, building upon his burnished national image, he sought sponsorship from a prominent New York gambler, who wagered Weston $10,000 (comparable to $182,000 today) to walk 1,200 miles from Portland, Maine, to Chicago in less than 30 days. The attempt became a national phenomenon. Widely covered by newspapers, the *Erie Dispatch* reported that 'Nobody talks about Congress. It's all Weston, Weston, the walkist – Weston, the pedestrian. He's the man.'[46] As Weston arrived in Chicago, after a journey of 29 days, a crowd of 50,000 people gathered to see his victorious finish. He was escorted to the Sherman House Hotel by fifty police officers and a thirty-piece marching band. His triumph was celebrated across America.[47]

Weston inspired a surge of competitive and performative pedestrianism across the United States, dubbed 'walking fever' by the national newspapers. Pedestrian teams were established by commercial companies. Towns constructed racing circuits and used roller rinks to host pedestrian events. Celebrities took up the sport, including Mark Twain. New inventions flooded the market, such as the pedometer and the 'walking shoe' (with built-in springs).[48] For the next twenty years, until it began to subside in favour of baseball, pedestrianism was at the forefront of an emerging sports culture in the United States. Weston was the first – but not the only – athlete-celebrity to emerge during the pedestrian craze. Summarising the 'walking fever' of postbellum America, Matthew Algeo, in his engaging account of pedestrianism, writes:

> Baseball was not the national pastime in the late 1870s and early 1880s. Pedestrianism was. It was the most popular sport in the United States. Its athletes were the highest paid, its contests the best attended and most profitable. When the Thomas H. Hall tobacco company began inserting trading cards into its cigarette packs in 1880, the athletes portrayed on the cards were pedestrians, including Edward Payson Weston, Dan O'Leary, Charles Rowell, and Frank Hart.[49]

As with the pedestrian culture of Britain, the attraction was manifold: a promise of riches, proffered by a vibrant gambling economy, and fascination among spectators with the sometimes absurd and theatrical (but also often thrilling) displays of walking prowess. The pedestrians of the time were stripped back to an existential and emotional core – pushing themselves along, struggling against the crushing weight of mental despair – with human suffering and courageous strife laid bare for the expectant crowd. These new sporting heroes were part of an emergent 'modern celebrity culture'[50] and Weston was among the most acclaimed.

Touring the United States, Weston would continue to set records – 100 miles in less than 22 hours (in 1870), 500 miles in just under six days (in 1874) – but he was soon threatened by upstart competitors, most notably the working-class Irish American Daniel O'Leary (1846–1933).

Emigrating to New York in 1866 – from rural hardship on a subsistence farm in County Cork, Ireland – O'Leary faced unemployment, overcrowded conditions and rampant anti-Irish sentiment. Along with thousands of new immigrants, he drifted west, eventually finding himself in Chicago. After first trying his hand in the lumber yards, he began working as a postman and then eventually a Bible salesman.[51] Long days pounding the city streets provided an unwitting regime of athletic training. Following the Great Chicago Fire of 1871, employment became precarious, until a chance conversation, in the fall of 1873, concerning the possibility of someone, somewhere, eventually surpassing the athletic feats of Weston. O'Leary is supposed to have remarked (no doubt apocryphally): 'Hold on, perhaps a foreigner might do it', and then – in a retort to gales of laughter and anti-Irish bigotry – 'Ireland has sent forth good men.'[52]

His career in pedestrianism began the following year, in 1874, with a 100 mile effort at the Chicago roller rink, in a modestly impressive time of 23 hours and 15 minutes. A second and more successful attempt later that year caught the attention of Chicagoan newspapers. While favoured by the local press as an 'adopted son' of Chicago, he elsewhere faced persistent anti-Irish sentiment as he began touring the eastern United States. In New York, during the spring of 1875, at P. T. Barnum's Hippodrome (later renamed Madison Square Garden), following yet another 100 mile victory, he told a reporter: 'I don't think I had a friend in the audience.'[53] A burning sense of resentment would drive O'Leary's impressive athletic feats – he was not just representing himself, but also his fellow Irish Americans.

O'Leary issued repeated challenges to Weston from as early as the summer of 1874. These challenges were roundly ignored – who did this Irishman think he was? Following his first six-day race in December of 1874 – during which he narrowly missed Weston's record – Weston once again demurred: 'Make a good record first and meet me after.'[54] This is exactly what O'Leary did. With stunning bravado, in April 1875, he broke Weston's 24-hour record (with a distance of 115 miles). Then only weeks later, he came within a hair's breadth of eclipsing Weston's six-day record. Weston – the most famous sportsman in America – could no longer avoid a match against this Irish 'upstart'.[55] As one local newspaper was to declare: 'This feat completely eclipses humbug Weston, and shows undeniably that Chicago's pet, O'Leary, can outlast the puffed-up Weston. Let Weston meet O'Leary, without any more nonsense, and take his punishment.'[56]

Described as 'The Great Walking Match for the Championship of the World', the head-to-head six-day race between Weston and O'Leary began on 15 November in the vast Interstate Exposition Building of Chicago. O'Leary quickly set the pace, leaving little doubt that he was the faster walker. His lead stretched out, longer and longer, mile by mile, as thousands of spectators hollered from the stands. A jumbled crowd packed the hall throughout the days and nights – adults and children, working men and upper-class ladies – the entire social stratum of Chicago displayed in fevered anticipation, surrounded by the aroma of roasted peanuts and stale beer.[57] O'Leary eventually won – continuing until midnight on the sixth day – covering a little over 503 miles – a new record for the six-day racing format. Embracing one another, Weston and O'Leary completed several valedictory laps together beneath cheering crowds: two American giants – the Muhammad Ali and George Foreman of the nineteenth century – resplendent together during this high-water mark of American pedestrianism.

During the mid-nineteenth century, pedestrianism had alternately dominated the sporting cultures of both Britain and the United States. There were, however, noted differences in style and convention. In the United States a strict 'heel and toe' requirement insisted that one part of a foot must always remain in contact with the ground – running was therefore not permitted. Weston himself claimed disdain for the ineffectiveness of running (although he was to later change his mind on this point). In Britain, a convention of 'go as you please' was more widely enacted. British athletes had begun to pioneer the sport of long-distance running (as opposed to walking). Newspapers and journals, on both sides of the Atlantic, debated the efficacy and moral aesthetics of these different styles. Which was more effective? Which was the purer embodiment of human movement?

These debates were fuelled by an increasing sporting competitiveness that had sprung up between Britain and the United States. The laying of the first permanent telegraph cable across the Atlantic seabed, in 1866, enabled near-instantaneous communication and ensured a new era of transatlantic sporting competition. Despite his early fame in the United States, it was not until 1867 (a year after telegramming commenced across the Atlantic) that the British press began to report on Weston, the 'great American pedestrian'. Throughout the 1870s and 1880s, the achievements of Weston and O'Leary were widely reported on by an often awed and sometimes sceptical British newspaper industry. The framing was often one of

'British vs American pedestrianism', with claims of historical and contemporary excellence for British athletes.

Transatlantic competition in pedestrianism was not unheard of before the 1870s. Two Americans in particular, William Howitt ('The American Deer') and Louis Bennett ('Deerfoot'), a member of the Iroquoian-speaking Seneca tribe, had travelled to the United Kingdom between 1845 and 1862 to compete successfully in foot races of up to 20 miles.[58] Bennett received the most notoriety, playing up to Victorian stereotypes of the 'savage red', sleeping in a bear skin and emitting great 'warrior whoops' during his athletic performance. British pedestrians – either visiting or migrating to the United States – had also demonstrated the sport in America since the 1830s. By the 1870s, however, there had yet to be any serious competition between British and America pedestrians over any of the now-established racing formats (100 miles, 24 hours and the six-day race). This changed in 1875. British newspapers had long doubted the achievements of Weston and O'Leary, with British sportswriter A. Easterling stating quite plainly, in December 1875: 'Not to mince matters, the reason we Englishmen only believe what we see of American prowess, is the extreme untruthfulness of American sportsmen.'[59]

The gauntlet was tossed down by English pedestrian champion William T. Perkins, for O'Leary to compete against him in two 100 mile races, one in the United States and one in Britain. O'Leary accepted this challenge, but before he could make arrangements to cross the Atlantic, Weston travelled to Britain, arriving on Christmas day in 1875, where he levelled his own challenge against Perkins. On 8 February 1876, the two men raced against each other in the Royal Agricultural Hall – borrowing the American innovation of indoor racing (British pedestrianism had to date taken place outside) – and, in front of a crowd of 5,000 spectators, Weston convincingly beat Perkins. The latter dropped out at mile 65, his socks soaked in blood, while Weston completed 101 miles in 21 hours and 55 minutes and then continued to reach 110 miles before the 24-hour mark.[60] Weston instantly became a sensation in Britain, where he continued to tour, race and give public lectures to enthralled crowds.

Still, not all were convinced about the superiority of American pedestrians. Writing in March 1876 about an upcoming attempt by Joseph Spencer to beat Weston's 100 mile record, *Illustrated Sporting and Dramatic News* declared:

> There seems now to be a fear amongst the writers of inferior status in London that the press and people of America will raise shouts of acclamation over Weston's achievements and indulge in a storm of derision against England. Nothing can be further from the fact … Knowing that we have a much better man than Weston, from 100 miles up to 500, we are not likely to fall into ecstasy on account of his doings …[61]

Unfortunately for the British, Spencer was also unsuccessful and found himself dropping out after 75 miles and 22 hours. *The Sporting Life*, in May 1876, bemoaned: 'There has been much discussion as to the relative merits of English and American walkers … [many] began to believe that we had no men in the country able to cope successfully against the American at any distance over fifty miles.'[62]

Unwilling to miss out on the action, O'Leary travelled to Britain in October 1876, where in Liverpool he immediately came close to his own world record for the six-day race (he covered 502 miles; his world record at the time was for 503 miles). Over the next year both Weston and O'Leary criss-crossed Britain, beating the best British pedestrians, and showcasing the six-day racing format to a British public that, since the time of the 'Barclay Match' craze, had largely lost interest in this particular long-distance format (sprint and middle-distance pedestrianism were now favoured by the British). Both continued their extended tour around Britain, yet with Weston studiously managing to avoid racing against O'Leary during 1876 and the earlier part of 1877. Unable to forestall any longer this obvious 'match of the ages', Weston agreed to race against O'Leary in London's Royal Agricultural Hall in April 1877, for the prize of £1,000 (equivalent to £144,000 today). Finishing before an estimated crowd of 20,000, O'Leary bested Weston in the six-day format – 520 miles to Weston's 510 – and in doing so set a new world record.[63]

The British press were ecstatic, but also shamed by the seeming superiority of American pedestrians.

Spurred by the exploits of these American interlopers, public interest in long-distance pedestrianism was briefly revived across Britain. Intending to settle the matter of British versus American pedestrianism, the 'Sporting Baron', Sir John Dugdale Astley, a British MP and keen sportsman, announced in January 1878 the 'long distance challenge championship of the world'.[64] Open to anyone, the event series would include five six-day races over an 18-month period. The champion of the first race would be awarded substantial prize money along with a silver and gold 'challenge belt' that the victor would be expected to defend in subsequent races. The race series became known as the 'Astley belt'.

The first Astley belt race took place in London, on 18 March 1878, where O'Leary (the sole American) beat seventeen British pedestrians and in doing so set a new six-day record of 520 miles.[65] O'Leary easily defended his record from New York pedestrian John Hughes at Madison Square Garden later that year, during the second Astley belt race. The British stepped forward once again for the third Astley belt, in March 1879, where reigning champion O'Leary was forced to retire after only 215 miles (there were claims, denied by O'Leary, that he had been drugged[66]). The new Astley champion, reaching a final distance of 500 miles, was Charles Rowell, from Britain, an ex-boatman and favoured athlete by members of the British aristocracy. The fourth Astley belt race returned over the Atlantic, to London's Royal Agricultural Hall, in June 1879, this time to include Weston, who had so far been absent from this championship race series – largely because he was engaged in a challenge to walk 2,000 miles across Britain within 1,000 hours (he was successful, by default setting yet another long-distance record). Former winners O'Leary and Rowell were both unable to race in the fourth instalment of the Astley belt series, and Weston, through a combination of running and walking, bested the other contenders to set a new six-day record of 550 miles.

The fifth (and final) Astley belt race took place in September 1879, once again in Madison Square Garden. Weston was there to defend his title. Charles Rowell, now recovered, was the British favourite. O'Leary had been in poor health since his attempt to win the third Astley belt and was unable to compete.[67] He was there, however, sitting in the stands to support his protégé, Frank Hart, an African American athlete from Boston. There were thirteen starters in total, including George Hazael, from Britain, Samuel Merritt from Connecticut, Fred Krohne from Germany and George Cunyon from Canada. These athletes were all considered sporting superstars, with lengthy and detailed biographical accounts published by expectant newspapers during the pre-race hype. Perhaps predictably, there was great interest in Hart, much of it shaped by underlying racial prejudice. An account in the *St. Louis Post-Dispatch* displays the racist tropes of the time, with paternalistic slave narratives concerning the supposedly child-like, uneducated and uncultured – yet 'crafty' – qualities of the 'Haytien negro':[68]

> Frank Hart, the colored boy who has just made hard-earned fame at Providence, R. I., by a walk of 362 miles in seventy-five hours, is a full-blooded Haytien negro. He is a round-faced, copper-colored, boyish-looking fellow, and looks uncomfortable in the good clothes that have been bought for him. He was a grocer's clerk in Boston, in which city his ability as a walker first brought him notoriety. He is twenty-two years of age, reads and writes, weighs about 130 pounds, and is credited with a great deal of shrewdness, pluck and modesty.[69]

It was a close match for much of this final race. Weston was berated for his seemingly odd antics, swinging a cane and lurching from side to side (it later transpired that he was concealing an illness), and Hart, nicknamed 'Black Dan' (after his mentor, Dan O'Leary), became the favourite despite this racial slur among the 9,000-strong crowd of New Yorkers. Rowell eventually triumphed, with 530 miles, completing a victory lap to the sound of 'God Save the Queen' from the band, while the roaring crowd jostled and slipped, partly restrained by a ring of policemen. Merritt, Hazael and Hart came second, third and fourth, respectively.[70] Rowell was presented a week later with the Astley belt, although American newspapers were more interested in the success and novelty of Hart, with the *Brooklyn Daily Eagle* commenting, 'there is nothing in a black skin or wooly hair that is incompatible with fortitude'.[71] Before cheering crowds at Madison Square Garden, in 1879, pedestrianism was seemingly unstoppable as both an American and British phenomenon. And yet, in many respects, it proved to be the beginning of the end.

New records would continue to be set over the next two decades. Daniel O'Leary established the prestigious 'O'Leary belt' race series in the United States and, until his death in 1933, he became a coach and mentor for talented athletes. Edward Payson Weston continued to embark on ever more impressive feats of endurance, including his famous 5,000 mile 'temperance walk' in Britain, in 1884, during which time he gave public talks about the moral and health benefits of eschewing alcohol. He was struck by a taxicab in 1927 and (with terrible irony) never walked again, before dying in his sleep in 1929. Frank Hart surpassed his mentor, O'Leary, and in 1880 set a new six-day record of 565 miles. He became the first African American athlete to be depicted on a tobacco trading card. As the golden age of pedestrianism waned, Hart's fame diminished, and he drifted into baseball, and with a brief sideline as an endurance coach (see Chapter 4), before his death in 1908.

Across the Atlantic, a rising star, George Littlewood, known as the 'Sheffield Flyer', in 1882 set the 'heel and toe' six-day walking record of 531 miles – this record still stands today and is the world's oldest athletic record. In 1888, he travelled to compete at Madison Square Garden, in a 'go as you please' race, setting an almost unbelievable six-day record of 623 miles. This would not be beaten for almost a century, when legendary Greek runner Yiannis Kouros ran 635 miles, in 1984. Littlewood still holds the British six-day record, but it was to be his last competitive race, as he limped home to the finish with a foot worn down to the bone. He returned to Britain and was feted as 'Littlewood the Lionheart' within the context of rising British sporting imperialism.

The nineteenth century was, then, a hugely significant period for the history of sport and leisure. Pedestrianism – as both nascent sport and wild entertainment – was at the heart of this revolution.[72] Alan Guttmann identifies seven characteristics of 'modern' sport that were crystallised during this time: the creation of sporting institutions (e.g., associations and governing bodies), secularism (i.e., sporting activity away from the confines of religious festivity and ritual), specialisation (i.e., the sporting professional or expert), equality (i.e., sport across social class, if not always gender or race), rationalisation (e.g., a scientific approach to training, nutrition etc.), quantification (e.g., statistics and measurements) and a fascination with record breaking (i.e., human progress and improvement).[73] Sport was becoming a rigorous, independent and rationalised *discipline*, in contrast to pre-modern conceptions of sport as informal activity or uncodified frivolity.

Pedestrianism – both athletically and culturally – was somewhat different to contemporary ultra-distance running. It was a highly professional and widely popular sport/spectacle, often drawing participants from working-class backgrounds who were looking to make a living, and it furthermore had peculiar idiosyncrasies of style and format. Yet this exciting period of foot-based racing also created many of the conventions of contemporary ultra-distance running – and it pioneered a number of approaches to endurance sport, such as pacing, nutrition and technique. More profoundly, many of those same emotional impulses – the fascination with witnessing personal struggle and humanity stripped back to raw existential emotion – can be found reverberating today. While the days of packed stadiums are long gone, a new era of live-streamed ultras and social media 'dot watching' has perhaps enabled something of a rebirth of this very same captivating spectacle.

Chapter 2

The mountains are calling

A lonely wooden signpost, standing high in the remote midnight darkness of Newlands Hause. Grazing sheep huddle together on surrounding fellsides, their smit-stained pelts quivering as they look up, with curious eyes reflecting back the bobbing light of multiple headtorches. It is an unremarkable place for an attempt on the world's oldest endurance mountain record. Cheers and laughter erupt from the small crowd of supporters, as Andy Berry, in T-shirt and shorts, races through to touch the post. Breathless for a moment, with hands on knees, he walks forward to embrace his partner: 'I didn't know what to expect', he recounts after, 'but I just looked for Jess and took it from there; that hug will live long in the memory.'[1] His journey to break the Lakeland 24-hour fell record had officially started at this very spot the night before.

The rules are simple. Starting and finishing in the same place, one must traverse as many fell summits over 2,000 feet as possible within 24 hours. To achieve the record, the runner must either exceed the total number of summits held by the current record holder, or reach the same number but in less time. There was added frisson for this attempt. The existing record was held by Berry's coach, Kim Collison, who was there to help ensure that his own 2020 record would be eclipsed: 'He was open and honest about places he could have had slightly better lines', Berry remarked of Collison, 'and where he felt better or worse. This allowed us, even on the day, to make decisions that bettered my chance of success.'[2]

Accompanied by an alternating team of pacers, his clockwise route took him in a circular loop around the Lake District, beneath blazing blue skies and through stifling heat – almost 100 miles in distance, over 78 fell summits, and with 12,200 metres of rugged and sometimes pathless ascent. Towards the end, with the orange gloam just beginning to cast shadows across the steep Wasdale valley, he was behind record pace – 'my brain was telling me it was hopeless and I was done'[3] – but spurred on by supporters and pacers, he pushed hard for the final few hours, clawing back time. Arriving at Newlands, Berry had matched Collison's 78 summits, but in the quicker time of 23 hours and 23 minutes, shaving more than twenty minutes off the record. He returned without fanfare on Monday morning to his day job as a plumber in County Durham: tired, but now also the latest link in a long and storied chain of fell running history.

The Lakeland 24-hour record stretches back more than 160 years, to a time in the Victorian era when the mountains were for the first time becoming an arena for human creativity and aesthetic experience. Running and endurance walking was a part of this change – from short 'up-and-down' community races at fairs and fetes, to arduous solo expeditions across long distances. Just as pedestrians were establishing the conventions of ultrarunning, so too were their hill and mountain running contemporaries pioneering a new culture of adventure-based athleticism.

The allure of the mountains was not predictable, nor was it guaranteed. In Britain and North America, the uplands had long been thought of as remote, untouchable and sometimes hellish. For New England settlers, perched on the hard-scabble edge of the White Mountains and Adirondacks, those towering peaks represented a devilish realm beyond Christian civilisation, described by William Bradford, governor of Plymouth Colony in the mid-seventeenth century, as 'hideous and desolate … full of wild beasts and wild men'.[4] Less than a century later, *Robinson Crusoe* author Daniel Defoe, in 1724, would describe the Lake District itself as 'barren' and 'frightful'.[5] They both reflected the view of their contemporaries: the mountains were to be avoided.

Such views were shifting towards the end of the eighteenth century. The philosopher and British member of parliament Edmund Burke is often credited with helping to change prevailing attitudes. In his 1758 treatise *A Philosophical Enquiry into the Origin of Our Ideas of the Sublime and the Beautiful*, Burke argued that a beauty of 'the sublime' (that is, of greatness or exaltedness) could be found in the terror and majestic wonder of the mountains, moors and other wild places of the world.[6] He was followed by the Romantic writers and poets, such as Blake, Wordsworth and Coleridge, who shunned the material and mechanised nature of industrialisation.[7] They instead placed an emphasis on the untameable majesty of the natural world, whereby innate beauty could be experienced through spontaneous feelings of awe and terror.[8] This movement would have profound influences, not just in Britain, but also later in the United States, with the Transcendentalist writers Ralph Waldo Emerson and Henry David Thoreau and writer-activist John Muir, who played a leading role in the development of the national parks, trails and wider American conservationist movement.[9] The Romantics and Transcendentalists did not just write about nature; they *lived* in it, *moved* in it – not out of any pressing need for work or survival, but for pleasure and a deep spiritual nourishment. From Coleridge to Muir, and Wordsworth to Thoreau, these dreamers and poets could be found tramping, for days or weeks at a time, across their most cherished landscapes.

As a philosophical sentiment, Romanticism was a response to the rationalism of the European Enlightenment and the creeping spectre of industrialisation. Yet as a cultural movement – and with some irony – the success of this movement was also dependent upon the fabric of technological and social innovation. It first took hold among the British gentry, who since the late seventeenth century had been embarking upon their 'Grand Tour' across the continent to Italy – a coming-of-age journey – although via means of comfortable stagecoach and with an accompanying throng of domestic servants.[10] These youthful aristocrats were drawn to the architecture and art of the Classical world, but they returned with stories and journal accounts of travel through the majesty of the Alps.[11] As Britain underwent the ructions of industrialisation, from the 1790s, the development of steam ships and rail began to make recreational travel feasible for an urban middle class. Inspired by those earlier literary accounts of nature – and alongside the growing cultural dominance of the great Romantic writers and artists[12] – these new 'tourists' were drawn to the supposed authenticity and bucolic mythology of the natural world.[13]

In Britain, the Lake District was the first region to become venerated as an area of sublime natural beauty. An 1820 guidebook, written by the Romantic poet William Wordsworth, encouraged thousands to make the trip, drawn by his stirring evocation of walking, reflection and quiet solitude. A similar movement was emerging in the United States. The Hudson River School artists began to romanticise the Hudson River and Catskills, in the 1820s, leading to the establishment of America's first tourist venue, the Mountain House Hotel, in 1824.[14] Similarly, the pushing back of the Western frontier opened up new tourist regions, from the 1850s onward, most notably Yellowstone, Yosemite and the Grand Canyon. In the popular imagination, these geological and ecological marvels were becoming sacred places, not just reflecting divine beauty, but also *American* beauty: raw, untamed and closer to Edenic paradise than the mountains of Europe.[15]

The Russian-British philosopher Isaiah Berlin would later argue that we should consider this cultural movement 'the greatest single shift in the consciousness of the West'.[16] According to Berlin, the Romantics and Transcendentalists challenged the cold rationalism of science and technology, elevating instead individual emotion and intuition, which in turn inspired a spiritual and cultural reorientation. This would be described much later, by the Canadian Charles Taylor, as the 'massive subjective turn of modern culture, a new form of inwardness, in which we come to think of ourselves as beings with inner depths'.[17] It was an intellectual and artistic revolution that not only reshaped our perception of nature – and our place in the natural world – but also redefined our conception of what it means to be human. It was this cultural movement – in the sense that it spurred the material and ideational foundation of

Victorian tourism – that would lead to the first 'modern' mountain running culture on either side of the Atlantic: English fell running.

Wordsworth died at his Lake District home, near Grasmere, in 1850 – an event heralded at the time as the passing of one of Britain's great poets. Only three years before, the construction of a railway line had been completed to nearby Windermere, which was blossoming into a resort town dependent upon tourism. The fame of Wordsworth and his contemporaries – including Samuel Taylor Coleridge, who had himself journalled extensive walks across Scotland and the Lakes – inspired a small boom in 'literary tourism' that would attract a burgeoning middle and upper class to the poetic landscape of natural Britain.[18]

The small village of Grasmere – described by Wordsworth as 'the loveliest spot that man hath ever found' – provided a particularly appealing destination, removed as it was from the lakeside promenade and opulent hostelries greeting those upon their arrival amid the clanking and hissing of the Windermere rail terminus. Buoyed by this influx of tourism, Grasmere began to host an annual village fete, held in early autumn, for locals and visiting tourists. From 1851 this included an annual sporting event: Grasmere Sports. Wrestling was the prime attraction, followed closely by equestrian events (the steeple chase and hack); the final event of the day was described as a 'foot race for boys'. In 1851, this was a short race around a field. Grasmere Sports only ran for two years, but was then relaunched in 1868, since which time it has been held continuously, barring a break during the First and Second World Wars.

It was in this new edition of Grasmere Sports that the first 'guides race' was held, so named after the Lakeland guides, who would escort visiting tourists across the fell sides. Writing about the second year of this race, in 1869, the *Kendal Mercury* wrote a report that is worth quoting in full:

> A novel attraction was next introduced called a guide's race, in which there were ten competitors. We did not hear the length of the course, which was from the wrestling field direct to the top of Silver How and back, whose rugged side seems well calculated to effectually bar

> the progress of any but the most hardy pedestrian. A fair start was made over walls, hedges, and ditches, and then, for a time, they were lost to view whilst crossing a larch plantation, but were presently seen to emerge from the opposite side as they wended their way up the steep mountain slope. A drizzling rain had now begun to fall which prevented them from being seen very distinctly from the starting point, though it was evident Dewier had the lead, and this proved to be the case as he was the first to the top of the mountain, but, being unsuitably shod for the nature of the ground, he was unable to descend so quickly as the others, and came much behind. The first to the winning post was G. Birkett, of Withborne, who was closely followed by W. Greenup, of Langdale.[19]

The event was recorded as drawing in a mixed crowd – with the 'local elite' and 'ladies' patiently observing the wrestling and racing beneath September drizzle – but it was the working-class guides who were to compete in these first 'fell races' (as they were becoming known within the local Cumbrian dialect).

Grasmere Sports was not the first fell race in Britain. Similar events had taken place at the Highland Games, in Scotland, in the 1840s, and the Lothersdale Show, in Yorkshire, from 1847. However, Grasmere Sports developed a tremendous reputation due to the huge and varied crowds that would travel to the Lake District every year for this flagship event, including members of parliament, visiting dignitaries, and, on one occasion, the Prince of Abyssinia.[20] There were concerns about the consumption of alcohol (which was only allowed indoors) and, by the 1890s, a gambling culture had started to take hold.[21] For the most part, however, Grasmere Sports was a successful and 'wholesome' event, perhaps somewhat in contrast to the livelier pedestrian races that were taking place in cities across Britain at the time. Lord Lonsdale – a northern British aristocrat, known as the 'Sporting Earl' – became an official patron and Grasmere Sports began to attract crowds of up to 10,000.[22]

The fame and success of the Grasmere guides race began to inspire similar professional races in the north of England during the late nineteenth century. Others of note included the Burnsall Classic, first reported on by a local newspaper in 1882 (although probably having taken place in previous years), and Kilnsey Crag, in 1898. These races were similarly attached to local sporting festivities.

They were professional races for several reasons. First, there was a significant cash prize for the winner. In the 1860s, the average wage for a skilled craftsman (e.g., a bricklayer or a carpenter) was 6½ shillings for a six-day week.[23] The attraction of these races was therefore obvious. In 1868, George Birkett won £3 (or 60 shillings) at Grasmere Sports – this was equivalent to around ten weeks' income for a skilled worker. Second, these races attracted wealthy Victorian tourists, including upper-class patrons. These patrons would have a personal guide, who would escort them during their holiday excursion over the fells, and the patron would place bets on their 'favoured man' in the annual fell race. This was not unlike the aristocrats who trained and stabled a horse for an upcoming equestrian event.

These races all remained outside the purview of the Amateur Athletics Association (AAA), formed in 1880 (see Chapter 3), which was hostile to professional sport. For the next century there would be a bitter division between amateur and professional sporting events in Britain (for many different sports, not just fell running). The AAA prohibited anyone who had *ever* participated in a professional event from *ever* competing in an AAA-governed sporting activity – it was essentially a lifetime ban on professional athletes from taking part in amateur events. As amateur athletic events became dominant over the course of the twentieth century, this would inevitably give rise to a sense of unfairness. It hardly seemed reasonable that 'professional' working-class athletes in the north of England would be blacklisted from national athletics because they had participated in a local village race.

The primary source of the grievance emanated from the fact that amateur events were not dissimilar in nature to their supposedly professional counterparts. The first amateur fell race was Hallam Chase, first held in 1863, near Sheffield, with claims to be the oldest continuously run fell race in Britain (Grasmere Sports had an interregnum during parts of the 1850s and 1860s). Rivington Pike, near Bolton, was the second amateur fell race to be established, in 1893.

These events were 'handicapped', with the fastest runners starting last. Yet a prodigious gambling culture developed around these events, with 'nobblers' attempting to trip runners or block their way; and runners themselves were known to take part in disguise, so as to be assigned a more favourable starting position.[24] While there were no cash prizes – and the events were therefore judged to be 'amateur' – non-cash prizes of a similar value to professional winnings were awarded and participants could take home a hefty haul through a side bet with the bookies.

While these early fell races were a forerunner of the independent and rather idiosyncratic culture of modern fell running, at the time they were not dissimilar to the wider practice of Victorian pedestrianism. Agricultural communities might have lacked the capacity to construct track stadiums, as in the larger cities of Britain, but they did have naturally formed racecourses lying at hand: the fells and hills of northern England. They were events that drew in a large crowd of spectators, alongside other attractions and sporting/community activities, and they were driven in part by the economic incentives of gambling and prize winnings (cash and non-cash). It was not until later in the twentieth century that a true culture of *recreational* fell running would take hold.

A full year before the first guides race took place up the side of Silver How – and during a decade when the fame of Edward Payson Weston was only just starting to grow across the United States – another race was taking place among the Tarahumara in northern Mexico. In March 1867, two Tarahumara villages, Bocoyna and Sisoguichi, came together to channel their local rivalry through a woman's race – known as an *ariwete*[25] – between their fastest female runners, four from each village. The Native American Tarahumara, also known more authentically as the Rarámuri, have since entered the Western imagination as a 'mythical' and 'secluded' tribe of runners, with legendry and supposedly superhuman endurance – although the truth is far more complex.

While this was the first Tarahumara race recorded by an American observer – in this case a reporter from the *New York Herald* – the roots of Tarahumara running are much older. Tarahumara running began as a form of persistence hunting, before later developing into competitive racing as part of local community festivity and as a form of rhythmic invocation akin to prayer or worship.[26] The Tarahumara were not alone. Foot racing had historically been important for many Native American tribes across North America, with deep spiritual, economic and social meaning attached to these running events.[27] It was European colonisation, the seizure of tribal land, displacement, and the destruction of native culture that smothered many of these ancient racing traditions. Living in a remote and mountainous part of rural Mexico, the Tarahumara were partly immune to European colonialism – for a time at least – and better able to protect their community traditions from outside interference.

The 1867 race is depicted as taking place midway between the two villages, with fourteen loops of 'three Mexican leagues' around an 'oblong mountain'. The inhabitants of both villages gathered together, bringing anything of value that could be wagered against the race, and according to the American correspondent, the villages 'were also sufficiently civilized to have a large quantity of the intoxicating drink – the Tezuina'. Stripped down to their petticoats, the eight women set off at 6.25 a.m. One of the women, from Bocoyna, had given birth ten days earlier and had bandaged her breasts for the race. With guards stationed at various points to ensure fair competition, the women spent the rest of the day racing around the mountain, while their respective communities drank, gambled and cheered their progress. As the final loop began, only three women were left:

> The multitude was now pretty well soaked with Tezuina, and the betting ran to the wildest extremes; everyone who had anything of value staked it on the race – hoes, plows and other agricultural implements, horses, cattle, sheep, pigs, goats, cats, dogs and whatever else there was of value changed hands. The men bet their clothes, while the women pitched in and bet their petticoats. All was a wild uproar...

Two women from Bocoyna were the victors, including the new mother, and they crossed the finishing line together in a time of

13 hours and 25 minutes. So how far did they run exactly? The news reporter claimed that the distance was 109 miles; however, there is some uncertainty about the exact distance of a 'Mexican league'. Traditionally, this meant the distance that a person could walk in an hour, most likely around 2.5 miles (so fourteen loops would be 105 miles – which is close to the reported distance). It is possible to look at a map of the terrain around the two villages. There is indeed an 'oblong mountain' situated between them, around which runs a dirt track for most of the perimeter. The distance for this loop is approximately 5.5 miles, giving perhaps a total distance of 77 miles, with around 2,500 metres of ascent. This seems more likely, unless of course these Tarahumara women were running at speeds that are faster than the best female ultrarunners today.

As far as we know, the race was not an unusual occurrence but was typical of Tarahumara racing culture at the time. Over the coming decades, through to the early twentieth century, there would be many occasions where Western visitors would be able to spectate and report on Tarahumara racing. There was intense American and British interest in the Tarahumara during the late nineteenth and early twentieth centuries, and hundreds of newspaper articles about the Tarahumara – most of which spent some time discussing their running prowess – and a full-length book account by the American explorer Frederick Schwatka, *In the Land of Cave and Cliff Dwellers* (1896). There were also early attempts to draw the Tarahumara into competition, either against European and North American athletes, or for the benefit of curious Western spectators. In 1906, for example, American railroad contractors organised a race for the Tarahumara, with a prize of $100 (at the time a small fortune for the Tarahumara). The village of Bocoyna selected their two fastest runners, both men, with the winner completing the 100 mile out-and-back, over rugged trails and mountain sides, in a time of 16 hours.[28] Newspapers ran breathless reports about the 'greatest runners on earth'. There were (exaggerated) claims that the Tarahumara were effortlessly able to cover 170 miles in a day. The Mexican government itself organised a long-distance trial – in order to prove the superiority of the Tarahumara – in which the runners reportedly covered a 600 mile mountainous trail route in less than five days.[29]

Given that the Tarahumara still race to this day, it is arguably the oldest racing culture still in existence, pre-dating a claim that is often made about British fell and hill running. Equally, the Tarahumara are not quite so secluded or mysterious as is usually depicted. Christopher McDougall's best-selling book *Born to Run* mistakenly gives the impression that the Tarahumara emerged from a hidden and mythical past to compete in the 1992 Leadville Trail 100 race (see Chapter 9). Rather, there was a period of around fifty years – from the 1880s to the 1920s – when Tarahumara runners were a prized and publicly paraded part of Mexican athleticism.[30] Tarahumara runners were to compete in a series of competitions in Texas during the 1920s and, following success in these events, two runners represented Mexico in the marathon at the 1928 Olympics in Amsterdam.[31] They came 32nd and 35th, to some disappointment, with claims that the marathon was simply too short a distance for their talent to be properly registered. Of course, the Tarahumara were themselves often happy to play into the legend of their athletic prowess. When offered an opportunity to compete in the 1928 transcontinental race – a rather ambitious 3,000 miles across the United States (see Chapter 4) – the Tarahumara demurred, supposedly disappointed when they heard it was only from the Pacific to the Atlantic (no doubt with a twinkle in their eye): 'If it had been there and back', the *Hamilton Spectator* reported, 'the Tarahumara Indians might have entered it for a warm-up.'[32]

While the Tarahumara are no doubt excellent and inspiring runners, we need to avoid falling into lazy racial or cultural stereotypes. Victorian and Edwardian newspapers depicted the Tarahumara as 'noble savages' with an almost animal-like speed and grace. Similar tropes exist today, with the supposedly simple lifestyle of the Tarahumara held up against the 'problem' of Western over-consumption and over-civilization.[33] These stereotypes have persistently depicted the Tarahumara – and other 'primitive' people – as 'impervious to pain and fatigue, as well as mysteriously in touch with nature'.[34] However, studies have been unable to detect any genetic predisposition towards endurance running among the Tarahumara. Rather, it is a nurtured quality, springing from day-to-day life in the mountains and from a unique running culture that emphasises the spiritual and communal aspects of running – not to mention the economic lure of prize-winning for poor subsistence farmers.[35]

In his excellent book *To the Limit*, Michael Crawley, a British anthropologist, recounts time spent with the Tarahumara and argues that their running feats are layered with a complex series of meanings that range from the spiritual and metaphorical – as a form of worship and praise for Tarahumara resilience – to economic necessity.[36] While we need to be mindful of this complexity, Tarahumara running is also of course rightfully celebrated. Throughout the twentieth and twenty-first centuries, it would continue to have a unique influence on American ultra-distance running. Most especially, this would connect to the Western preoccupation with somehow 'escaping' from civilisation and the search for a more authentic life in nature.

Though separated by an ocean and a vast cultural divide, the Lakeland guides and the Tarahumara held something in common: they were native to the mountains, with the landscape providing a natural space for everyday sporting and cultural activity. Visitors and tourists would travel to behold the wonder of these fleet-footed mountain people but, for most of the late nineteenth century, outsiders themselves were spectators rather than participants in these local and community-run races. Yet, in the nineteenth century, another development was taking place among a more privileged and often wealthier class of mountain athlete. Driven by imperial and masculine ambition – and the notion of technological, moral and civilisational superiority – a new breed of European and American explorers were pushing the boundaries of achievement in the mountains.[37]

The so-called 'golden age' of Alpinism is usually credited with beginning in 1854, when Alfred Wills, a High Court judge from Britain, made a claim to the first ascent of the Wetterhorn. Wills likely knew that the Wetterhorn had already been summited more than a decade before, by two Grindelwald guides, but the widespread celebration of his achievement, and a series of guidebooks published by Wills, led to the formation of the Alpine Club in a London hotel. It was a narrow group of men, most of them Oxford and Cambridge graduates, distinguished by independent wealth and overt class privilege.[38]

A rush to make the first ascent of unclimbed Alpine peaks would ensue over the coming decades. While this new culture of Alpinism was a distinct adventure sport in its own right – that is, it was mountaineering – it was also part of a larger cultural turn whereby the boundaries between 'sport' and exploration were to become blurred. As the number of unclimbed Alpine summits and routes began to diminish during this 'golden age', there was a desire to seek new challenges that would test the limits of Western ambition. This would take mountaineers to the far reaches of the Andes, the Himalayas, Patagonia and the North and South Poles – new frontiers of both mountaineering and colonial ambition – but there was also a desire to formulate endurance records and routes in more familiar and accessible locales. For example, Sir Martin Conway – a British MP, academic and president of the Alpine Club (1902–1904) – lamented the loss of 'mystery' in the Alps. In his 1895 book, *The Alps from End to End*, he devised a trans-Alpine endurance route that would enable a return to the 'habits of the Alpine pioneers'.[39] As potential first summit ascents became scarcer, there was a natural urge to go further – and faster – on more familiar ground.

The Lake District became a proving ground for this generation of British Alpine climbers. It is here where the boundaries between mountaineering and hiking/running became blurred – just as they are sometimes today. The seemingly first attempt at a continuous circuit of the high fells was undertaken by the Alpine mountaineer Rev. T. M. Elliott, from Cambridge, in the early 1860s. Departing from Wasdale Head, he completed a 15 mile route with 6,500 feet of ascent, over the Scafell massif and the ridge line running from Great Gable through to Red Pike and Stirrup Crag, in around 8.5 hours.[40] While this effort received little newspaper coverage, it was no doubt spread via word of mouth to fellow members of the Alpine Club. Elliott was killed in Switzerland in a mountaineering accident five years later.

Over the next half century there was a flurry of attempts to devise ever more ambitious circuits around the Lake District fells. In the spring of 1870, following Elliott, Thomas Watson, with a local guide from Borrowdale, completed the first circuit of the 3,000 foot Lake District peaks. Many others followed over the coming decades, including, in 1871, Charles Pilkington, a notable pedestrian and future president of the Alpine Club (an early example of the crossover between endurance athletics and mountaineering), who completed an impressive 60 mile loop over the major Lakeland fells, in a time of 21 hours and 10 minutes. These attempts were informal and uncodified but were gradually taking shape into something that resembled a Lake District 24-hour fell record. In 1893, Cumbrian climber John Wilson Robinson and long-distance walker G. B. Gibbs completed a longer 'round' (as these attempts were becoming known) that started from Keswick – in awful winter conditions, using alpenstocks in the ice and snow – in a time of 23 hours and 25 minutes. Both had revealed in separate pieces of correspondence the notion of making an attempt on 'the record'.[41]

By the late 1870s a proto-version of the Lake District 24-hour fell record now existed, running as a rough loop that would take in the high Lakeland summits of Bowfell, Scafell Pike, Skiddaw and Helvellyn.[42] There were approximately a dozen attempts at this fledgling record between 1870 and 1900, with varying routes, distances and successful fell summits. While one of these attempts involved a team of Lakeland locals – the 'brothers Tucker', in 1878 – it was otherwise an elite group of middle-class professionals who travelled to the Lake District for these early endurance efforts.

We can speculate as to why this might have been the case. These long-distance attempts carried with them a significant risk of injury and a period of fatigue. Working-class locals relied on good physical health to make a living – in agriculture, labouring and guiding – and had little in the way of economic security. They would likely have been unwilling to risk a loss of income from a period of convalescence. Unlike the guides races, which were just starting to be established, there were no prizes, no winnings and little external benefit, other than the nebulous prestige or personal satisfaction that would result from setting a new record. In contrast, members of the Alpine Club had independent wealth, sedentary working lives and, if necessary, the means to seek expensive medical treatment. With a successful career built in the professions, they were also more likely to be motivated by public status and fame among an elite set of peers.

These nineteenth-century attempts had been somewhat informal, but it was Dr Keith Wakefield who provided a clearer sense of what a Lake District fell round should involve. In 1904 – and then for a second time, in 1905 – he made two successful circuits, setting a new record of 23 summits in 22 hours and 7 minutes, covering 59 miles and 23,000 feet of ascent. He described his objective as 'to ascend the greatest possible number of peaks over 2,000 feet, and return to the starting point within twenty-four hours'.[43] These are the principles that today still guide the 24-hour Lake District fell record.

Wakefield was a local GP, from a prominent Kendal family, and he later spent time serving as a medical missionary in the Grenfell Missions (1908–1914) and in active service as a medic on the Western Front. His record was beaten in 1916 by a working-class pedestrian, Cecil Dawson, from the Lancashire cotton towns around Manchester. Dawson had pioneered long-distance fell walking across the Pennines and in North Wales, with rebellious excursions over private land, often in defiance of patrolling gamekeepers. He was unusual in this respect – he came from an 'inferior' social class to Wakefield – and it is perhaps for this reason that his record was rejected by the Fell and Rock Climbing Club (FRCC). The official reason given related to the inappropriateness of setting a record during wartime, but the FRCC also implied – as was claimed in a later account – that they 'would not recognise anything in the nature of racing on the fells'.[44] This was an odd remark given that Wakefield's previous record had clearly been set with speed in mind. One can only wonder if this decision would have been made if Dawson had been from a more 'acceptable' class background.

Class divisions would persist – as would the patriarchal nature of British mountaineering (women were excluded from the Alpine

Club until 1974) – although following the end of the First World War there was a great expansion of long-distance efforts in the British countryside. The Rucksack Club, formed in Manchester in 1902, became an important organisational vehicle for this growing sporting endeavour, often with an emphasis more on hiking than climbing or mountaineering. Their most prominent member, Eustace Thomas, a prosperous electrical engineer based in Manchester, helped to pioneer this new wave of long-distance adventurism.[45] He completed and helped to define a number of successful routes, especially over that great rugged backbone, the Pennines, which runs through the industrial heart of northern England. In 1918, Thomas set new records on Cecil Dawson's Colne–Buxton traverse, over 50 miles in less than 18 hours, and the 40 mile Derwent Watershed, in 11 hours and 39 minutes. He then turned, in 1919, to the mountains of Wales, traversing in turn the 2,500 foot peaks of South Wales and the 3,000 foot peaks of Snowdonia.[46] To this day, all of these remain established and competitive routes for long-distance runners, walkers and orienteers in Britain.

While Thomas would perhaps be most famous for becoming the first person to summit all 4,000 metre Alpine peaks – and for designing the 'Thomas stretcher' – his notable achievement in Britain was to beat Wakefield's 24-hour Lake District fell record. A protégé and friend of Wakefield, Thomas brought a scientific and engineering intensity to his preparations – including a vegetarian diet, something that resembled a modern training programme, rubber-soled shoes, lightweight clothing and careful analysis of the route.[47] He made several attempts, beginning in 1919, before setting a new record in 1923. Not only did he complete Wakefield's original circuit in a faster time of 21 hours and 25 minutes, but he continued on from Keswick, extending his attempt out over the fells of the Grassmoor range, to complete a round of 79 miles and 30,000 feet in 28 hours and 25 minutes. Notably, Wakefield himself accompanied Thomas for a large part of this attempt. It was the first example of that unwritten fell and ultra running code – exemplified by Kim Collison's support for Andy Berry exactly 100 years later – whereby previous record holders will help aspirants in their attempt to break the existing record.

Over the course of fifty years, then, the Lake District – and other parts of Britain – became the playground for a new culture of long-distance mountain endurance attempts. Compared to the more celebrated activities of pedestrianism, or even the guides races, these acts of athleticism often received little newspaper attention or national acclaim. It was a niche and exclusive form of 'serious leisure', performed by a small group of privileged men. Women would have notable but unacknowledged success in the great mountain ranges of the Alps and the Andes – with mountaineering legends such as Lucy Walker and Annie Peck – but in Britain this new craft of mountain endurance would remain a male endeavour. The Lake District 24-hour fell record would continue to become more formalised, especially when, in 1932, a Keswick guest house owner, Bob Graham, would extend the record and in so doing create what has since become the most iconic mountain running route in Britain: the Bob Graham Round (see Chapter 5).

Given the large and active mountain-sport communities that now exist across the Western and Mountain states of America, it seems remarkable that at the beginning of the nineteenth century much of this territory was unknown, unmapped and unclimbed. Large parts were not yet even incorporated into the United States. The nineteenth century was therefore predominantly a period of expansion and exploration, during which time Americans would encounter the mountains as part of a new and growing frontier. The mountains of Britain and Europe were a familiar and well-trodden landscape, enabling creativity and experimentation by athletes in search of rigorous Alpine training and new endurance challenges. In contrast, for non-indigenous Americans and European settlers, the American West provided a 'blank canvas' upon which – and unfortunately at the expense of pre-existing Native American cultures – a new tradition of mountain athleticism and exploration would eventually be written. It is hard not to see this thread of adventurism and the unknown woven into the landscape and culture of contemporary American mountain sports.

The first significant expeditions to explore and map the lands lying beyond the Appalachian Mountains were commissioned by President Jefferson during the late eighteenth and early nineteenth centuries. Early forays included naval expeditions to map the coastal line of present-day Washington and Oregon, with the naming of notable peaks, such as Mount Hood and Mount Saint Helens, in 1792. Overland expeditions included those by explorers such as Lewis and Clarke, in 1805, across North Dakota and Montana to the Pacific Ocean, and those by army lieutenant Zebulon Pike, in 1806, along the Front Range of Colorado.[48] Lieutenant Pike was himself drawn by the lure of mountain climbing and he attempted to scale several peaks during this expedition, although not Pikes Peak itself (which he named 'Highest Peak' – it was later renamed in his honour). These official early expeditions to reconnoitre the American West grew less frequent, but commercial interests – particularly among fur trappers – ensured the continuation of exploration and mapping. The creation of a clear and defined land route across the continental United States came with Lieutenant John C. Frémont and his journey over the Sierra Nevada in 1844. His first expedition took him over Carson Pass – named for Frémont's fur trapper scout, Kit Carson – near Lake Tahoe, and down to Sutter's Fort in Sacramento, a route than runs roughly parallel to and slightly to the south of the modern-day Western States trail route (see Chapter 7).

By the middle of the nineteenth century, then, as these explorers continued to push westward, most of the great mountain ranges of America were still largely unmapped and unclimbed. The western ranges were perceived to be remote and dangerous, hardly a location for the mountain running cultures that were emerging in Victorian Britain. The completion of the transcontinental railroad in 1868 enabled thousands of settlers to begin seeking new economic opportunities in the American West, but as a *New York Times* editorial stated in 1871, 'vast tracts of the national domain yet remain unexplored. As little is known of these regions as of the topography of the sources of the Nile or the interior of Australia.'[49]

While the American West still represented the unknown – and was only partially settled – on the Eastern seaboard a new approach to the mountains was in development. Inspired by the European Romantics, Ralph Waldo Emerson, a Unitarian minister, established the Transcendental Club in 1836. Believing that our understanding of life can only be gained through the observation and experience of untainted nature – which he understood to be a reflection of the divine – he bemoaned the discord 'between man and nature, for you cannot freely admire a noble landscape if laborers are digging in the field hard by'.[50] Emerson became a keen if rather modest hill climber, seeking spiritual joy and knowledge in a natural world that he believed needed to be protected from the creep of industry.[51] His protégé, the poet and essayist Henry David Thoreau, would take this passion to new heights (quite literally) in the 1840s and 1850s. He travelled extensively around the eastern United States, climbing and often camping on the mountains of New England, and then detailing his experience in essays that were widely read by the public. A new generation of American outdoor enthusiasts were inspired by the writings of Thoreau. Gradually, interest would pivot away from the celebrated majesty of the Alps – a favoured holiday destination for wealthy Americans – to the magnetic pull of the great American mountain ranges.[52]

In the second half of the nineteenth century this gradual encounter with the American mountains was fuelled by the formation of mountaineering and hiking clubs. This would have a profound impact, not just for the sport of mountaineering, but also as a precursor to the development of trail running. As the next chapter outlines, the first American trail races were either organised or inspired by these new sporting clubs in the early twentieth century. The first such organisation was formed in 1863, in western Massachusetts: the Alpine Club of Williamstown. It was modelled on the British Alpine Club, but notably it allowed both men and women to be members – remarkably, with most men away fighting in the Civil War, nine of the first twelve members were women. This trend of female involvement would be replicated by other American mountaineering clubs. As Barbara Cutter argues, mountaineering clubs promoted female independence and physical toughness, which laid down important cultural foundations for the later suffrage movement in the United States.[53]

Following Williamstown, other clubs emerged in the 1870s, in Portland, Maine, and in Denver. Yet it was the Appalachian Mountaineering Club (AMC), formed in 1876, that would have the most significant impact and would grow to be one of the largest hiking/mountaineering clubs in the United States (second only to the Sierra Club).[54] Centred around MIT (Massachusetts Institute of Technology) and Harvard University, the first AMC president, Edward Charles Pickering, a noted astronomer and physicist, spent his free time visiting and exploring the White Mountains and the Adirondacks. Pickering gathered around him a group of like-minded professionals and academics to pioneer 'serious leisure' in the outdoors. Inspired by European mountain culture, they sponsored their first two-week camping trip in 1887 and, in 1888, established America's very first mountain hut, on the col between Mount Madison and Mount Adams.

American mountain tourism had existed before this – with the first mountain hotel opening in the Catskills, in 1824, and with early trips by awed travellers to Yosemite from the 1850s – but this was the first time that actually *climbing* these mountains became a part of American leisure culture.[55] In the same way that the Alpine Club in Britain was a vehicle for first ascents in the Alps – and then later in the Andes and Himalayas – AMC members also travelled further afield, with Charles E. Fay in particular making a large number of first ascents across the Canadian Rockies in the 1890s.[56] All of a sudden, the mountains had become a playground and source of life-affirming inspiration for a small group of privileged American hikers and mountaineers.

As immigrants made their way across the continent to settle in the American West – with San Francisco growing from a small fishing village of 1,000 residents, in 1848, to a bustling metropolis of over half a million by 1880[57] – so too were the conventions of amateur mountaineering brought to the West Coast. The AMC provided a ready-made template for the new clubs that were to emerge along the Pacific seaboard.

The Oregon Alpine Club (OAC), founded in Portland, in 1887, by entrepreneur and wilderness advocate William Gladstone Steel, was driven by his ambition to develop a tourist industry in the Oregon Cascades. A journalist, originally from Ohio – the child of Scottish-born abolitionists active in the Underground Railroad – Steel was driven by a desire to make the outdoors accessible for a wider American public. While the OAC faltered, due to a large but often inactive membership, it was reformed under a new name, the Mazamas (a term for 'mountain goat' that comes from the indigenous Nahuatl). Membership was restricted for this new club to those that had climbed a glaciated mountain. Two hundred and fifty climbers gathered for the Mazamas inaugural 1894 meeting in Government Camp, at the base of Mount Hood, before ascending to the summit the following morning. Steel was a flamboyant and ambitious figure, organising mass spectacles – including fireworks and music on Mount Hood – and he helped to popularise West Coast mountaineering as a serious but also fun and anarchic pastime.[58] He went on to play an advocacy role, including by helping to establish Crater Lake as America's fifth national park, in 1902. Mazama members themselves would go on to be competitors in the earliest American trail races, including at San Francisco's Dipsea race (see Chapter 3).

Further down the West Coast, in California, a related but slightly different impetus led to the formation of the Sierra Club. Founded by John Muir and twenty-six other delegates, at a Stanford University meeting in 1892, the declared intention of the Sierra Club in their founding document was to 'explore, enjoy, and render accessible the mountain regions of the Pacific Coast'. Like other clubs, it had a membership drawn from a well-educated set of middle-class professionals – academics, writers, scientists and businessmen. Driven by the instincts of Muir – who had himself been strongly influenced by the Transcendentalist writings of Emerson and Thoreau – the Sierra Club was uniquely animated by a desire to preserve the natural landscape.[59] The Californian wilderness, especially Yosemite, faced a particular threat from over-commercialisation and overdevelopment, much of which was linked to tourism, agriculture and mining. The Sierra Club was therefore conceived as an environmental protection group rather than strictly as a mountaineering and hiking club. While members of the Sierra Club would go on to pioneer Alpine-style climbing across the Californian mountains – and in other parts of the United States – the club quickly became nationally prominent as an environmental advocacy group. This included lobbying for the creation and expansion of national parks across the United States, and more practical work to create and maintain a network of trails that would permit travel without undue damage to the natural landscape.

As the nineteenth century drew to a close, a remarkable shift had occurred in both Britain and North America. The mountains were no longer a place to be avoided, but a romanticised landscape that now provided challenge, inspiration and aesthetic experience. A new and growing industry – tourism – was providing a physical and cultural infrastructure that would continue to attract climbers, mountaineers, hikers and runners. And yet, while mountain landscapes had been drawn into the orbit of civilisational imagination, they would also remain 'edge' spaces – a place for adventurism and escape. Such themes would continue to resonate over the twentieth century with the creation of contemporary running cultures – including, as the next chapter recounts, the genesis of American trail running and so-called 'mountain marathons'.

Chapter 3

Marathon mania

Independence Day – 4 July 2015. A crowd lines the street of a small Alaskan coastal town, whipped by a steady breeze that sweeps in across the grey expanse of Resurrection Bay. Celebrations like this are taking place across the whole of the United States for the national holiday – well, perhaps not *quite* like this. The crowd is tense, peering up at the white-capped Kenai Mountains, which loom like jagged sentinels above the town. Suddenly a dark-haired, shirtless man appears, racing down a scree slope, bounding over the lower talus field and tearing along the main street. Then there are others. Some collapse to the ground, most stagger around in exhaustion, a small number are carried away for medical assistance. Nearly all are scratched, bleeding and filthy. The crowd hollers and cheers, film crews beam the spectacle to a live audience around the world, and for a moment the sleepy town of Seward takes centre stage in the glamorous world of mountain running.

This is the annual race up the steep side of Mount Marathon – a race dating back to 1909 – and the Spanish winner, Kílian Jornet, has just set a male course record. In another breathtaking display of athleticism, the female course record was broken only hours before, by Swedish runner Emelie Forsberg.

Two months later – 5 September 2015. A clear day in the Scottish Highlands, with only a gentle breeze, and the early autumn sun beating down. Crowds gather on the rocky summit of Ben Nevis, cameras clicking, as the first runners crest the summit plateau. Finlay Wild, Rob Jebb, Ricky Lightfoot – British fell running aristocracy, resplendent in the heraldic splash of their club vests. They turn for the descent, a daring plunge over scree and boulders, more than 1,000 metres down to the bustling jamboree of Fort William. Finlay Wild wins again – his sixth consecutive victory at 'the Ben' – a local Scott and rising star, who six years later will come within minutes of Kílian Jornet's (at the time) supposedly 'unbeatable' record on the Bob Graham Round. This is the blue-ribbon event of British mountain running, dating back in some form to 1895, with a roll-call of past winners that stretches across the pantheon of British fell running.

Mount Marathon and Ben Nevis – two mountains, two races. Both these events emerged at a critical and formative moment in the history of sport. Pedestrianism was fading away, gradually becoming eclipsed by a new culture of amateur athletics. For competitive running, this would result in a greater number of participants, but a smaller crowd of spectators – and little in the way of professional or commercial activity. The economic basis for professional 24-hour and six-day racing was evaporating – and in some instances it would be actively banned by anxious authorities – and with it any real interest in ultra-distance competition (see Chapter 4). Yet from within this tumult and growth, new racing formats and disciplines were emerging – most notably, trail running and so-called 'mountain marathons'.

The shift to amateur athletics had begun with a philosophical and cultural movement known as 'Muscular Christianity'. The term had been floating around in public discourse during the 1850s, reflecting concerns with the seeming degeneracy and effeminacy of young men, but it was first developed as a coherent ethic in the writings of Thomas Hughes (1822–1896) and Charles Kingsley (1819–1875). Hughes and Kingsley were both successful writers, keen sportsmen and privately educated upper-class elites; they were also Christian Socialists and Chartists, with a complex politics that was simultaneously bold and utopian, while also steeped in the gendered and racial prejudices of colonial Britain. Their ideas gained traction in the upper echelons of English schooling, before later exportation to Canada and the United States. Theodore Roosevelt would become a vocal adherent. As argued by Hughes, in his 1861 novel *Tom Brown at Oxford*, sport was necessary to promote Christian morality, physical fitness and 'manly' character.[1] Hughes reflected a Victorian obsession with health – seemingly threatened by newly decadent lifestyles – but he also channelled a colonial desire to 'ensure the virility of the "British race" and the strength of the British Empire'.[2] Kingsley would later expound on these themes:

> In the playing field boys acquire virtues which no books can give them; not merely daring and endurance, but, better still temper, self-restraint, fairness, honour, unenvious approbation of another's success, and all that 'give and take' of life which stand a man in good stead when he goes forth into the world, and without which, indeed, his success is always maimed and partial.[3]

Kingsley and Hughes had a profound impact on the integration of sport into elite education. Athletics clubs were first founded at the Universities of Cambridge and Oxford, in 1857 and 1860, but by the close of the nineteenth century, athletics had become a major feature of school and collegiate curricula. Competitive teams were becoming regularly attached to prestigious educational institutions in both Britain and the United States.[4] For bright young minds, trained to succeed in a world of capitalist endeavour and imperial rivalry, a structured programme of athletics was perceived as ideal for the nurturing of masculine values relating to toughness and competition.

The young men that were a product of this elite education would carry these sporting attitudes with them into their post-collegiate lives. Mincing Lane Athletic Club (MLAC, 1863), founded in the wealthy heart of London's spice and tea trading district, was the first in a wave of amateur athletics clubs. It was followed by the Amateur Athletic Club (AAC, 1865), established by Old Etonian John G. Chambers, himself a prominent organiser of athletic competition during his formative years at Cambridge University.[5] Membership was restricted to 'gentlemen amateurs'. Across the Atlantic, William Curtis, Harry Buermeyer and John C. Babcock – who had recently founded a gymnasium in the financial and commercial district of

Manhattan – drew inspiration from this rising tide of English amateur athletics. They themselves were hardly upper-class elites, but rather grizzled Civil War veterans, who were at the forefront of an emergent American sporting culture, itself characterised by a deep-seated sense of frontier toughness and American exceptionalism. Together they founded the New York Athletic Club (NYAC, 1868),[6] with the local elite drawn to their ideology of character-building, masculine sport. The club would become the first among a tremendous surge of amateur athletics associations across the East Coast.

As Steven Pope argues, these clubs were attempting 'to draw class lines against the masses and to develop a new bourgeois leisure lifestyle'[7] – and in so doing, they were also developing a new code of amateur sport. NYAC co-founder Curtis provided a definition of amateurism that would become widely accepted:

> [An amateur is] any person who has never competed in an open competition, or for admission of money, or with professionals, for a prize, public money, or admission money, and who has never, at any period of his life, taught or assisted in the pursuit of athletic exercises as a means of livelihood.[8]

For a time, these clubs remained small and exclusive, but there were attempts among a burgeoning middle class to gain social distinction and prestige by replicating upper-class amateur sport. The number of amateur associations grew – and these clubs also began to (partially) relax their membership criteria. MLAC was re-badged as London Athletics Club (LAC), acknowledging a growing presence across London, and by 1874 it had 900 members. With success and size, these amateur athletics clubs came together, in the 1880s, to better regulate inter-club competition and create governing bodies that would oversee amateur sport for the next century: in Britain, the Amateur Athletics Association (AAA, 1880); in the United States, the Amateur Athletic Union (AAU, 1888). This new amateur sporting landscape would become dominant in the sport of athletics. While pedestrianism was still popular in the 1880s, it would not remain so for long in the face of a sustained amateur onslaught.[9]

The dominance of amateur athletics came to fruition, in 1896, with the first modern Olympic Games. The revival of this ancient

Greek sporting contest had been conceived by Baron Pierre de Coubertin, a French aristocrat and academic. He was concerned that French colonial power was threatened by the sporting virility of young men in Britain, Germany and the United States. Coubertin wanted to inspire a similar movement in France, based upon his belief that 'true education must deal with the muscular, the intellect, and with morality, all integrated in the same activity'.[10] Held to great acclaim – and with tremendous patriotic pomp – the 1896 Olympic Games launched a new type of athletic competition: the marathon.

Over the next decade there was an explosion of interest in this new endurance discipline. The first American marathon took place that same year, in New York, organised by the Knickerbocker Athletic Club.[11] The Boston Marathon was launched only a year later, in 1897. Amateur races quickly began to appear across the major cities of North America and Britain, organised and embraced by a growing number of amateur athletics clubs. Many of these new races were dubbed a 'marathon', although this was essentially a shorthand for endurance racing, and the distance of these races could vary considerably, from 10 through to 25 miles (the marathon was not standardised until 1921). In 1908, London hosted the fourth edition of the modern Olympic Games – and a year later the first full-length amateur marathon in Britain was established, in Manchester, followed shortly thereafter by the now-defunct Polytechnic Marathon in London.

As amateur athletics continued to grow in popularity, amid the international fervour surrounding the Olympic Games, it was diversifying and becoming shaped by important dimensions of class and ethnicity. The marathon was particularly attractive to lower middle-class participants, who had for several years been forming their own athletics clubs. These athletes often worked in technical trades – as machinists, carpenters, printers and so on – and they were able to reimagine the surrounding urban landscape as a ready-made training ground. Given the ethnic and cultural diversity of these cities – as with New York and London – sports clubs often reflected existing social dynamics. This could include fierce rivalries, such as those between Irish and Italian diasporas. Irish-heritage athletes would encounter particular success on both sides of the Atlantic, winning twenty-six medals between them for Britain, the United States and Canada in the 1908 London Olympics – a success that was especially pertinent given the context of Irish nationalism and the tense (sometimes violent) campaign for home rule.[12]

This new juggernaut – the 'marathon craze' – was replacing the old world of pedestrianism: now it was about the city marathon, local neighbourhood races, club rivalries, pavement pounding, Olympic prestige, a circuit of national and international championships, an emphasis on times, splits and personal bests, and a distinct aura of masculine bravado. Pamela Cooper illustrates just how successful and diverse the marathon had become within the circles of mostly working-class and lower middle-class urban amateurism:

> On 26 December 1908, a marathon sponsored by the New York Journal had more than 700 applicants; two-thirds of them were rejected because they were not members of the Amateur Athletic Union. Only 106 actually started the race, 53 finished, and Irish-born Matthew Maloney of the Trinity AC won in 2:36:26.2. The list of finishers shows mostly Irish surnames with several Italians appearing towards the back of the pack. Their affiliations were mainly middle-class clubs; 19 were not even sport club members. The marathon suddenly had become a popular event, the sport of the lower-middle-class and of minority groups.[13]

And yet women were entirely excluded from this new athletic culture. This was due in part to official prohibitions by the AAU and AAA, both of which considered the female body unsuitable for athletic competition, but it also stemmed from a values system that promoted sport as an expression of masculinity. American athletes were driven to address a perceived 'crisis of masculinity' (echoing a theme that can be found throughout the social history of sport), typified by Theodore Roosevelt's call, at the Chicago Athletic Club in 1899, for the 'strenuous life' wherein male virility was seen to be threatened by the absence of martial struggle and the closing of the American frontier. In Britain, there was a not dissimilar desire to express the superiority of patriarchal British imperialism and colonialism – for British athletes to strut the stage of international competition, and for everyday participants to play their part in the vigour of the British Empire. On both sides of the Atlantic, athletics provided a whetstone against which male competition, aggression and physicality could be sharpened.

In the space of several decades, then, athletics had been radically transformed. It was from within this new culture of amateur sport that American trail running would emerge.

It all began in San Francisco. The Sierra Club, following its formation at Stanford University in 1892, began almost immediately to hold organised hikes out across Marin County. This was an accessible locale, a short distance from the city, via ferry across the bay, and then through to Mill Valley on the newly constructed Sausalito-Tomales railroad. It was perfect for busy middle-class professionals seeking a weekend dose of nature-based therapy. Trips included long hikes out on the flanks of Mount Tamalpais – the highest point on the peninsula – and occasional overnight camping. It was a verdant paradise, slightly removed from, yet on the very doorstep of, this booming maritime metropolis.

At around the same time, the Olympic Club opened the doors of its first permanent clubhouse, in 1893. The San Francisco Olympic Club had been founded in 1860 by two brothers, Charles and Arthur Nahl. Both were German heritage, professional artists, who achieved distinction with their depiction of the American West and the Californian Gold Rush. They were also exceptional gymnasts. Their personal training ground – literally their backyard – would serve as the initial site of the Olympic Club. Over the following decades it would grow to include many different athletes – including boxers, golfers, hikers and amateur runners – and notable public figures such as media magnate and presidential candidate William Randolph Hearst (1863–1951). The Olympic Club was to remain an exclusive association; by the turn of the twentieth century it had a membership that reflected the upper strata of San Franciscan society. Yet, much like the city itself, it was culturally and ethnically diverse. In 1880, almost half of all those living in San Francisco were foreign-born, with notable Irish, German and Italian communities. As mineral wealth flooded into the city, the nouveaux riches were looking to emulate the cultural and social lives of a British-born upper class. This included sporting excellence and clubbable membership within exclusive associations.[14]

In 1904, two keen hikers from the Olympic Club – Italian American Alfons Coney and German American Charles Boas – decided to hold an unofficial race against each other. They would run from the Mill Valley train station, past the mill itself, over a creek, then up the steep (and now infamous) Dipsea Steps (numbering around 300 at the time – there are currently over 600), through woods and along narrow trails, out over the sides of Mount Tamalpais, to the Lone Tree and the highpoint of Cardiac Hill, and then down to the Dipsea Inn, nestled beside the lapping waves of the Pacific. The route was a little over 7 miles, with around 2,000 feet of rolling hills. Boas won – with money changing hands among the crowd of betting spectators – although there is no record of his finishing time. Regardless, the informal race made something of a stir.

A week later, Coney, Boas and their fellow hikers formed a new club, the Dipsea Indians. Members were still required to be affiliated with the Olympic Club. Timothy Fitzpatrick, an Irish American judge, was appointed as 'Grand Chief' to oversee and implement plans for an annual race. Two important decisions were made. First, the course would be marked, but runners would be free to choose an alternative route, which gave some leeway for judgement and creativity. Second, the race would be handicapped, with runners assigned a starting place based on their perceived ability. Runners with less ability – and this was decided by a committee – would be given a head start. In theory, anyone had a chance of winning the race. Over subsequent years, both children and the elderly would be counted among the list of race winners.[15]

In November 1905, 84 male runners lined up to begin the first official Dipsea race – this was a number that exceeded almost any marathon taking place in the United States during that era (Boston Marathon only had ten finishers that year). Given the prominence of the Olympic Club and the standing of the men involved, there was intense newspaper interest. Reporters from major newspapers in California were on hand to observe America's first 'trail' race – at the time still described as cross country – and in the following days it featured as a leading sports story, including this account by the *San Francisco Chronicle*:

> It was the most wonderful contest of the kind ever seen in California. Never in the history of athletics in the State has such an event ever before taken place. It is a question if such a gruelling event has ever been pulled off in any part of the world. The athletes went a little over nine miles, but in that distance they had to climb to an altitude of 1680 feet, and then come down to the waters edge. Not only was it a course of one mountain, but in the distance there were some three or four; none, however, was as high as the last, where the runners had to pass the Lone Tree. From that point it was all down hill to the sea, and when that was reached there were two miles of a stretch through soft sand.[16]

Crucially, the race had been opened to participants outside of the Olympic Club and it attracted a range of athletes from the surrounding area, including high school and college runners, and other amateur athletic associations. The winner (based on the handicap system) was John Hassard, a 17-year-old from Oakland High. In second place, with the fastest actual time, was local mail carrier Cornelius Connelly, another Irishman, who ran for the Emerald Gaelic Athletic Association, finishing in 1 hour 4 minutes and 22 seconds. There were 71 finishers in total. The event finished with a bonfire and potlatch on the beach, attended by 500 runners and guests.[17]

The race would continue in much the same fashion throughout the early twentieth century. The number of finishers remained relatively constant – usually somewhere between 40 and 80. In 1961, the number of finishers was 61. Yet three months later, in December of that year, President Kennedy called on Americans to become a 'nation of athletes' and not a 'nation of spectators' – an echo of Roosevelt's 'strenuous life'. It was a patriotic call to athleticism that contributed to the 'running boom' of the 1960s and 1970s (see Chapter 6), and by 1970 the number of Dipsea finishers had risen to an incredible 941. Runners were typically of European descent, barring a small number of exceptions, such as the entry of a seven-man

Japanese team – the Showa Athletic Club – in 1928, and the first African American finisher, Fred McWilliams, in 1922.[18] While it had been established – and continued to be led – by middle-class Americans, the Dipsea race proved to be an attractive outlet for working-class athletes, especially Irish and Italian Americans living in the bustle of the San Franciscan metropolis. However, governed by AAU rules, it was an exclusively male race.

Nancy Dreyer, a nurse from Berkeley, was the first woman to run the Dipsea race unofficially, in 1950. This was a full sixteen years before Roberta Gibbs became the first woman to complete the Boston Marathon (also unofficially). AAU rules changed in 1971, after which time women started to become official entrants to the Dipsea race. An annual 'Dipsea hike for girls' had been launched in 1918, although it only ran for four years. It was named a 'hike' – although it was in reality a race – so as to avoid AAU proscriptions concerning female competition. The first annual hike had 148 finishers, that year exceeding the number of finishers for the better-known Dipsea race. The organiser, George James – who maintained the rather anachronistic tradition of kissing the female winner of the competition – was to give an excited account following the first hike:

> [It] was a sight to remember, seeing these young ladies in the flower of youth, with clear eyes, cheeks flushed a picture of health, coming down the stretch, some strong while others began to wobble but all game to the core – a fitting tribute to a clean life and outdoor athletics.[19]

Despite his gendered and patronising tone, James was essentially a progressive when it came to female involvement in sport. In other social circles, the Dipsea hike was controversial, with newspaper articles and letters from men that questioned the impact of hiking on female 'beauty'. One female participant, Emma Reimann, wrote a reply to the *San Francisco Examiner*:

> Mr. Stanlaws doesn't know what he's talking about. He ought to see the group of us that have formed an athletic club, with Professor Edward B. Sparks as director. We go out almost every week the year round, and I don't think he'd find anything to complain about ... As to making the skin coarse, I prefer sunlight to the rouge box any day.[20]

Reimann went on to set a female course record in 1922. Her time of 1 hour 12 minutes and 6 seconds would not be beaten until 1969 – it was also faster than ten of the men competing in the Dipsea race that year.[21] This would be the final female hike. It was cancelled as a result of pressure from local clergy and physicians, who were concerned about immodesty and the physical strain placed on the female body.[22]

In contrast, the official Dipsea race was thriving. It continued to draw a mixed crowd of athletes from across California, becoming an important annual sporting event for inter-club competition. Several Dipsea runners would go on to represent the United States at the Olympic Games. It also attracted a continuing number of hikers and outdoor enthusiasts, including members of the Sierra Club and the California Alpine Club (CAC). Both clubs played an important role in developing and maintaining the trail network of Mount Tamalpais, so it was only natural that their members would be drawn to the race itself. The varied nature of trail running – sitting at the interstices of athletics and hiking – was a characteristic of the Dipsea race from the start.

Was this the very first trail race? Almost certainly. The term 'trail racing' was already in wide use throughout the nineteenth and early twentieth century, both in Britain and the United States. Rather than referring to foot racing, trail racing was a term used specifically in Britain for hound and horse racing on scent-marked countryside trails. Throughout the twentieth century, it was also used widely in Canada and the American West to describe skiing down a marked course. The language and concept of racing along a marked trail was therefore already in wide circulation and applying it to running was a natural evolution of the term. The Dipsea race was itself initially described as cross country, and this language would persist for decades, but in relation to running it gradually adopted and indeed helped to pioneer the term 'trail racing'. Perhaps the earliest reference to the 'Dipsea trail race' came in a 1912 article, published by the *San Francisco Call and Post*.[23] No doubt the newspaper was picking up on language already in use by runners and hikers in the Mount Tamalpais area.

The term made sense. The Dipsea race was different to cross country, which takes place on flatter and more runnable terrain, such as woods and fields that are adjacent to towns, schools and colleges. In contrast, the Dipsea race went out over a steeper and more remote landscape. Cross-country racing was also linked predominantly to collegiate competition, whereas the Dipsea race sprang from a combined culture of hiking and amateur athletic competition. Because hiking clubs played such a critical role in building and maintaining an American trail network – including the trails out over Mount Tamalpais – it made sense for these participants to begin describing the Dipsea race as a 'trail race'. The term 'trail racing' therefore sprang from several sources: it borrowed from language already in use to describe horse/hound and ski racing; it expressed an urge to capture the unique character and landscape of the Dipsea race; and it acknowledged and celebrated the marked 'trail' as a distinctive feature of the American outdoor landscape.

Following the early success of the Dipsea race, there were efforts to replicate the trail racing format in other parts of the United States. As word of the Dipsea race began to spread, California was the first and most obvious location for a second trail race.

On 29 April 1908, less than three years after the establishment of Dipsea, a race was organised up Mount Wilson, in the Sierra Madre range overlooking Los Angeles. Mount Wilson had long been a favoured hiking destination for local residents – partly inspired by the opening of the observatory in 1904 – and several attempts had been made for a speed record to the summit. The race was organised by local businessman Charles J. Fox, the editor of the *National Police Gazette* (an illustrated sporting magazine), and Eugene Estoppey, a champion runner, of Swiss extraction, who had placed sixth in the 1899 Boston Marathon. Estoppey would later achieve fame as an ultra-distance runner, which included participation in the transcontinental race of 1928 (see Chapter 4). The 'marathon craze' was taking over Los Angeles, with the establishment that year, also by Estoppey, of the Los Angeles to Venice marathon. The 'Mount Wilson hill climb' as it was usually known – although it was also referred to in 1908 as a 'trail race' by the *Los Angeles Times*[24] – began with 20 runners lining up, ready for the 7 mile, 2,000 foot climb to the top, where they would then turn around for the rapid descent back to the start. It was witnessed by hundreds of spectators, with marshals lining the route to offer assistance and encouragement. Irish American and serving soldier Joseph King, from San Francisco's Olympic Club, won the race in a time of 1 hour and 25 minutes. Local and ethnic rivalries were clearly on display: King was photographed wearing a vest emblazoned with crossed Gaelic and American flags, alongside Estoppey (who placed fifth) sporting the Swiss national flag.[25]

The race was considered a great success – matching the number of competitors in the 1908 Los Angeles Marathon – and it was won the following year by Edward Dietrich, who had also been victorious at that first local marathon.[26] The newspaper accounts surrounding these two very different events make for fascinating reading. A Californian running scene was beginning to develop around a tight clique of competitors. This new Californian athletic fraternity included successful Olympic Club and Dipsea runners, such as Cornelius Connelly and Joseph King, who both travelled down to compete against the best that Los Angeles had to offer. The marathon and the hill climb were held in equal regard as a test of running prowess. Towards the end of 1908, Estoppey – for money – would run up and down Mount Wilson three times (21 miles and 6,000 feet of ascent). And then, in 1909, he was challenged to a 120 mile race, from Los Angeles through to San Diego, by the Austrian mountaineer Paul Reinwald.[27] This race did not eventually take place, but it illustrated that there was an interest in experimentation away from the strictures of amateur athletics.

In 1909, the second year of the event, coverage of the Mount Wilson hill race was dominated by a story that made syndicated news across the United States – of a female 'hermit' who ran the race in an unofficial capacity:

> As the last registered contestant left the foot of the trail Thursday morning on the second annual Mount Wilson race, the hundreds of spectators were startled by the appearance of a woman, 50 years of

> age, garbed in skin-fitting tights and wearing a crimson blouse; deftly offset with a baby-blue headgear of fluffy material which streamed down her back and dangled almost to her heels … Her name was ascertained to be Mrs Marie A. Riedeselle, a well-known character about the Santa Anita canyon, who lives as a hermit and thrives as a vegetarian … After posing for her picture, she was sent away by the starter with the usual 'formalities'. She left the foot of the trail at 8:45 o'clock and negotiated the distance to the top in 2:05 … Judges at the summit asserted that she finished quite strong and in much better condition that many of the male contestants.[28]

Female runners were unable to compete officially – as was standard with all AAU events – and Riedeselle blazed a precedent as perhaps the first woman to run not just a trail race, but also to run unofficially in an AAU-governed race. She is a compelling figure. An accomplished cyclist, Riedeselle won a competition in 1893 for designing practical bicycle clothing for women, following which she lived in the mining camps of Klondike, Alaska, where she designed and sold cold weather clothing.[29] Riedeselle then moved to California for a life of seclusion and self-sufficiency. In 1907 she gave the following account to a curious reporter:

> I suppose you wonder why I live out here all alone. It does seem strange, but, ah, this is the life to live! It is the life of a free woman, unchecked and free from the trammels of a sordid civilization which binds its devotees to the petty conveniences of life.[30]

It is doubtful that Riedeselle considered herself a 'trail runner', or even a 'runner'. Yet her moving and articulate statement of the good life – and her fierce independence – certainly encapsulate what would become defining values in the rugged adventurism of American trail running.

Despite propositions for other similar events – including in Yosemite – the Dipsea and Mount Wilson races were to be the only trail races established in California during the early part of the twentieth century. This was in contrast to the more successful growth of track and road running events across the state and other parts of the United States. The post-Olympic 'marathon craze' seemingly provided a sufficient and convenient outlet for prospective athletes.

As amateur athletics grew and developed – with increasing inter-state and national competition – there were attempts elsewhere in the United States at experimentation. The concept of a 'mountain marathon' was particularly inspiring to many American athletes. It was a ramping up of difficulty and athletic grit. Marathons were hard. Mountain climbing was hard. Running a marathon up a mountain? Well, that was just a logical way to push athletic achievement. From the 1910s through to the 1930s a small number of these mountain marathons were established across the United States. Typically, they were not trail races – they usually followed roads or rutted dirt tracks that were traversable by automobile – nor did they extend as far as the modern marathon distance. Organisationally, they slotted into the annual AAU calendar – which meant that women were excluded – and they were part of a rapidly expanding schedule of 'marathon' races. By the 1920s, it was commonplace for elite runners to criss-cross the country and represent their local athletic club at prestigious races in different states.

The Cheyenne Mountain Marathon – a true mountain-running event – was held only once, in 1926, despite plans to make this an annual event. It continued a fascination with Native American running – something that had been initiated in the nineteenth century with the Tarahumara – and it was billed explicitly as a contest between 'Indian' and 'white man'.[31] The course ran for 6 miles along the newly constructed highway, up from Broadmoor to the summit of Cheyenne mountain, with just under 3,000 feet of climbing, reaching a total elevation of over 9,500 feet. The race had been organised by local millionaire Spencer Penrose, with the aim of testing the mountain endurance of Native Americans against the best competitive marathon runners in the United States. Twelve runners toed the start line, of whom eight were Native American (from the Hopi, Zuni, Acoma and Pueblo), three were European Americans, and there was an additional sole Swiss runner. The Native American runners triumphed, taking the first eight places. The winner, Pohoquaptewa, a Hopi from Arizona, had already been cementing regional fame during the 1920s, with successive victories at the New Mexico Gallup Marathon, and a brief but intriguing reference to setting a record on the 'Pikes Peak run'.[32] An official Pikes Peak race did not exist at the time – with the exception of a famous automobile event (also established by Spencer Penrose) – but it is likely that unofficial records for the Pikes Peak ascent were being documented locally.

Official races up Pikes Peak began to be organised from the 1930s. The first race took place in 1936. It was a one-off event, held to celebrate the takeover of the summit automobile road by the Forest Service (until this time it was a private toll road, also owned by the rather wealthy Penrose). Twenty-seven locals, including two women, started this ascent-only race, which ran up the steep and winding Barr Trail to the summit. Lou Wille made it to the summit first, in just over 3 hours – one of only 19 finishers – with 21-year-old Agnes Nellesen topping out in 6 hours as the first woman.[33] Wille would be back, more than two decades later, to compete in the revival of the (modern) Pikes Peak Marathon in 1956 (see Chapter 6).

A second Pikes Peak race took place in 1938 – now officially called the 'Pikes Peak Marathon' – and this time it drew in a more established group of athletes from across the United States. It was only a 12 mile course, but with serious elevation gain, running up from Crystal Creek, along the highway and a short stretch of trail, before cresting out at the summit. With a total ascent of 5,280 feet (exactly one mile), it was dubbed a 'vertical mile race' by excited newspaper pundits. The race was widely covered across the sporting print media, with *TIME* magazine providing a particularly colourful first-hand account:

> Clyde Ormsby, Colorado steelworker, removed his false teeth just after the starting gun, gave them to a highway patrolman. Gordon Mace of Estes Park, greased from head to toe, collapsed. John Sutak, onetime Colorado College footballer, sandwiched between signs advertising 'Sutak's Peanuts,' sprinted ahead of the field, dropped out from exhaustion after two miles. An ambulance followed the procession, picked up those who fell. For those who survived, barrels of water—placed a mile apart—served as combination drinking troughs and bathing pools ... First to break the tape was Boston's 119-lb. Francis Darrah, a seasoned distance runner at 25, whose time of 2 hr., 8 min., 14.6 sec. was the fastest ever made on foot up the mountain.[34]

The race would run for only two years, before falling into abeyance due to the onset of the Second World War.

As marathon running boomed across the contiguous United States, something rather more modest was taking place in Alaska. During the Fourth of July celebrations in 1909, in the small town of Seward, local dog musher Al Taylor accepted a wager to run an out-and-back to the summit of the unnamed mountain overlooking the town:

> Taylor, dressed in his Sunday-best white shirt, woolen trousers, and leather boots, ran up the dusty street and into the woods. Within an hour he reappeared. Shouts erupted from the bar patrons, who flooded outside to cheer Taylor on. Watches were checked and the verdict given. He missed the goal. By minutes. A dusty, tired, and thirsty Taylor sauntered into the bar and bought drinks for the house.[35]

This was the first unofficial 'race' – dubbed a 'marathon' by Seward locals – and a year later the unnamed peak became known as Marathon Hill, later evolving into Mount Marathon. The course might lack anything comparable to the distance of an actual marathon – it is only around 3 miles – but it climbs for almost 3,000 feet, largely off-trail, with a descent that involves glissading down snow fields, over loose shale, mud slides, and a rocky waterfall near the finish. The first official race was held in 1915 – and it has run continuously since this time.

Until 1950 the race would only attract a handful of local competitors, never more than eight, and all were men. But gradually the reputation of the race would begin to grow, drawing in runners from across Alaska, other parts of the United States, and eventually attracting international athletes. Women would enter in 1963 – nearly a decade before they were allowed to officially compete in AAU-organised marathons – when three locals participated: Ann Wemark, Madeline Hicklin and Jane Trigg.[36] Race officials protested, but the rules did not specifically prevent women from running. They all finished, and the door was opened for women to compete, although the first official women's race did not take place until 1985. Even in this remote location, the 'marathon craze' of amateur athletics could be found playing a formative role in shaping a new and exciting sporting culture.

Across the Atlantic, the growth of amateur athletics posed a dilemma for professional fell racing in Britain. To attract a higher calibre of athlete – including aspiring Olympians – and to be part of mainstream athletic culture, it was necessary to abide by AAA amateur rules. Yet most professional fell race organisers and runners in the north of England were not willing to do this. The practice of awarding a cash prize pre-dated the rules of amateurism. Why should they listen to a distant organisation, established by Old Etonians, down at Oxford University? They themselves already attracted large crowds and a good calibre of racer; there was no pressing need to do anything different. Yet this meant that professional fell runners faced the prospect of a lifetime amateur ban by the AAA. Ultimately, for working-class athletes in the north of England, it was no choice at all. Professional fell races provided local kudos and prize money. If this meant not being able to run in these new amateur events, well then, so be it. The institutionalisation of amateur running in Britain therefore ensured that professional fell running would remain a small, idiosyncratic and isolated sporting culture – this was of course in contrast to American trail and mountain running, which had emerged within this new culture of amateur athletics.

While the beating heart of English fell running was to be found in these professional races – and this remained the case until after the Second World War – elsewhere in Britain a parallel tradition of amateur fell running was slowly beginning to develop. Given the changing landscape of athletics, it made sense for these new races to be established under now-dominant AAA amateur rules. The dozen or so fell races founded in the first half of the twentieth century were nearly all amateur – the most famous of these would be Ben Nevis.

A nineteenth-century tourism boom in the Scottish Highlands, partly prompted by a high-profile visit from Queen Victoria in 1873, encouraged intense interest in the ascent of Ben Nevis.[37] The construction of the West Highland railway line to Fort William, in 1894, and the creation of a public bridleway to the summit, helped to ensure that Britain's highest peak was accessible for visiting tourists. Interest in scaling the mountain quickly became a celebrated challenge, inevitably leading to speculation about 'the record'. On 27 September 1895, 27-year-old William Swan, a local Fort William resident, made the first official timed ascent of Ben Nevis:

> Mr William Swan, tobacconist here, ascended Ben Nevis with the object of establishing a record. The day was exceedingly hot and unsuitable for mountaineering, but, notwithstanding, Mr Swan managed to reach the summit, and, after drinking a cup of Bovril, returned to Fort William in the incredibly short space of 2 hours 41 minutes. This is believed to be a record.[38]

Newspapers began to document the Ben Nevis 'mania' that gripped public imagination: the fastest person, the oldest, the youngest, the first woman. Excited coverage ensured that these feats were shared and celebrated by a fascinated audience.

Over the next three years a small number of prospective challengers made the journey to Fort William for a serious attempt at beating this new record. Competitors included Lieutenant Colonel Spencer Acklom (1897), fresh from serving in the Himalayas, and William MacDonald (1898), a skilled tradesman, sent by his local working-men's athletic club, Leith Gymnasium, to claim the record on their behalf. Competing versions of masculine and class pride were on the line, from the staunch colonial military figure setting out to demonstrate the vitality of his training and upbringing, to the scrappy working-class boy laying a claim to fleet-footedness over local Scottish hills. MacDonald was ultimately the faster of the two, setting a record in 2 hours and 27 minutes, beating Acklom's time by almost a 30-minute margin, although there was some dispute about the exact starting and finishing location in Fort William.[39]

A formal race was proposed to finally 'settle the matter', although this was perhaps more about cashing in on heightened publicity rather than a concern with the integrity of the record itself. On 3 June 1898, the Lochiel Arms Hotel offered a gold medal to the winner of a race up Ben Nevis. Upon hearing this news, the genteel Acklom, no doubt steeped in the culture of upper-class amateurism, dismissively remarked: 'True sportsmen contend for sport, not reward.' He refused to participate. Despite this supposed 'reward', the race was held under Scottish Amateur Athletic Association

(SAAA) rules and became part of an emerging calendar of amateur athletic events in Britain. Ten competitors took part in this first official competition – all men – leaping forward at the sound of the starting shotgun. A reporter from the *Glasgow Daily Mail* witnessed the account firsthand:

> An interested crowd witnessed the start, and followed with the eye the progress of the sprint up the mountain side. Although dull, the weather was otherwise favourable, but there was a good deal of fresh snow on the higher reaches of Ben Nevis as well as an occasional bank of fog, which, doubtless, hindered the climbers to some extent. Considerable diversity of opinion prevailed as to who the probable winner would be, as those who took part in the race included well-known athletes and harriers from Edinburgh and other places in the south.[40]

The winner, Hugh Kennedy, a Fort William gamekeeper, crossed the finishing line in 2 hours and 41 minutes. Another win for local Scottish pride.

There would be several variations of the Ben Nevis race over the next three years, before interest waned and the race became defunct. It was eventually relaunched in 1937, and then relaunched *again* in 1951, growing within the decade to a roster of over 100 runners and with spectating crowds in their hundreds.[41] While these early record and race attempts were dominated by men, there were notable efforts by women to defy the gender proscriptions of the time. This included Lucy Cameron in 1902, followed later that year by Elizabeth Tait, who set a record for the ascent of 1 hour 59 minutes and 30 seconds.[42] This record would stand until 1955, when it was beaten by 16-year-old Kathleen Connochie, the first female competitor to take part in an organised Ben Nevis race – a highly symbolic moment for the much later history of the sport (see Chapter 6).[43]

Just as Ben Nevis – the mountain – stands astride the British Isles, so too would this historic race continue to play a dominant role in the developing culture of mountain running.

As the old world of pedestrianism faded away, the marathon had now become perceived as the ultimate test of endurance. British fell running was changing and adapting to this new world of amateur athletics, while American trail and mountain running represented experimentation at the outer edge of this new and dominant athletic culture. While the early twentieth century was a remarkable period of growth and change – one of several 'running booms' that would punctuate the history of athletics – the diarchy of amateurism and Olympian sport was smothering any real interest in extreme acts of endurance. Elite endurance athletes were largely, and understandably, drawn to the tempting lure of marathon glory.

And yet, away from the limelight of Olympic competition, there would prove to be a small number who sought to keep the flame of ultra-distance athletics burning.

Chapter 4

Hard times

Picture the scene: 5.30 a.m. on a grey and blustery Thursday morning, 1 May 1903. A crowd gathers around Westminster Baths in London. Shivering in the gloom, groups of men in starch-white athletic attire stretch and hop around on rain-slicked cobbles, their pale faces glancing up at dark clouds. Even at this early hour, hundreds of intrigued spectators are milling around. Automobiles honk through the throng, searching for a space to park. Traders and bill-boarded hawkers call out to prospective customers.

At 6.25 a.m. the athletes are ushered to the Palace of Westminster, where a start line is marked out below Big Ben. A jostling crowd has formed – as many as 30,000 according to some reports – lining the streets and sides of London Bridge.[1] Minutes later, at 6.33 a.m., a well-known boxing referee, Bernard Angle, shouts 'Go!' – and just like that, led by a procession of mounted police, 87 athletes are off with swinging arms and a fast-walking trot. Most are dressed in knee-length shorts, long-sleeved jerseys, tight-fitting leather caps and rubber-soled plimsolls.[2]

So begins the amateur London to Brighton racewalking event, organised by young stockbrokers based in the financial heart of the city. The race is taking place on a 53 mile route that for much of the next century will in various guises be the pinnacle route of ultra-distance athletics, as a testing ground for both elite runners and amateur walkers. The competitors were right to be worried, it did indeed rain again later that day – a deluge for more than half of the race – but the victor, E. P. Broad, arrives at Brighton Aquarium a little over 9 hours and 30 minutes later, escorted by police cars and watched by crowds and local officials. It is a rather modest amateur racewalking result – hours slower than the existing running record.

Only a month later, a professional running race would take place on that very same route, incentivised by a cash prize from the *Evening Standard* – fifty guineas for the winner (around £8,000 today) – with a 5 a.m. start beside Westminster Bridge, once again in the pouring rain.[3] The race favourite, Len Hurst, was out to prove something – and he did, sailing to the finish in 6:32:34, a new record that would stand for two decades. A bricklayer by trade, Hurst had been blacklisted from amateur sport at the age of fifteen, in 1887, for taking part in a local prize-giving event. His 'professional' status had tragically barred him from Olympic qualification in 1896.[4] Seething with frustration, he entered the inaugural Paris Marathon – the world's first city marathon – an event open to professionals, held only three months after the official Olympic marathon.[5] Hurst triumphed, finishing in 2:31:30. It was a world record, 27 minutes faster than the Olympic champion that year, but one that would remain entirely unrecognised by official governing bodies. Hurst was Britain's finest distance runner – who would compete in everything from the marathon to the six-day race – but he was also trapped within a small and diminishing circuit of professional running.

The fact that there were *two* London to Brighton races, only a month apart, highlights the fissure that was ripping through the world of athletics. There were now separate athletic ecospheres – professional and amateur – each with differing codes of conduct and varying dramatis personae.[6] As a sporting discipline, ultra-distance athletics had long been inseparable from professional pedestrianism. Yet the final race of the pedestrian era had taken place that same year, in 1903, with a six-day relay race in Philadelphia. It would be the last such race for a long time – 24-hour and six-day racing would not be revived again until the 1980s. Meanwhile, amateur athletics was ruthlessly focused on the marathon and other Olympic-standard formats.

The first half of the twentieth century – a period marked by hyper-nationalism, war and economic hardship – would be a low point for ultra-distance athletics: neither a recreational sport, nor a focus for elite competition. In Britain, there would be a flicker of interest in the amateur discipline of racewalking. Meanwhile, in the United States, attempts would be made to revive professional ultra-distance running. These moments of revival were occasionally spectacular, even historically significant – as with the transcontinental races of 1928 and 1929 – but there was no longer any public appetite for ultra-distance athletics in a world of packed football and baseball stadiums.

Generational memories would fade, the extraordinary feats of pedestrianism would drift into legend and, by the middle of the century, ultra-distance athletics would be largely extinguished.

As a renowned violinist with the Newcastle Orchestra, Tom Payne was perhaps an unlikely figure to help briefly revive ultra-distance athletics and shepherd it into an era of mass-mediated sport. The footage is remarkable, in a 1920 newsreel clip, filmed by media giant and pioneer of cinematic journalism British Pathé, at the London to Brighton racewalk on 30 September.[7] This was not the first time that the London to Brighton race had been captured on film – Pathé journalists were there the year before at the 1919 race (also won by Payne) – but the 1920 finish was spectacular. Payne, a short and wiry man, with spectacles and a receding hairline, is filmed as he arrives in Brighton with a characteristic racewalking chicken trot. Surrounded by a mob of well-wishers at the finish – a pipe-smoking, fedora-wearing AAA official vigorously shaking his hand and grinning into the camera – Payne sobs and shakes, confused and overcome by the attention. It was the birth of a new media age: Payne was the first ultra-distance athlete to be captured on film. For the first time, distant followers of the sport and a curious public were able to witness the raw emotion of a race finish.

First shown in European and American cinemas from 1909, newsreels were quickly becoming a dominant form of media, and would remain so until the advent of television in the post-war era.

Newsreel topics would vary, from political news and world affairs, to sport and entertainment.[8] By the 1920s, significantly more people were viewing sport through newsreels than they were in person at events themselves. As Mike Huggins argues, they provided 'powerful ideological reinforcement of wider cultural sporting attitudes', most particularly by framing sport as a masculine and gladiatorial contest: a spectacle for baying crowds, seasoned with codes of amateurism and sportsmanship.[9] And yet, the 1920 depiction of Payne cut against these dominant ideas within sport: he was portrayed not as gladiator but as fragile survivor – a media framing that has particular resonance for contemporary depictions of ultrarunning.[10]

This was a significant shift in the media depiction of ultra-distance athletics. Newspaper accounts had traditionally focused on the competitive and statistical aspects of racing – how fast and how far – yet these newsreel accounts of racewalking were beginning to shift attention to the emotive experience of the competitors. Distance and speed might be important, but the personal story of the competitors was also brought into focus. Later that decade, depictions of the transcontinental races (see later in this chapter) would similarly try to capture the experience of runners – such as their sweltering struggle across the Mojave Desert, or participants laughing together in a moment of downtime[11] – rather than focusing on the up and down of the race itself. Ultra-distance athletics was becoming seen as idiosyncratic adventure and heroic struggle rather than as traditional competitive 'sport'.

In 1920, Payne was himself at the pinnacle of his career: sponsored by the makers of Phospherine, a health tonic made famous by soldiers during the First World War, and with a recent biographical pamphlet detailing his sporting success and martial credentials as a former serviceman.[12] Yet he was also about to see an enforced end to his career. A year later, in 1921, he performed a musical act that involved bursting through a large paper recreation of the Brighton finish line. Dressed in shorts and a running vest – and under the billing of 'World-Famous Musician-Athlete – he proceeded to play the violin before a paying audience.[13] Shockingly, the AAA considered this a breach of amateur rules and Payne was banned from amateur athletics, until his readmittance a decade later, in 1931.[14] By this time, approaching his fiftieth year, he had passed peak athletic ability. Despite this rather abrupt end, a rundown of Payne's career provides a fascinating insight into the nature of ultra-distance athletics during the fifteen years of his dominance.

By the time that Payne developed an interest in athletics, the 1903 London to Brighton stockbrokers' race had helped to kickstart widespread interest across Britain in amateur racewalking. While those aspiring to Olympic running glory focused their efforts on the marathon and sub-marathon distance – and elite runners, like Len Hurst, competed in a blacklisted circuit of professional racing – on the periphery of mainstream amateur athletics a small group of endurance specialists continued a tradition of long-distance walking. These were not 'running' events. Rather, a 'heel to toe' gait was expected and usually enforced by race officials, with a set of rules that had been codified by the AAA in 1880.[15] It was at the time almost the only way in which endurance athletes would compete on foot over distances that exceeded the marathon.[16]

As a budding young musician in the early 1900s, and with a limited income, Payne began to walk regularly from his home in South Shields to orchestral practice in Newcastle. This 28 mile round trip saw him unwittingly build up a deep and consistent base of training. Persuaded in 1906 to enter one of the new race-walking events, the Spencer Cup, a 24 mile circuit around South Shields, he finished in second place. This result was considered outstanding for a novice. His athletic career soon began with gusto: Payne began to win and set records on a series of newly established racewalks. Most notably these included Manchester to Blackpool (48.25 miles), the Bradford 'Whitsun' Walk (40.5 miles) and the famous London to Brighton (53 miles). Following the format of the 1903 stockbrokers' race, these events typically pulled in a starting list of somewhere between 50 and 100 competitors, and they were organised by local athletics clubs, walking associations and voluntary committees.

The participants themselves were mostly from among the urban middle classes, such as clerks and cotton merchants, all of them kitted out in the latest sporting apparel and seeking to apply modern regimes of training and nutrition. Spurred by the introduction of racewalking into the Olympics, track events also began to be organised from 1908. Payne himself set a non-stop 24-hour walking record of 127 miles, in the 1909 track race at White City Stadium in London (a world record for non-stop walking that still stands today).[17] Like many athletes of the time, Payne's sporting career was interrupted by the outbreak of war in 1914 – all races were cancelled – although he returned in 1917 to notch up a series of wins before the eventual end of his athletic career in 1921.

Racewalking during the early part of the twentieth century was fascinating. It appealed for the first time to recreational athletes – in contrast to professional pedestrianism – and participation was largely driven by 'an urban middle-class who were guided and inspired by public-school practices' whereby 'sport was seen to have important social and moral attributes'.[18] It was this morality that often expressed deeply held ideas of masculinity and social class. Punishing athletic events were an opportunity for men to show 'good character' through physical and mental fortitude.[19] The Boer War at the turn of the twentieth century – followed by the outbreak of the First World War in 1914 – fomented a culture of martial manliness, in both Britain and the United States.[20] School educators and sports officials argued that athletics programmes and events would help to hone a tough and disciplined generation of men, better suited for nationalistic ambitions relating to industrial and military dominance.[21]

Payne's 1921 biographical pamphlet drives home this point. A chronological portrait of his athletic career is interspersed with testimonials from former servicemen about the health benefits of Payne's sponsor, Phospherine, which claimed to bestow athletes and soldiers alike with the ability to survive 'unequalled rigours, hardships and perils'.[22] Channelling the spirit of the times, a 'brotherhood' of the Centurions was formed at a London hotel in 1911 to celebrate and recognise those who had successfully walked 100 miles within 24 hours. The name, of course, referenced the numerical mark of distance, but it also played on references to a Roman militarism that was romanticised across imperial Britain. The club badge depicted a Roman legionnaire, standing boldly, legs astride, with sword, shield and crested helm: athlete/soldier, soldier/athlete. Tom Payne was awarded Centurion badge number 18.

The Union Stock Yards in Chicago at the turn of the twentieth century must have been an overwhelming place: a vast, sprawling complex of animal pens, abattoirs and meat packing facilities. It employed 25,000 workers, who between them butchered, packed and shipped over 400 million animals per year.[23] Incredibly, it was processing almost all the meat consumed by an American public that was only just then beginning to develop a taste for hamburgers and hotdogs.[24]

We will never know what 22-year-old Frenchman and recent immigrant Albert Corey thought as he stepped into those yards in 1903, but given a deep self-confidence and bluff exterior, he no doubt strode confidently into that clamour of mechanised slaughter. The meat industry would provide a living for Corey – he was there as a strike breaker to undercut industrial action – but it was amateur athletics that would bring him national acclaim in his new and adopted country.

Having joined the French army in 1896, Corey had been encouraged by his superiors to develop an undoubted talent for endurance running.[25] By the time he arrived in Chicago, essentially having deserted the armed forces, the heady days of indoor pedestrianism at the Interstate Exposition Building in Chicago were gone. They had been replaced by a competitive amateur athletic culture that had coalesced around the Chicago Athletic Association. Turning up unannounced for their marathon training on 10 August 1904, he impressed them not just with his easy running style, but with claims to have run the 1900 Paris marathon and set a 100 mile record in 1899 – 'I have lots of records', he confidently told them in broken English.[26] There is some doubt now about the veracity of these claims, but at the time it was enough: he was on the team. Three weeks later he won two silver medals at the St. Louis Olympics, in the marathon and the relay race.[27]

Corey would distinguish himself as a successful marathon runner over the next half decade. Yet in Chicago there was still a flicker of interest in ultra-distance running – after all, this was the home of Daniel O'Leary, a hub of American pedestrianism that had been second only to New York. Chagrined at the uncertainty surrounding his claim to a 100 mile world record, Corey began to set his sights on achieving a verified North American record. Indoor multi-day racing had effectively ended in the United States, so Corey began to target an old pedestrian road record: the '100 mile' Milwaukee to Chicago route (it was actually between 90 and 95 miles). Notably, he also sought approval from the official custodians of amateur sport, the AAU, who agreed to witness and verify his attempt.

Corey's first effort, in December 1905, was a solo record attempt, accompanied by pacers, a supporting automobile crew, and Walter Liginger from the AAU.[28] It proved to be a disaster. The roads were in a terrible state after heavy rain – thick mud that coated his shoes like cement – and as he struggled along, his pace slowing and spirits fading, the supporting automobile ran out of fuel. Pushing ahead, Corey found himself lost for several hours in darkness. He finished in a little under 24 hours, but with typical bullishness declared: 'I am confident that I can do the distance in sixteen hours or less.'[29] The next attempt, in September 1906, was organised in the form of a two-man race, between Corey and Alphonse Thibeau, a talented French-Canadian runner living in Chicago. Liginger reprised his role as the official AAU representative. Because this was an actual race – albeit only between two competitors – it was the first time that the AAU were to sanction an ultra-distance race (something they would not do again until the ultrarunning revival of the 1960s). The race also included a link to the old world of pedestrianism: Frank Hart, now a running coach, was there to provide support and encouragement.[30] Unfortunately, once again, muddy roads and a failing automobile conspired to end the attempt. Both Corey and Thibeau dropped out together at Racine, after a little over four hours. Finally, on his third attempt, in October 1907, racing against local rival Sidney Hatch, Corey succeeded in breaking the record. He finished in a time of 18 hours and 33 minutes – credited as a world amateur 100 mile record (although slower than professional pedestrian records) – with Corey breezily telling reporters at the finish that the run was 'child's play'.[31]

Corey and his record attempts were typical of ultra-distance running in the United States during the first half of the twentieth century. Incredibly, given the racing culture of pedestrianism only decades before, there were few organised races that went beyond the standard marathon distance. The Olympic Games had sparked a new era of amateur athletics, but it also quickly normalised the maximum distance that endurance athletes were expected to run. Unlike in Britain, racewalking had not taken off as either sport or recreation. If you wanted to challenge an existing ultra-distance record, then you had to organise the attempt yourself – there were simply no scheduled or recurring ultra-distance races that one could compete in. A hidebound AAU was not normally interested in supporting races of this distance. It was only Corey's status as an Olympic medal winner that persuaded them to observe and ratify his record attempts.

Sidney Hatch faced a similar dilemma – he had endurance talent, but no ultra-distance races to channel this ability through. Born in the rapidly expanding suburbs of Chicago, 21-year-old Hatch competed alongside Corey at the 1904 Olympics. Over the following decade he would compete at the highest level across the United States, including three top ten finishes at the Boston Marathon. Rather than embodying the cliché of obsessive track athlete, Hatch was relaxed and creative, experimenting with cross country and pushing the distance as he trained on the dirt tracks and trails around the outer the edge of the city.

A year after competing in the 1908 London Olympics (his second and final appearance on the international stage), Hatch leapt at the opportunity to compete in a 100 mile race organised by the American Roller and Cycle Club in Chicago. The aim of the race was to beat Corey's 100 mile amateur world record. It all came together quickly. In July 1909, a small group of elite Chicagoan runners were selected – seven of whom would actually compete in the race – and a date was set for a little less than two weeks hence.

They trained as a group, taking long runs out together in the surrounding countryside.[32] Hatch was considered the favourite, although Charles Lobert, another competitive marathon runner, fancied his chances and cheekily told reporters that he would beat Corey's record.

The race started at 1.32 a.m. (presumably timed to allow an early evening finish for the expectant crowds), with the athletes running loops around a grassy field at Riverview amusement park, the site of a popular shooting range and magnificent wooden horse carousel. As dawn broke, Hatch pulled ahead of his Illinois Athletics Club teammate Olaf Lodal (a Danish marathon runner who would compete in the 1912 Olympics). Hatch had run a steady first half, holding back in the middle of the pack, but maintaining a relentless pace as the other runners dropped or slowed. With machine-like precision, stopping only twice for a total of six minutes (for a rub down and food, at miles 50 and 84), he clocked both the 50 mile (6:45:28) and 100 mile (16:07:43) world amateur records.[33]

Hatch continued with his successful amateur marathon running career over the next few years – and with his daytime job as a mail carrier – but in 1916 he made another 100 mile record attempt. This time it was to be on the Milwaukee to Chicago route: that winding network of rutted mud roads upon which Corey still held the record. As with Corey a decade before, the AAU sent a representative to ratify the attempt. On a chilly Tuesday evening, on 18 October – just days before a snowstorm that would sweep in across the Midwest – Hatch set off from Milwaukee City Hall at 8 p.m., watched by 2,000 spectators and accompanied by a pacer and, for the first mile or two, 'a score of school boy athletes'.[34] He was dressed in matching flannel trousers and long-sleeved shirt – looking much like a man out for a run in his pyjamas – and he wore mittens to protect his hands from the unseasonable weather. Stopping only three times and relying entirely on hot lemonade and orange juice for nutrition, he ran for most of the night into a bitingly cold wind. Surpassing even his own schedule, he came into Chicago accompanied by mounted police and the ever-present AAU automobile, in a time of 14:50:30. The route itself was only just over 95 miles, but with a little fudging the AAU declared that a route detour had lengthened the distance – and just like that, Hatch now had a new 100 mile amateur world record. It was an incredible performance. While slower than the professional world record of 13:26:30 – set on an indoor track by British pedestrian Charles Rowell in 1882 – given the weather and the state of the roads, it was a stunning achievement.

Corey and Hatch were exceptional in the sense that their ultra-distance efforts went largely unnoticed – greater attention and public prestige was attached to their successes in the marathon and Olympic Games. There was no longer any widespread interest in ultra-distance competition. That was to change briefly in 1928, and for a moment there would be a very real prospect that something akin to professional pedestrianism might be revived.

Charles C. Pyle was hardly known for his lack of ambition. A colourful and flamboyant figure, he revelled in the booming optimism of 1920s America. There was a sense of newness and possibility: radio and cinema, automobiles and electrical appliances, celebrities and mass market consumerism, jazz and art deco. It was a period defined by a break with the old — described by Susan Currell as a 'rift between tradition and modernity'[35] – and seemingly anything was possible. Surfing the crest of this heady, intoxicating decade, Pyle, a natural charmer and publicist, with a background as an entrepreneurial theatre-owner, was able to create an entirely new profession for himself: that of the 'sports agent'. Jim Reisler captures the physical and performative presence of Pyle at the height of his persuasive powers:

> Powerfully built from having been an athlete himself – a boxer and bicycle racer despite a heart condition – the 46-year-old promoter radiated both importance and confidence. The 6′ 3″ Pyle had sandy, gray hair, a pencil-thin mustache, and looked like a heftier version of the actor William Powell. C.C. dressed well, always wearing a pin-striped suit and usually a hat, which he used to his advantage – dominating most rooms he entered and commanding attention. And Pyle talked and kept talking in a kind of rat-a-rat that mixed bold dreams, bravado and the promise of a big payoff just ahead.[36]

Pyle was an American archetype: Gatsby-like, both dreamer and hustler – a remarkable sleight-of-hand conjurer – holding his creations together through sheer force of will.

He made his mark in 1925 when he began representing iconic football player Red Grange, following which he brazenly launched his own short-lived professional team, the New York Yankees, and even his own football league – both aimed at challenging the dominance of the NFL (without success). In 1926, he then signed French tennis prodigy Suzanne Lenglen – who pioneered the short tennis skirt and headband – for a lucrative tour around the United States.[37] No doubt inspired by the success and worldwide fame of the Tour de France, Pyle began in 1927 to hatch his next venture, bigger and more audacious than anything before: a transcontinental foot race from Los Angeles to New York.

There was a mixture of incredulity and awestruck anticipation when Pyle, always the showman, made his announcement in Hollywood. Such a race would be dangerously mad, and many were sceptical, including Clarence De Mar, seven-time winner of the Boston Marathon. Yet in 1927, seemingly anything was possible. The *Los Angeles Times* captured the prevailing view:

> His latest scheme, that of conducting a 3000-mile sprint across the continent, sounds much crazier that anything yet suggested and therefore will probably develop into the biggest success of all his schemes. Pyle gets an idea that something can be done and then goes ahead and proves it while those who think he's crazy pay the bills.[38]

Pyle proceeded to open invitations to prospective runners. Sticking it to the 'crusty' amateur rules of the dominant AAU, this would be a professional race with a hefty prize pot: $25,000 for the winner and successively smaller amounts for the other finishers.[39] It would be a stage race, over eighty-four days, with runners stopping every evening to rest and have their time for that section recorded – and the runner with the lowest cumulative time over nearly three months of racing would be the winner.[40] The course would follow newly constructed Route 66 – at the time still mostly an incomplete and rutted dirt track – from Los Angles to Chicago, and then along a network of roads to the finish, with a 26-hour relay at Madison

Square Garden, New York. The plan was to fund the race through sponsorship and an array of sideshow schemes designed to extract money from the expected crowds en route. Pyle was rubbing his hands in anticipation, as he outlined with typical salesman panache to *TIME* magazine:

> We'll run through hundreds of towns, cities and villages. Spectators by the thousands will be attracted to these places to see the race pass through. That will mean money for local merchants and advertising for the towns. It will help the sale of everything from mouse traps to grand pianos. Each town will be assessed so much by me for advertising, or we won't run through, but through a rival town. Then we'll sell a million programmes, easy. You can't tell the runners without a programme. I'll get a hundred thousand for the advertising in that. I'll have a travelling amusement show with the race. Admission will not be free. I'll make money on that too. In fact, it's about the easiest thing I've ever seen.[41]

Pyle's scheme was taking place at an interesting juncture in American cultural history. Twenty per cent of American households now owned an automobile – and tourism was booming. The race deliberately appealed to not just the vacation industry but also a growing romanticism for the American road, which itself was rooted in a nostalgic nod to the pioneer spirit of the Old West.

Inspired by international newspaper coverage, 199 runners from various parts of the world signed up for the transcontinental race. Some were already runners of established fame, such as Finnish-American William Kolehmainen, holder of the marathon world record (set in 1912). Given this pedigree, he was understandably considered race favourite by the American press. The starting line also included British-Rhodesian Arthur Newton, perhaps the greatest ultra-distance runner of the interwar period. Newton already had impressive credentials. The 55 mile Comrades Marathon had been launched in 1922 to commemorate South African soldiers who had fallen in the war. Newton had won the race every year between 1922 and 1927, barring 1926 when he finished second – an impressive tally of five victories.[42] In 1924, he stunned the endurance running world when he threw down the gauntlet at the London to Brighton race, a route chosen by Newton because of the prestige it carried.

He completed two solo runs, just weeks apart, and both were record breaking. The second of these attempts, in 5:53:43, demolished Len Hurst's 1903 record by almost 40 minutes. It was following these victories, in 1927, that Newton received an invitation to compete in the transcontinental race as an honoured guest and big-name draw.[43] Alongside Kolehmainen and Newton, there were other former Olympic competitors and medal holders, all of whom would now be classed as professional runners and barred from future amateur competition (including the Olympics). Money speaks – Pyle truly was gathering around him a field of the very best.

Remarkably, these giants of endurance running only constituted a small part of the field. Lining up against them were a collection of the unknown and seemingly unhopeful. Finnish-American Johnny Salo and British-Italian Peter Gavuzzi shared something in common: both worked aboard ship, doing much of their training in repetitive loops on deck. Salo and Gavuzzi were talented but at the time entirely undistinguished runners. Joining them was Andy Payne, a part-Cherokee farm boy, a local star, but unknown beyond his hometown in Claremore, Oklahoma. Philip Granville, a champion racewalker of Jamaican-Indian extraction, had travelled down from his adopted home in Canada. As a former winner of the Manchester to Blackpool racewalk, he was seen as the most viable prospect by those north of the border.

Five African Americans added to the diversity of the field. Eddie 'the Sheik' Gardner was a talented prize-winning runner from Seattle, so named because of a trademark towel that he wrapped around his head. Gardner was largely unknown beyond his home state of Washington. Yet, in a personal coup, he received sponsorship and backing for the race by black newspaper the *California Eagle*, which aimed to challenge a prevailing stereotype that African Americans were physically unsuited for distance running (Finns were seen as the endurance specialists of the time – a racial stereotype linked to the supposed strength of the 'northern European race').[44] Incredibly, Tobie Joseph Cotton, Jr was only fourteen when he began training to compete in the race. His father, a Los Angeles auto mechanic, had been crippled during an accident when a jacked-up truck fell and crushed his spine. The eldest of eight children, Cotton saw the race as a prospect to bring in much needed income. His family would act as a support crew: a cobbled-together van driven by his 13-year-old brother, food and water from an even younger brother, and their incapacitated father as coach and physio. Sammy Davis, from Atlantic City, was the third African American to enter the race. He had been a star athlete at school, followed by time serving in the First World War and then as a professional boxer. Davis was physically fit but had no specific background in long-distance running. He was encouraged and sponsored to enter by Lou Greenberg, an old friend and sports editor in Atlantic City, who believed that Davis would help to promote the city as a tourist destination.[45]

The final two African American runners received little coverage during the race and dropped out before the finish. They were not alone. A majority of the Pyle runners were entirely unsuited for the race, with little training or lingering health problems: many were desperate or naive, incentivised by the huge winnings at stake. Eight prospective runners were rejected during the pre-race medical check as unfit to compete – and of the 199 starters, only 55 would actually make it to the finish.[46]

The race began at 3 p.m. on Sunday 4 March – a time and day chosen to maximise crowds and revellers at the starting line. Race favourite Kolehmainen burned ahead to claim a massive lead, only to drop out with a strained groin on day 3. Almost a quarter of the runners had dropped out by day 7, as racers battled through the heat of the Mojave Desert. Arthur Newton, running at his familiar and steady training pace, had risen through the ranks to take overall lead, with Andy Payne in second. On day 9, the sunburnt runners crossed the Colorado River and slogged up into the biting cold of the Mohave mountains, where poor tent accommodation at night had them shivering and struggling to recover. They headed across the red and lavender deserts of Arizona, then up through the dense pine forests surrounding Flagstaff. It was here where disaster struck Newton on day 16: he was forced to retire with a torn Achilles tendon. Unwilling to part with this celebrity-athlete, Pyle hired Newton as an 'official advisor', and he spent the remainder of the race supporting the other competitors as team coach.[47] Echoing a theme that would be found elsewhere, the *Los Angeles Times* attributed Newton's injury to his age:

> Newton had the experience, the fortitude and the will to conquer the 3400-mile trail. But he didn't have the legs. His years were against him. He held every amateur running record from 29 miles to 100 miles, but at 44 years of age the old pins wouldn't hold up. It takes youth to supply the reserve strength necessary for such a grind.[48]

The race continued down past the Native American reservations of New Mexico, to Albuquerque, where it was refused entry by the local mayor. This was to become a recurring problem for Pyle, and a financial black hole was beginning to swirl at the heart of the race: it was simply not making money. As they entered the Texas Panhandle on Day 34, having covered 1,152 miles, the race was becoming more clearly defined. Gone were the celebrity athletes, such as Newton and Kolehmainen. Rather, the race was led by Arne Souminen, a cerebral medical doctor from Detroit, followed by Andy Payne and Peter Gavuzzi. Trailing a little were Johnny Salo, Eddie Gardner, Philp Granville and a small number of other runners, with the remainder of the field way out back. Yet as the runners crossed Texas, the race was still wide open – they all knew that anyone could drop out at any moment. Sure enough, Souminen's race finished on day 39 with a pulled tendon – and Payne and Gavuzzi were now together in a virtual tie at the front.

The Texas crossing was not without incident. As the only southern state through which the race ran, Jim Crow laws required black runners to be housed in segregated accommodation. Racist agitators patrolled the route, hooting and hollering at the sight of black and white athletes running and working together. One confrontation almost became violent. Eddie Gardner's black trainer, George Curtis, found himself surrounded by a crowd threatening to burn his automobile, as the mob leader shouted, 'they ain't got no reason racing n*****s against white folk'.[49] Thankfully, Curtis managed to extricate himself from the situation before it degenerated further. A prize of $1,000 had been raised in Oklahoma for the first runner crossing the state line, with the expectation that this would be local boy and race leader Andy Payne. It was actually Eddie Gardner who was leading on this particular section, driven perhaps by boiling resentment at the harassment, but sadly he pulled back after being followed and receiving death threats concerning his imminent victory. Payne crossed into Oklahoma to receive a hero's welcome – no doubt dampened by the treatment of his racing compatriot – with schools and businesses closed as a state-wide holiday was declared along the route.

And on the race went. Over the sparse plains of Oklahoma, into Kansas, and then Illinois. As they entered Chicago on day 64 – having covered more than 2,000 miles – there were only 70 runners remaining. It was a daily grind that must have felt unbearable at times, especially for those at the back. Yet something remarkable was happening. As the prize money slipped out of sight for almost all of them, they became a tight group: journeymen and comrades, bound together, with one burning objective – to finish.

Payne and Gavuzzi continued to lead, usually running together, with Salo trailing in third. They moved down from Chicago into Ohio, and once again disaster struck. On day 71, Gavuzzi was forced to retire by a concerned race doctor. With painful abscesses in his mouth – something that Gavuzzi attributed to a high-sugar racing diet – he was no longer able to take on sufficient nutrition to retain a healthy weight. For this small and softly spoken working-class British-Italian – less than 500 miles from an historic victory – it was a tragic end. Barring disaster, the race now belonged to Payne. Across the pastures and industries of Pennsylvania, through to New Jersey and New York, the 55 remaining runners arrived in the city of New York on 26 May – day 85. They then completed a 26-hour lap around Madison Square Garden, with Payne taking home $25,000 for first place, and Salo $10,000 for second. Financially, the race had been a disaster – Pyle was forced to borrow money to pay out the prize winnings – but it left an undoubted mark on the sporting consciousness of America. Against all odds, they had done it.

Pyle was now essentially broke – but his dreams of dominating a new culture of athletics were undeterred. Shortly after the race, he hosted reporters at his expansive Vanderbilt Hotel suite, in New

York, where he outlined madcap plans to cash in on an emerging 'golden age' of running:

> I am going to write a treatise on chiropody in English, who he who runs may read, and I am going to give away one copy with every purchase of C.C. Pyle's Patent Foot Box, which will contain remedies for every one of the 3,000 maladies of the human foot. I will make vast sums out of this because this country is going marathon. We are just entering the golden age of the foot.[50]

Pyle was right – there would be a boom in running and eventual commercial interest in everything foot-related – it just so happened that he was forty years too early. As Pyle would continue to find, there was simply no real economic foundation for a commercial business in the running market.

Given the financial failure of the 1928 event, this might have been the end for transcontinental racing. Yet, undeterred, Pyle and many of the same runners returned in 1929 to reprise this extraordinary feat. This time the race would run from New York to Los Angeles. Returning runners included Salo, Gardner, Granville and Davis. Andy Payne had returned to Oklahoma to invest his winnings on the family farm and train as a lawyer; his racing days were done. In contrast, Gavuzzi and Newton had struck up a professional running partnership. They agreed to work together during the race, with any winnings split equally between the two of them.[51] Over 100 runners started on 31 March, each paying a $300 entry fee (a new scheme by Pyle to make this race more financially viable). They were all working-class men – from backgrounds that included drycleaning and carpentry – striving for tantalising riches in the only way that they knew how: through professional running. Gardner and Newton dropped out relatively early in the 1929 race, leaving Gavuzzi (supported by Newton in a customised van) and Salo to battle it out to the end.[52]

The 1929 race ended in ignominy after 79 days and almost 526 hours of running. In order to avoid the frustration and danger of racing through downtown Los Angeles traffic, the runners were told to make their own way to Wrigley Field, where a final track marathon would commence when all runners were present. Gavuzzi had a ten-minute lead at this stage, but on arrival he found that the marathon had started without him. His lead had disappeared! A frantic Gavuzzi attempted to catch Salo, but without success. He came second, falling short – in a race of more than 3,600 miles – by only 2 minutes and 47 seconds.[53] It has been suggested over the years that Pyle engineered the finish in order to generate media acclaim with an American win. In some respects, it did not matter: there were no prize winnings waiting for either Salo or Gavuzzi. Pyle had been declared bankrupt during the race and despite various promissory notes he never paid out any of the winnings.[54]

While some of the 'Pyle runners' would continue to race on a small professional circuit throughout the 1930s – most notably in Canada – the transcontinental races sounded the death knell of professional ultra-distance running in the interwar period. Not only had they been a financial failure, but America was now plunging into a recession that would for a time dampen public interest in athletics and erode the already unreliable market for sporting exhibitionism. The world had moved on from professional pedestrianism and the term 'ultramarathon' had not yet been popularised. It would take an entirely new generation of post-war athletes to rekindle the dying embers of ultra-distance running.

Chapter 5

Trailblazing

Chelsea Clinton does not normally post on social media about ultrarunning – but this was somewhat exceptional: 'Incredible story: Jasmin Paris becomes the first woman to win 268 mile Montane Spine Race – breaking record by 12 hours! AND she expressed milk for her baby along the way. Inspiration.' It was a moment of unusual – but justified – high-profile attention for women and the sport of ultrarunning. Only hours before, in January 2019, Jasmin Paris had taken part in a post-race interview on BBC breakfast television. With a typical mix of modesty, shyness and steely determination, Paris, a 35-year-old veterinary scientist based at the University of Edinburgh, explained to the bemused interviewers how she manages 4 a.m. training runs, alongside work and her 14-month-old daughter, while also retaining a competitive drive. 'I was going out to be competitive', she admitted, 'I thought there was a chance I could win the race.'[1] This was a huge understatement. As she chatted to the BBC – looking rested and fresh-faced after having returned home the previous evening – the second placed runner, and previous record holder, Eoin Keith, was still out on the course, a full 15 hours behind Paris, and only now approaching the finish.

The Montane Spine Race is arguably Britain's most celebrated annual event in ultrarunning. Despite a small number of actual competitors – there were 137 starters in 2019 (of whom 12 were women) – the 'brutal' reputation of the race attracts significant media attention. Held in the depths of winter, with only eight hours of daylight, the route runs the length of the Pennine Way: 268

miles, 11,000 metres of ascent, over bleak moorland and broken hillsides, which are either frozen solid, covered in snow or thick with mud. With a little luck, competitors are able to enjoy the streaked half-light of winter, coffee-coloured heather and rolling hills, down narrow valleys, and through sleeping villages that glitter with frost-rimmed magic. Often it just rains – heavily.

The 2019 race began with typical understatement: in the small village of Edale, on a Sunday morning, with anxious-looking runners and a huddle of supporters and volunteers. In semi-darkness, participants start by climbing over Kinder Scout and along high moorland that plunges northward through the heart of the country. Jasmin Paris – unaware that she will soon become the focus for global media excitement – is running at the front of the race with two Spine veterans: Eoin Keith, from Ireland, and Eugeni Solé, from Spain. They arrive together at Checkpoint 2, in Hawes, after 108 miles and 28 hours. Keith takes a little longer at the aid station, while Paris and Solé – not wanting to waste precious daylight – push forward. Their lead over Keith will continue to grow. Arriving at Middleton in Teesdale – Checkpoint 3 at 142 miles – it is now 10 p.m., on Monday, and they are heading into their second night. Both wisely snatch a couple of hours of sleep. Paris also takes the time to express breastmilk: 'I had to express because you can't really go cold turkey, you end up with loads of problems.'[2] It is an extra layer of self-care, but also a necessary task that will later capture public imagination and catapult Paris to international fame.

Paris and Solé leave together again, curving around for a climb over the highest point in the race, Cross Fell, and down to Alston – Checkpoint 4 at 173 miles – by mid-afternoon on the Tuesday. It is here where Paris begins to draw on her immense talent for endurance. The race is one of strategy, attrition and mental resilience, where good decision making is more important than raw athletic power. 'It was really cold up there on the last day, way below zero and very windy. I was wearing six layers, three pairs of leggings, every item of clothing that I had', Paris was to explain later. 'Eugeni had slightly less gear than me, which is a risk he took.'[3] It proved to be a costly decision. Paris begins to stretch out her lead along

Hadrian's Wall and past the Sycamore Gap – two hours ahead by Checkpoint 5 at Bellingham (215 miles) – where she snatches around 40 minutes sleep, before the final stretch over the Cheviot hills on the Scottish/Northumbria border. Determined, and unwilling to risk losing her advantage, Paris makes good progress, past the final mountain hut, and then down to the finish in Kirk Yetholm. It has taken 3 days, 11 hours and 12 minutes – she has slept for a total of three hours. The finishing photographs will be shared in newspapers around the world: Paris, smiling with joy before the camera, holding her red-cheeked daughter, Rowan, who has a somewhat befuddled look in snowsuit and rabbit hat.

The drama is not over. Solé has been trailing, not far behind, but struggling and shivering in the cold. Only six kilometres from the finish – two and a half hours behind Paris – he hunkers down in the refuge hut and activates his emergency beacon. Medical support soon finds him. He is cleared to continue, but shortly afterwards makes the decision to withdraw. Eoin Keith – steady, assured, methodical – is 12 hours back yet now suddenly destined for second place.

The Montane Spine Race is always dramatic and interesting, but it was the story of Paris – a breastfeeding woman, demolishing the male course record by 12 hours – that would be broadcast around the world. Her success as a woman was not surprising to Paris. 'In my own experience, the longer I race, the more competitive I can be with men', she explains after the race. 'The longer you go, the less it is about strength and aerobic power. It's about what is in your head and about looking after yourself, being able to multitask and juggle things.'[4]

The Montane Spine Race takes place over Britain's oldest long-distance trail route: the Pennine Way. Conceived in 1935 – finally completed in 1965 – the Pennine Way was modelled on earlier efforts in the United States to construct the Appalachian Trail and other long-distance routes. These trails hark back to a time in North America and Britain when an entire generation dedicated themselves to making the outdoor world accessible for future generations. The emergent practice of hiking was at the forefront of this cultural revolution – with profound implications for our approach to recreation and conservation in the natural world. Critically, the culture of hiking would continue to shape off-road running for generations to come.

Hiking was certainly not a new pastime. In Britain, there are accounts of recreational rambling from the beginning of the nineteenth century, and in the United States from around the 1830s. But it was during the first half of the twentieth century that hiking clubs would flourish dramatically in both their size and cultural impact. The 'club' aspect of organised hiking was paramount: this was not a solitary pursuit, but something to be done with others in a structured and supported way. Clubs brought people together to learn from one another and enjoy a shared, comradely experience. These club participants often combined hiking with other pastimes, such as conservation, botany, natural history, geology and bird watching – it was therefore often a middle-class form of recreation.

Helen Walker argues that there were several reasons for the success and growth of hiking clubs: a concern with health and vigour (including the cultural innovation of the supposedly healthy tan), a relaxation of Victorian propriety (which enabled young men and women to mix more freely together in outdoor spaces), and mounting social anxiety concerning the need to physically prepare for war and conflict.[5] The result was that tens of thousands of people, on both sides of the Atlantic, began to tramp around in stiff boots and khaki clothing, with a rise in popularity that eventually led to the 'hiking craze' of the 1930s.[6] It was during this decade, in 1933, that a young Duke of York – later to become King George VI – would himself give a public declaration on the joy of hiking.[7]

The history of this outdoor hiking movement is complex and varied. Growing popularity was often driven by youth organisations – such as the YHA (Youth Hostels Association), Scouts and YMCA (Young Men's Christian Association) – but the social patterning of involvement was consistent across Britain and North America. In Britain, hiking clubs were predominantly found in northern industrialised cities with easy access to local countryside, such as

Manchester, Sheffield and Leeds, but also in London and the outlying shires of the capital. The extensive British railway network – which provided subsidised day-return tickets for young hikers – enabled easy access to hiking routes for this group of outdoor enthusiasts. In the United States, hiking clubs were first established in New England, California and the Pacific Northwest – areas with large cities and accessible mountain landscapes – followed later by the Midwest. The pattern was consistent: in urban centres, Americans and Britons sought escape to a natural world that was tantalisingly close to the outskirts of the city.

This 'escape' from civilisation was an echo of the Romantics and Transcendentalists, writers and artists these middle-class young people were intimately familiar with, due to their upbringing and schooling. Writing retrospectively, in 1937, Lewis Paton, himself a keen hiker – and by then an influential school headmaster – sought to capture the ethos that had animated his generation:

> We were rebels against all stuffiness and all snobbery. On the pleasure beach one has to pay for everything … and the child learns to think of joy in terms of money. We learned to think of joy in terms of comradeship, health, adventure and God's out-of-doors. We were out for a holiday from the obsession of the everlasting cash nexus, the artificial, and all the sophistications of an all-dominating civilisation.[8]

It was not just a reprieve from civilisation, but also a celebration and stewardship of the natural world, with an intellectual framing that understood walking as a spiritual and restorative act of self-improvement. Sunday walks were at times combined with a religious service. As Philadelphia's Batona Hiking Club stated in a 1934 newsletter: 'commune with nature and you will receive messages of hope, beauty, cheer, and courage that will not let you grow old'. Walking provided not just physical health, then, but also inner nourishment. This belief was echoed across the Atlantic by Alfred Wainwright, who in the 1930s was beginning to explore the summits and valleys of his beloved Lake District:

> Up here, you are near to your Creator; you are conscious of the infinite; you gain new perspectives; thoughts run in new strange channels; there are stirrings in your soul which are quite beyond the

> power of my pen to describe. Something happens to you in the silent places which never could in the towns, and it is a good thing to sit awhile in a quiet spot and meditate.[9]

And yet, while there was a persistent spiritual undercurrent, the act of walking could also be deeply political: access and conservation were dominant and controversial issues in both Britian and the United States.

In Britain, the need to protect ancient byways and footpaths dated back to the eighteenth century, during which time parliamentary Enclosure Acts had begun to parcel up common land for private ownership.[10] The first society to preserve these footpaths, the Association for the Protection of Ancient Footpaths, was set up in the vicinity of York, in 1824, followed by the Manchester Association for the Preservation of Ancient Footpaths, in 1826.[11] Despite efforts to preserve access, by the early part of the twentieth century the moors and hills of Britain, which had historically been used as public commons for grazing, were almost entirely in private hands, predominantly used for game shooting and animal husbandry. Patrolling gamekeepers sought to impede access – often violently – and there were to be no national parks in Britain until after the Second World War.

This was a source of bitter resentment to city dwellers, many of whom would gaze up out of grime-choked valleys to the surrounding countryside, furious that they were denied access by wealthy landowners. In 1931, rambling clubs came together to advocate for access by forming the National Council of Ramblers' Federations (NCRF). This was followed shortly after by the historic mass trespass on Kinder Scout in 1932 – organised by communist activists in the British Workers Sports Federation (BWSF), although opposed by the NCRF, which disapproved of direct action. The trespass saw around 400 people walk across Kinder Scout, the highest point in the Peak District, where they were forcibly resisted by the Duke of Devonshire's gamekeepers. Five of the trespassers faced harsh jail sentences. Before his sentencing, one of the incarcerated, 19-year-old student Arthur Gillet, responded to a question from the judge about whether he was ashamed of his actions: 'No sir. I would do it again tomorrow.'[12] The notoriety of the trespass led to renewed campaigning. It is often credited with leading to the creation of Britain's first national trails, including the Pennine Way (which was proposed only three years later) and the eventual National Parks legislation of 1949.

While British communists and ramblers battled gamekeepers, hiking clubs in the United States were also trying to ensure wider access to the natural world. Here too, there was a concern with private ownership – leading to a much earlier push for national and state parks that would provide an eventual template for similarly protected spaces in Britain – but it was also about creating accessible routes through an often trackless wilderness. Waymarked routes and trails would open up these areas but also prevent bushwhacking hikers from damaging fragile ecosystems. While the pace of trail building accelerated considerably during the first half of the twentieth century, it had an origin that dated back to the earliest days of organised American mountaineering. In 1876, the year that the Appalachian Mountaineering Club was established, the club proposed the creation of twenty trails. It created a division to oversee this work. William G. Nowell, the AMC's Councillor of Improvements, outlined the expected standard of these new trails: 'First, that all paths should be made a good width, from six to eight feet; second, that they be cleared of all under-brush and trip-roots; third, that holes in them be filled, so far as practicable.'[13] These new trails were to be marked with the club logo – an 'A' – acting as blazes that would mark the way. Following the precedent set by the AMC, hiking clubs engaged in a sustained effort to establish a network of trail routes across the United States.

It was in the twentieth century that much grander plans began to bear fruit: to establish truly long-distance walking routes. These would be corridors of nature – pilgrimage routes in defiance of an industrialised and capitalist age – running like spiritual arteries through the congested body of a rapidly privatised landscape. A High Sierra route had been proposed from as early as the 1890s – this would eventually become the John Muir Trail (with work beginning in 1915) – followed by proposals for the Long Trail (1910), the Appalachian Trail (1921) and the Pacific Crest Trail (1932).

Inspired by this wave of activity, something similar began to take shape in Britain. Plans were hatched for the Cleveland Way and the Pennine Way in the 1930s, with further National Trails to be proposed and developed from the 1950s onwards. At the same time, a surge of interest in hiking during the 1930s led to more clearly defined paths and a growing familiarity with the mountains of Britain. Author and illustrator Alfred Wainwright first ventured to the Lake District in 1930. Many more trips would follow, leading eventually to the publication of his renowned set of Lakeland guidebooks in the 1950s and his detailing of England's 'Coast to Coast' route. Wainwright's guidebooks would become the basis for not just successive generations of hikers, but also endurance runners and record-worthy routes. This would include the notorious 'Wainwrights' – a continuous 352 mile circuit of all 214 Lake District peaks mentioned in the guidebooks.

There was, then, a flurry of activity during the first half of the twentieth century that, as Silas Chamberlin argues, 'created a close-knit community of men and women with a shared culture of hiking and trail building'.[14] Over many decades they erected the physical and mental landscape against which ambitious runners and long-distance walkers would test themselves. This included a remarkable and early experiment in what we would now call 'ultra-distance trail racing': the Mount Baker races of 1911–1913.

Bellingham Bay is a case study in rapid American growth and expansion. Situated on the Pacific coastline, near the Canadian border, it was founded as a small lumber settlement in 1852. A brief gold rush and the discovery of substantial coal deposits drew in commercial investment, with all the attendant trappings of a thriving industrial and business venture. The settlement blossomed into a series of mid-sized towns, which were incorporated as the city of Bellingham in 1903. From lumber shacks to city, in the space of fifty years. The pace of industrial growth was incredible: shipping, railroads, bridges, mines and endless construction, all against the backdrop of the conifer-clad, snow-topped range of the North Cascades and the lower-lying Chuckanut Mountains. Industry meets wilderness: as it would turn out, the perfect set of conditions for a long-distance mountain race.

The Mount Baker Trail Club was formed in 1907, tasked with overseeing construction of a trail network along the flanks of Mount Baker, which loomed over the city at more than 3,000 metres.[15] In May 1911, another organisation – the Mount Baker Club – was formed to organise hikes out into this ever more accessible backcountry. Yet, for an ambitious community, with an appraising eye on the growth of American tourism, more needed to be done to raise the profile of their majestic mountain range. In a poetic speech at their inaugural meeting, newly elected club president Arthur J. Craven outlined his vision for the connection of civic life to the outdoors:

> One touch of nature makes us all akin. In the shadows of the woods along the trail, on the slope of the icy mountain, where things look large and human differences grow exceedingly small – you will find no wealth there, but rugged strength, patience and manliness – no aristocracy or rank, except with those who have learned to carry their own packs and to try to be kind and helpful to their fellows.[16]

Craven was a lawyer, originally from Indiana, where his father worked as a pastor. With views no doubt informed by this upbringing – at a time when an evangelical revival was sweeping across the United States – Craven believed that civic action and human kinship were enhanced by the transformational experience of our time within nature. In an echo of the Transcendentalist movement, he saw the surrounding landscape not as a resource to be exploited, but as a place where personal virtue and spirituality might be cultivated. Under Craven's leadership, the club debated proposals to promote access to the burgeoning trail network around Bellingham. And then, only a month later, on 29 June, they announced their decision: they would organise a competitive race to the summit of Mount Baker.[17]

A date was set for 9 August, and work began immediately to devise a suitable route, with local mountaineer Charles F. Easton performing a recce and publishing a trail map in the *Bellingham Herald* for prospective racers.[18] Anticipation grew. Organised groups began taking the train to the trailhead at the town of Glacier in order to explore the sides of Mount Baker. A team of three local luminaries, plus their guide, made a 'record breaking' summit attempt on 15 July, in an admittedly rather modest time of 37 hours. All of this was simply a prelude to what was already becoming recognised as a daring and historic race. 'I am confident that the climb will be one of the most closely watched events of the kind that ever took place in America', declared Henry Enberg, local pharmacist, photographer and member of the organising committee. A little overconfident perhaps, but a confidence not entirely misplaced. Washington senator Wesley Jones was to later claim that the race had even been a topic of discussion for President Taft and Congress. Jones was also to boast – not just immodestly, but no doubt inaccurately – that if he had been available that day, then he himself would have been the race winner.[19]

The race format was eventually agreed upon at a committee meeting on 20 July – and it was rather unusual. Racers would assemble for a pre-race briefing at 9 p.m., on Wednesday 9 August, before a 10 p.m. start outside the Chamber of Commerce in Bellingham. They would each wear a bib number, so that their progress could be verified by judges along the route. Following the starting gun, competitors were expected to travel independently from Bellingham by means of a 'race aid' – conceived initially as any combination of horse, wagon, train or automobile – which would take them either by railroad to the town of Glacier (44 miles) or along rutted tracks to Heisler's Ranch (26 miles). They would then ascend by foot to the summit of Mount Baker, using either the new and undeveloped Glacier Trail (14 miles) or the better-known Deming Trail (16 miles), each with 3,000 metres of ascent, before returning the way they came. Much of the excitement stemmed from the uncertainty surrounding the choice of route and transport. Automobiles were potentially quicker – with a shorter route to traverse – but were notoriously unreliable and had to travel over tracks that were in a miserable state. The Deming Trail itself was longer than the ascent route from Glacier, but it was flatter and more 'runnable', with a shorter (yet steeper) snow climb to the summit.

The race was not just a test of physical endurance, but also one of competing strategies and technological innovation. It was a remarkable confluence of ideas: Edwardian conceptions of technological futurism, nature-based spirituality, rugged individualism and machismo.

As the competitors gathered that evening, the sun was beginning to drop behind Bellingham Bay and the lapping waves of the Pacific. The race had been billed as a 'mountain climbing contest', and the fourteen competitors that evening were somewhat different to those on the starting line of a city marathon. These men were loggers, miners, ranchers and farmers: woodsmen and mountain goats, possessed with intimate knowledge of the terrain, rather than endurance runners honed through formal athletic training. At the sound of the gun, they dashed towards their waiting transport. Eight runners chose the automobile to Deming Trail. Six opted for the train to Glacier. After an hour on the train, 19-year-old race leader Harvey Haggard, a packer for the local Poison Mine Company, arrived at the Glacier trailhead. Stripped down to his underclothes and carrying a Crisco candle – a light source favoured by local miners – he made his way upward through the conifers. The night was clear with a large moon, the frosty air ensuring that snow-packed trails remained firm underfoot. The trail itself would have been largely imperceptible, hardly used, and only recently marked with trail blazes. As Haggard ascended into 70 mph wind, he crested the summit dome at 5.18 a.m. It turned out he was 19 minutes ahead of 25-year-old Joe Galbraith, a rancher and logger, and former high school star athlete, who was the lead runner on the alternative Deming Trail.[20]

Galbraith had arrived at Heisler's Ranch in only 54 minutes. Leaping out of the automobile, he made his way quickly along the marked trail. The Deming Trail stretched along a flattish valley floor, with the jagged silhouette of the Twin Sisters looming overhead to the south. He covered the distance in 3 hours and 27 minutes. Reaching Mazama Lake – a glacial depression at the start of the climb to the summit – he rested and ate breakfast at the camp of a forest ranger.[21] Family and friends were there to support him, and after 45 minutes he resumed, this time paced by his brother. Galbraith eventually arrived at the summit for 5.46 a.m., only to find that Haggard had passed through more than 20 minutes before.

After four minutes of enforced rest – during which the judges recorded the summit time – the runners turned for their respective descents. Haggard was clearly in front at this stage, but a great deal would hinge on the uncertainty of their return transport. The sun was rising, the growing warmth melting the lower snow fields as they raced home. Haggard arrived at his onward train first, at 9.01 a.m., having completed the 28 mile round trip in a little over 10 hours. Galbraith reached his waiting automobile at 9.40 a.m., behind and seemingly destined for second place. Unfortunately for Haggard, disaster struck as he lay resting in the return train. A short passage from the *Bellingham Herald* captures the almost unbelievable drama:

> At 7 minutes past 9 o'clock, with the train going terrifically, an 1,800 pound red bull, the property of Dan J. Loop, a rancher living near Glacier, burst from the thick underbrush alongside the track ... The engine had just time to emit a startled scream from its whistle, when the impact came. The bull, flung high in the air, fell a distance ahead of the engine, was ground under the wheels, lifting the front trucks of the locomotive from the rails. As if reluctant to leave the track, the engine and the special coach, both now derailed, ploughed along for ten rods, tearing up the iron ... Haggard, lying on the bunk as naked as the day he was born, hit the ceiling of the coach, was slammed into a corner and bounced back amongst the seats.[22]

Thankfully, nobody was seriously injured in the crash (apart from the poor bull, which was roasted and eaten in the final race celebrations). A valiant Haggard flagged down a horse and carriage, travelling down the tracks until he was able to transfer to an automobile. Yet Haggard had lost the race – and he knew it. Galbraith arrived to cheering crowds, his Ford Model T, nicknamed 'Betsy', careening around the corners into Bellingham.[23] Arriving at 10.28 a.m., the entire trip had taken Galbraith 12 hours and 18 minutes. He took home a $100 prize purse, a silver trophy and a 'handsome buffalo robe'.

The race was reprised in 1912 and 1913. With growing notoriety, it was to attract runners from across the country, including Swedish-American Paul Westurlund, fresh from his debut at the Dipsea Race.[24] Runners encountered difficult and dangerous conditions, battling through rain, snow and thick mist.[25] Westurlund arrived at the summit first during the Bellingham race, but with a broken rib, and clothes frozen to his body. Disoriented, he had fallen hard on the glacier during the ascent. Yet it was Haggard who returned this year with a vengeance, outpacing Westurlund for the second half of the race and lowering the record to 9 hours and 51 minutes.

Changes were made for the 1913 race. It would begin at 5 a.m. and participants were required to return in a different direction (i.e., ascending via the Deming Trail, but then returning through Glacier, or vice versa). Heavy snowfall and poor conditions saw the race organisers make another crucial mid-race change: runners would only be required to reach the saddle of Mount Baker, rather than complete the final climb to the summit. In the confusion of the race, this change was not communicated to all runners. Westurlund was victorious in a time of 9 hours and 39 minutes, but only because second-place finisher John Magnuson had mistakenly made the full summit climb. The race that year was also marred by possible tragedy – Victor Galbraith had gone missing. His cousin (and 1911 winner) Joe organised a search party in the early afternoon. Fighting through a blizzard, the party found Victor trapped in a 40 foot crevasse, shivering and delirious in his thin running clothes.[26].He was safely stretchered back down to Mazama camp.

Plans for a 1914 race were eventually shelved, although not because of concerns about safety. Having been taken over by the local Booster Club – a committee of businessmen tasked with the economic development of Bellingham – it was decided that the Mount Baker Race was not sufficiently profitable. Race numbers had declined to only nine runners in 1913, and while the crowds were large – anywhere between 5,000 and 20,000 – the race was losing the city money. A more modest two-day affair of family entertainment was proposed as a replacement,[27] and so ended America's first trail ultramarathon. It had achieved everything hoped for by the Mount

Baker Club. The surrounding trail network had been built up, and a road constructed through to Mount Baker itself. The surrounding backcountry was now more accessible and better known. While Bellingham was to become a favoured destination for a new wave of American tourism, sadly this brief experiment in mountain athleticism ended without fanfare. However, elsewhere in the United States, efforts were already afoot to develop truly long-distance hiking trails and to experiment with speed records and possibly even racing over these new routes.

'Long Trail is Being Considered as Possible Marathon Route' – so read this extraordinary byline in the *Bennington Evening Banner*, a Vermont-based newspaper, in July 1926.[28] Having first been proposed in 1910 by James P. Taylor – an associate principal at a school in Saxton – the final sections of the Long Trail were only now being completed by the Green Mountain Club (GMC). Stretching the length of Vermont, from the Massachusetts state line to the Canadian border, the Long Trail was unique: a point-to-point trail – a gnarled and tangled mass of roots, rocks and hills – running out over the carpeted forest of the Green Mountains. Construction of this unique route had been a mammoth undertaking.

The GMC had itself been founded by Taylor with construction of the Long Trail specifically in mind. It was a group stuffed full of the local elite – lawyers, businessmen, educators, clergymen and a future governor – ambitious local leaders, much like in Bellingham, all with the cultural and economic prospects of Vermont weighing on their mind. In 1926, with the final stretches of the 273 mile trail finally near completion, there was discussion among the GMC executive committee of a possible 'marathon' race along the route. With close ties to nearby Boston, they no doubt saw the potential to tap into this thriving hub of American athletics.

And so stepped forward Irving Appleby: First World War veteran, former member of the Canadian Black Watch, now a local milk salesman. Making the journey largely alone – dressed in a cotton shirt, khaki trousers and sturdy leather boots – he started out at the beginning of July from the northern tip of the trail. Walking for 16 hours over the course of a day, he would prepare an evening meal, wrap himself up in an army blanket by the fire – sleep for six hours – and then cook breakfast before starting out again.[29] Donning a poncho, he battled through torrential rain and over river crossings in spate (surrounded by an incessant cloud of insects) to reach Bennington, having traversed the full route in 12 days and 5 hours. There was a brief moment of local excitement. James P. Taylor himself was to declare that this could be an ongoing competition, 'where hiker after hiker tries to better the record already made'.[30] Then, little more than a month later, the backlash commenced.

In August, two teenage female hikers, Lila Stearns and Elsie Olund, had declared their intention to hike the entirety of the Long Trail. They were experienced hikers, with recent excursions over long distances in the White Mountains and the Appalachians, so were waved off with public fanfare and great anticipation.[31] Yet after four days on the trail, a newspaper furore erupted: they were missing! A search was frantically organised, with Appleby stepping forward – via public letter – to lead the search for 'these poor kids', who tragically lacked his self-declared masculine fortitude and skill: 'I would probably rank among the very strongest and hardiest men in America.'[32] Farcically, the search ended before it began: the two hikers were perfectly safe, having dropped down from the Long Trail at Hell Hollow Brook, two days into their effort.[33]

Prospects to turn the Long Trail into a 'racing route' suddenly soured. Only a week later, an editorial in the previously supportive *Bennington Evening Banner* declared:

> There is no doubt that Mr. Appleby accomplished a remarkable feat in covering the entire length of the Trail in so short a time and no one wishes to detract from him his glory. Nevertheless, The Long Trail is not meant for a marathon track. It is a beautiful pathway through the heart of the Green Mountains and should be enjoyed leisurely.[34]

Appleby returned in 1927 to lower his record further, this time accompanied by racewalking champion F. C. Jameson.[35] While his companion was forced to drop out due to exhaustion, Appleby pushed through to finish in 10 days and 10 hours.[36] To Appleby's consternation, the GMC, swayed by public opinion, had started to turn against the prospect of speed records. Demanding proof – which they must have known he lacked – the GMC refused to ratify his record. Appleby returned *again* in 1928 – this time with a photographer – and *again* the GMC refused ratification. Meanwhile, through-hiking on the trail was booming. Appleby himself was now employed to guide groups of Bostonian tourists out over the trail.[37] In 1927, the first female through-hikers – the so-called Three Musketeers – completed the entire trail in 27 days. To resolve matters, the GMC rushed through a resolution stating that speed records undermined the spirit and intention of the trail: from now on, they would ratify 'end-to-end' hikes, but not records based on speed.[38] Ratification or not, public interest in speed records was always going to remain strong, and ultimately the GMC was fighting a losing battle. Public interest in speed records would naturally carry over to the even grander long-distance trails that were still under construction.

As economic depression consumed much of the world – followed by the destructive conflagration of the Second World War – the collective comradeship of hiking and rambling groups was beginning to fade. Trail construction continued, only more slowly, and a social shift saw hiking and rambling gradually evolve into an individual rather than necessarily group activity. Millions embraced walking on both sides of the Atlantic, in the 1950s and 1960s, but many of these new participants were motivated by ideas of self-sufficiency, rather than the organised group excursions that had been such an important component of hiking in the pre-war years. As guidebooks and outdoor gear began to flood the market, increasingly there was no need to rely on the experience of established hiking groups, and by the 1970s membership of these historic clubs had shrunk considerably.[39] This trend was perhaps inevitable, but the gradual opening of long-distance trails also played a key role in fostering the mythology of solo hiking and self-reliant journeys of discovery.

The Appalachian Trail finally opened in 1937. It had taken nearly two decades of intense work, by multiple hiking clubs and thousands of volunteers, along a route that now stretched for over 2,000 miles. This mammoth effort had been coordinated by an organisation founded in 1925, known as the Appalachian Trail Conference (ATC).[40] Even by the late 1940s, problems were still being ironed out. For example, following the establishment of a nudist colony between Greenwood Lake and Lake Wawayanda, hikers were told they could still use this short section, but would be required to do so naked; the local hiking club, Union County, sagely chose the option of a permanent diversion.[41] Attention to trail building had also languished during the war and several sections were suffering from threadbare maintenance. And then, suddenly, there was Earl Shaffer.

The son of a welder, Shaffer scratched a living in his home state of Pennsylvania during the Depression, before enlisting in 1941 and serving for the duration of the war. Tragically, his childhood friend and hiking companion Walter Winemiller was a casualty at Iwo Jima in 1945. Learning of the news, Shaffer penned a heartbreaking entry for his diary: 'Miss your voice, the touch of your hand. My buddy, my buddy. Your buddy misses you.' Leaving the army shortly after, Shaffer resolved to hike the entirety of the Appalachian Trail. His intention was to 'walk the army out of my system, both mentally and physically'.[42] He was part of a generation that sought a way to overcome the trauma of conflict. Many retreated to the solitude of white picket fences and the hum of suburbia; others embarked on journeys of discovery – physical and metaphorical – in search of something deeper within themselves. Shaffer chose the Appalachian Trail.

Starting out on 4 April 1948, without fanfare or announcement, he made his way northward from Mount Oglethorpe, in Georgia (the original southern terminus). Largely underprepared and underequipped, he began covering an average of 17 miles per day, relying on corn bread for nutrition, a poncho for clothing, and sleeping in a lean-to at night.[43] For three months his progress was entirely unnoticed – as he battled rattlesnakes and copperheads en route – but in June that summer he sent a letter to the ATC notifying them of his attempt. Newspaper reporters began to track him down. Emerging to replenish supplies in Caratunk at the end of July – tanned, whip-thin and with the flash of a grin – he said that the 'first two weeks are the hardest. After that you get hardened up'.[44] On 5 August he summitted Mount Katahdin. It had taken him 124 days.

The ATC had not intended for hikers to traverse the entire trail in one continuous push. Articles in the *Appalachian Trailway News* even raised doubts about whether such a feat was possible. An unbelieving ATC secretary interrogated Shaffer – surely this was fabricated – but a collection of evidence, including hundreds of photographs, soon assuaged the doubters. Shaffer was ratified as the first through-hiker on the Appalachian Trail. It was by default a record, yet already newspapers were chattering about the prospect of more to come. As the *Baltimore Sun* wrote, only a day after Shaffer's final summit:

> So, unless someone else comes along, it looks as though Mr. Shaffer is the champion of the trail. The beauty of it is that, since nobody else had accomplished the feat ahead of him, all Mr. Shaffer had to do was get there … The next poor fellow who tries will have to do it in less than four months if he wants to become famous.[45]

Like the first tumbling boulder in a rockslide, Shaffer was the prelude to an interest in long-distance solo hiking and speed records that would only grow and grow.

In 1951, Gene Espy began his northbound trek. A recent college graduate from Georgia, he pioneered some of the better-known conventions of self-supported through-hiking, including mailing supplies to himself along the route. Arriving at one of the sturdy wooden huts built along the trail – Smith Gap Shelter in Pennsylvania – he was surprised to meet Chester Dziengielewski, a working-class machinist from Connecticut, who was making the very first southbound trek. They shared an evening meal together, before heading in opposite directions: they were the second and third successful finishers on the Appalachian Trail. More would follow. Martin Papendick finished the Appalachian Trail later that year (southbound). Much like Shaffer, he was a war veteran, seeking solitude and solace in the wild. The two remained in contact and exchanged letters about their experience. Papendick was also preparing for his next big challenge: the Pacific Crest Trail.

The Pacific Crest Trail (PCT) had first been proposed by Clinton C. Clarke in 1932. Running from the Mexican border through to Canada – over more than 2,500 miles – the envisaged route would traverse remote and at times trackless areas of the Sierra Nevada and Cascades. A successful oilman and Scout leader, Clarke envisaged the PCT as a challenging and remote mountain route, rather than something for the typical 'recreational' hiker: 'for building sturdy bodies, sound minds, and active, patriotic citizenship'[46] (an echo of the masculine nation building that was so predominant in the United States and Britain at the time). Unlike the Appalachian Trail, which skirted through populous areas, trail building was also much trickier here. Between 1935 and 1937, Clarke led a series of expeditions – involving relay teams of Scout and YMCA members – to map and define the route. At times it used existing trail network, such as the 428 mile Oregon Skyline Trail (which had been completed in 1920), but it also charted a course through areas of complete wilderness.[47] In September 1937, the route was declared largely mapped – although actual trail building would continue until 1993 – and it was expected that hiking the PCT would take around 10 months over a two-year period (i.e., two full summers of trekking, with a break during the intervening winter).[48] More than a decade later, in 1952, Papendick confounded this expectation. Hiking north to south, following the rough route of the PCT, he began his journey on 4 July and finished on 1 December – it had taken him 151 days. While he published an account of his trek in *Appalachia*, this record was almost entirely overlooked at the time. It would not be until the 1970s that public attention would be drawn to the exploits of through-hikers on the PCT.

War veterans like Shaffer and Papendick were not the only people to seek healing and self-discovery on the long-distance trails of America. In 1954, Emma Gatewood began her southbound Appalachian Trail hike from Mount Katahdin. She was sixty-six years old, from Ohio, and the survivor of a brutally violent marriage that had ended in the early 1940s. Entirely unprepared and often lost, she was persuaded that year to return home by forest rangers. Back again in 1955, she began this time on 3 May from Mount Oglethorpe.

With little more than a shower curtain to keep the rain off, she headed north, often sleeping on a bed of leaves at night and relying on berries for food.[49]

By June, reporters began to excitedly track her progress – and on 8 July the story was picked up for syndication across hundreds of newspapers. Sitting down for breakfast that morning, Americans read a variation of the same headline: 'Grandma Walking Appalachian Trail'.[50] Inspired by the story, readers began to show up on the trail to offer her supplies and assistance: the phenomenon of 'trail magic' was born. Finishing on 25 September, she was the first woman to through-hike the entire trail – and to her surprise, she was now also a national celebrity. She appeared on America's first morning chat show, the *Today Show*, where she was interviewed by David Garroway. 'I've had all the walking that I'll want for a long time', she declared,[51] but she came back the following year to hike the trail again. Further hikes would ensue – including the 2,000 mile Oregon Trail in 1959 – with 'Grandma Gatewood Day' declared on her arrival in Portland. Her fame was to continue, with trips to Hollywood for television and radio appearances throughout the 1960s. Her incredible legacy was to challenge the mythology that surrounded long-distance hiking. While these trails were capable of providing escape and adventure, they were not just for war veterans and grizzled mountain men – they were for everyone.

Britian's first national trail – the 268 mile Pennine Way – had been directly inspired by the Appalachian Trail. First proposed by the journalist Tom Stephenson in 1935 – as a 'faint green line' that would be engraved by the 'feet of grateful pilgrims' – he also intended the route to leverage public access to otherwise private moorland. Planning began in the late 1940s and the route was eventually officially opened in 1965. It immediately saw a flurry of attention from a whole range of people, including a team of eight firemen and, hiking alone, a 17-year-old Boy Scout, all within months of the official opening.[52] Serious attention from runners was an inevitability. In May 1969, Holmfirth Harriers would be the first among several athletic and fell running clubs to attempt a relay record (aiming for a time of 48 hours). Slowed down immediately by poor weather and visibility, they decided to end their attempt at Blackstone Edge. Solo record attempts soon followed. The initial running record was set in 1971, by Bill Bird, from London-based Ranelagh Harriers, in four days and eight hours – a record that would soon be bested by northern fell running natives Alan Heaton, in 1973, and Joss Naylor, in 1974[53] (see Chapters 6 and 7).

While the concept of a marked national trail was a novelty in Britain, setting records on established routes already had a long and distinguished pedigree: most notably the 24-hour Lakeland record and other notable lines, such as the Welsh 3000s (see Chapter 2). Yet in the same year that the Pennine Way record was first set, 1971, a new organisation was launched in Cumbria: the Bob Graham 24 Hour Club. Proposed by Fred Rogerson, the aim of the club was to define and celebrate attempts on a route that had been established decades before by Robert Graham. The club hoped to raise the profile of Graham and his achievement, while also establishing a route – the Bob Graham Round – that would pose a difficult but viable 24-hour challenge for any long-distance fell runner.

Robert Graham was a working-class Cumbrian native, born near Carlisle in 1889, who had found himself drawn into the growing pursuit of rambling and fell walking in the early decades of the twentieth century. Little is known about his early life, with different accounts stating that he worked as a gardener and then perhaps later as a fruiterer.[54] There is no doubt, however, that he was a working man from a modest background. He moved from Carlisle to Keswick, in the heart of the Lake District, so as to be closer to the fells and mountain culture that had become such a feature of his life. This was a crucial period in the evolution of fell walking. It was gradually shifting away from the elite spheres of Victorian gentility to a more democratised practice among a wider middle class, although class prejudices would linger for decades. The later exploits of Graham would, shamefully, be doubted, partly because of his background, but also due to his place outside the hallowed halls of the exclusive Alpine Club.

Described as 'powerfully built, modest, kindly',[55] Graham made ready use of the fells that towered above his new home in Keswick. The length and duration of his excursions increased, with recollections from a friend that Graham 'and a group of "elite" enthusiasts would regularly walk 50 miles over the fells in all directions and all weather'.[56] Graham's involvement in fell walking was emerging at a time when there was an intense flurry of interest in the Lakeland 24-hour record – with successful attempts to break the record already having been made by Keith Wakefield (1905), Cecil Dawson (1916) and Eustace Thomas (1923), all of whom were still active on the scene. It was this world of long-distance adventure that Graham was gradually becoming involved with, despite a class background that in previous decades might have seen him excluded from this clique of mountain men.

In May 1932, Graham was to help his friend Frederick Spencer Chapman target the 24-hour record. A Cambridge graduate and renowned Arctic explorer, Spencer had recently been attached to the British Arctic Air Route Expedition, as a photographer and ornithologist, to map and explore the uncharted parts of Greenland. Only five years later, in 1937, Chapman would become the first person, along with his sherpa, to climb the 7,000 metre Himalayan peak Chomolhari. Extraordinarily, Chapman was also to spend three years in Malaysia during the Second World War. Trapped behind enemy lines, he lived in the jungle and raided Japanese supply lines. Believing these attacks to be part of a much larger commando force, the Japanese had 2,000 soldiers combing the wildness in search of what they believed to be an elite squad of phantom soldiers. After evading this persistent hunt, Chapman was successfully evacuated from Malaysia at the end of the war.[57]

A decade before his exploits in Malaysia – and waved off by Keith Wakefield – Chapman made what is now known as an anticlockwise round. This involved heading from Keswick to the Newlands Valley, and then across the Great Gable range to Wasdale. Travelling from Wasdale over Scafell to Bowfell, Chapman was on track to break the record – and almost took fell running history in a different direction – but he encountered thick mist and inclement weather.

Following the loss of his compass and ensuing navigational delays, compounded by a knee injury from his Greenland expedition, his progress began to slow.[58] He eventually circuited across to the Helvellyn range and the northern fells before descending into Keswick, having summitted thirty-nine fells in a little over 25 hours. It was an impressive attempt, but ultimately a 24-hour record failure. Chapman was assisted by a team of eight pacers, including Bob Graham himself and the (at the time) 24-hour record holder, Eustace Thomas.[59] This was a tight clique of men, brought together across class boundaries by a shared passion for long-distance walking at an elite level.

Graham would have been paying close attention as he supported Chapman's round. He was already preparing for his own attempt, which was to take place three weeks later. It would be Graham's second attempt, after a failed effort the year before.

Sunday 12 June. In the muggy quiet of a warm summer night, at 1 a.m., Graham unobtrusively set off from Keswick with only one pacer. Breaking with the tradition of past record attempts – all of which had gone anticlockwise – Graham instead headed straight up the silhouetted flanks of Skiddaw. Relying on fruit pastilles and water for the first two legs, they arrived at Dunmail for around 9 a.m., where they had tea, boiled eggs, buttered bread and 30 minutes' rest. Then across the Langdales – with a hot and hazy sun beginning to beat down on them – to Bowfell, along to Scafell, and down the sharp descent into Wasdale, arriving at 4.45 p.m. More eggs, with milk and soda, then onwards after another 30-minute break. A change of pacers and up over Yewbarrow to Great Gable and Honister – at the time still a working slate quarry – arriving a little after 9 p.m. to sip on hot powdered milk (supplied by bemused miners finishing work for the evening). Then, with a final pacer – his fourth companion for the day (two of whom had been out for Chapman's attempt three weeks prior) – out over the final three fell summits in pattering rain, down for the valley run from Newlands to Keswick. A small group of friends and family stood waiting, as Graham trotted in, to reach the Moot Hall, a little after midnight, in a total time of 23 hours and 39 minutes, over 42 fell summits. He was awake at 6 a.m. the following morning to cook breakfast for friends and supporters.

It was a new 24-hour Lakeland record, deftly claiming a title that had been held for almost a decade by his friend Eustace Thomas. Given the low-key nature of the attempt – and Graham's seemingly 'ordinary' background – many were sceptical. A small number of newspapers did report on Graham's new record, but most of these articles spent the larger part of their column discussing Chapman – the famous 'Greenland Explorer' – and the details of his failed attempt the month before, the failed exploits of a Cambridge graduate clearly perceived to be of more interest to readers than the evident success of a Cumbrian working man. Bob Graham was celebrated by those close to him, but otherwise mostly overlooked by the wider public. It would not be until the formation of the Bob Graham 24 Hour Club that his achievement would be publicly celebrated and – over the ensuing decades – replicated by thousands of runners.

The interwar hiking craze and multi-decade effort to build a trail network – and even grander long-distance routes – would have a profound impact on outdoor recreation and sport. As a new post-war settlement began to unfold, outdoor activities had become normalised for vast swathes of a North American and British public. Those early pioneers had built the cultural and physical foundations upon which an outdoor athletic culture would continue to thrive. For those setting speed and endurance records, such as Bob Graham in the Lake District, or Earl Shaffer on the Appalachian Trail, it was less about pure aerobic power in a traditional athletic sense – as Jasmin Paris would echo many decades later – and more often about mental resilience and self-reliance. That ability to deal with the unknown, and to move efficiently through the natural world, would remain defining features in a sport that, in the 1950s, was on the cusp of evolving into something that would more closely resemble contemporary mountain, ultra and trail running.

Part II

Running revolution

Chapter 6

A nation of athletes

An incredible photograph emerged in the aftermath of the 1967 Boston Marathon – an iconic sporting image that would herald a moment of profound change. A female competitor, wearing a grey sweatshirt and bib number 261, is lunged at from behind by three men, who appear to hold her back. Surrounding runners look on in confusion at this violent and disturbing scene – a woman's athletic achievement threatened by male aggression. Runner 261 is Kathrine Switzer, the first woman to officially run the Boston Marathon. One of the men, John Semple, a race official, screams and swears as he tears at her bib number.[1] Despite appearances, the other two men are helping Switzer: her boyfriend, a former All American football player, is pushing Semple away (he eventually tackled him into the nearby bushes), and her coach is yelling 'leave her alone, let her finish'.[2]

Prior to that moment, women had only ever completed the Boston Marathon unofficially. Roberta Gibbs had been refused entry the previous year, with the dismissive comment that women were 'physiologically incapable' of running the distance. She ran the marathon anyway – the first woman to do so – in an unofficial time of 3 hours and 21 minutes. A year later, Switzer noted that the race rules did not specifically prohibit women from running – it was assumed that they wouldn't or couldn't – and she gained entry by registering under the gender-neutral designation of 'K. Switzer'.

Despite the fracas, Switzer completed the Boston Marathon that day. She was not the first woman to complete a marathon – officially or unofficially – but her subversive act was successful for several reasons: (i) it was so brazenly public, (ii) she fitted cultural ideas of femininity (and was therefore visibly breaking down barriers for women), and (iii) AAU discrimination against her was so blatant.[3] In the ensuing controversy, the AAU brought in a rule to *officially* ban women from competing in long-distance AAU-governed races.[4] It was, however, too late for those wanting to cling to the status quo: the clamour for athletics to fully democratise could no longer be ignored. Fierce campaigning – including with financial support from cosmetics company Avon[5] – led to the overturning of the AAU ruling in 1971, and, in 1984, the first women's Olympic marathon. The Switzer incident was a watershed moment in athletics, then, yet it was neither surprising nor unexpected: a quiet revolution had been taking place for over a decade.

The post-war decades were a period of renewal and rising prosperity. In the United States, there was a mass exodus, from both cities and rural backwaters, to the comfort and domesticity of the suburbs.[6] Similarly, in Britain, reconstruction was driving the creation of so-called New Towns and huge swathes of modern semi-detached housing. Single-family households quickly became the norm, rather than the busy multigenerational or shared family homes of the previous century. These households were hungry for new family leisure interests. This was accompanied by rapid changes in lifestyle: household appliances, mass car ownership, television and calorie-rich diets, coupled with more sedentary working lives and urban planning that prioritised car travel.[7]

As early as 1952, doctors and policy makers were concerned about these profound changes: that year, the National Institute of Health declared obesity the number one health issue in the United States.[8] Similar concerns were echoed in Britain, with the formation of a committee in 1957, by the Central Council for Physical Recreation (CCPR), to examine the ways in which sporting participation might be encouraged among the general public.[9] Part of this concern with health and fitness was bound up with widespread anxiety during the Cold War. As historian Shelly McKenzie argues, throughout the 1950s and 1960s there was a 'complex rhetoric' that 'envisioned children as future parents, citizens, and soldiers whose moral, mental, and physical capabilities were key to maintaining the superiority of the nation both at home and abroad'.[10]

There was another side to suburbanisation: increased leisure time and a new focus on physical education within school curricula. Throughout the 1950s, for example, Little League Baseball doubled in size every year as it swept across small town and suburban America.[11] Britain also saw a huge interest in sports participation – such as swimming, basketball, netball and badminton – alongside a rapid expansion of youth teams (for boys) in football, rugby and cricket.[12] For the first time in history, the idea of *doing sport* was slowly becoming encultured across an entire generation of young people.[13]

Concerns about obesity and the physical decline of society came to a head in the early part of the next decade. In Britain, the Wolfenden Report was published in 1960: it advocated the creation of a sports council to promote and support the sporting lives of not just children, but also adults.[14] The report inspired a governmental focus on sport, with a slow but steady expansion of leisure facilities, coaching and funding. A year later, in May 1961, President Kennedy expressed similar concerns in a speech to football fans in New York: 'We look instead of play, ride instead of walk ... our national sport is not playing at all, but watching. We have become more and more, not a nation of athletes, but a nation of spectators.'[15]

Kennedy followed these remarks with presidential initiatives on sport and physical health, including, in late 1962, the issuing of a challenge: that a US marine should be able to hike 50 miles in no more than twenty hours. The 'Kennedy March', as it became known, would prove to have an electrifying effect upon America.

By the end of the 1960s, then, the sporting lives of Britons and Americans had been utterly transformed. Active involvement in sport was now commonplace – and this would filter through to endurance running. Inevitably, these changes would have a profound and formative impact on the disciplines of mountain, ultra and trail running.[16]

After more than a decade of war and austerity, the summer of 1951 was a joyous and celebratory moment across Britain. Desperate to move towards a more optimistic future, the Labour government launched the Festival of Britain, a series of exhibitions and events designed to showcase artistic, scientific and sporting ingenuity across the nation.[17] Millions attended. The festival was deliberately contemporary, eschewing the drab brown and green tones of pre-war Britain for a fresher and bolder palette of 'futuristic' colours.[18] At 7 a.m. on 11 August, the official 'festival race' began: 48 runners departed from below Big Ben in Westminster, heading south for Brighton. They were slowed by heavy rain and a strong headwind, but after 52 miles the winner, Lew Piper of Blackheath Harriers, raced into Brighton for a finishing time of 6 hours 18 minutes and 40 seconds.[19] The stockbrokers' racewalk still occurred most years on this route, but this was something else entirely: it was a true London to Brighton *running* race.

Buoyed by this success, the race organiser, Ernest Neville, decided to make it an annual event. More ambitiously, he wanted to use the race as a springboard to spread the gospel of distance running and to provide a competitive focus for the small endurance running community. Fast approaching his eightieth year, Neville had been at the heart of ultra-distance athletics for almost five decades. He first walked the London to Brighton route at the age of fourteen, in 1897, after watching pedestrian Edward Knott clip along the route before awed spectators. Neville himself entered the racewalking scene as a young man in 1903, with a string of accomplishments that were as much administrative as athletic, including the establishment of the Centurions in 1911 (see Chapter 4) and the active promotion and support of various racewalking events across the UK. He had been involved in almost every aspect of racewalking for half a century, including as official racewalking judge at the 1936 Berlin Games.[20] Now in his twilight years, this septuagenarian from a leafy Surrey suburb was turning his attention to distance running.

In December 1952, Neville and a small group of friends convened the Road Runners Club (RRC). The aim of this new organisation was to support distance running as a leisure activity. Many of the early members were competitive runners, with notable race times on track and road, but the animating spirit of the organisation was that *anyone* and *everyone* should be able to run for recreational purposes. The primary focus of the RRC committee was organising the blue-ribbon London to Brighton race every year, along with a triannual newsletter of carefully typewritten text. Over time this evolved into a full-colour magazine, known simply as *Roadrunner*. The RRC was a dominating presence throughout the 1950s and 1960s, with an influence that would be manifold.

First, the RRC helped to standardise and normalise the idea of running and racing on the road. Running tracks were not commonplace, nor were they always accessible for everyday training. In contrast, roads were *everywhere* – and members were encouraged to make use of them. In terms of racing, the RRC acted as a coordinating body to support an emerging roster of road races. This included the standardisation of distance measurements on the road, advice on event management, and working with the authorities to ensure that road races could be held safely and responsibly. A race insurance scheme was launched – though thankfully accidents were minimal – and Neville worked with the Ministry of Transportation to clarify concerns about traffic management during road races.

Second, the RRC slowly built a running community that was both competitive and recreational. The newsletter contained advice on training, such as extended discussions on the need to include speedwork in marathon training, or the incorporation of salt into ultramarathon nutrition.[21] The early newsletter editions printed all the recent race results of individual club members, with most competing in a varied collection of sub-marathon, marathon and occasionally ultramarathon distance races. The times were impressive – a sub-3-hour marathon was standard for most members – but as the membership expanded there were a growing number of more 'modest' finishes. Even in the early years there was an international component to membership. The great South African runner and Comrades Marathon legend Wally Hayward was listed in the 1953 membership results, including his records that year (while visiting

Britain) for London to Brighton, the Bath 100 mile, and a 24-hour world track record (159 miles and 562 yards).[22]

The RRC did not itself initiate the 'running boom' of the 1960s and 1970s, but it did start to lay the groundwork for mass participation in recreational running. Future RRC presidents would include some of the most noted athletes of post-war Britain, among them Ron Hill, Don Ritchie and David Bedford. RRC members also looked abroad to the Comrades Marathon as – alongside London to Brighton – another pinnacle of international distance running.

Slowly, in the 1960s, the RRC would also begin to draw in athletes from across the Atlantic, where in the United States a similar running revival was just beginning to take place.

It is a freezing morning in the Bronx, 8 March, with frosty blue skies just beginning to cloud over into a leaden afternoon. Sedgwick Avenue: in a decade, this New York arterial will be overshadowed by the brute arch of the Cross Bronx Expressway and clusters of stacked tenement buildings, on the cusp of fame as the birthplace of hip hop. In 1959, it is still a battered row of brickwork buildings – a bustling channel of industry and commerce – running up alongside the glimmer of train tracks and the Harlem River.

An African American man appears, lean and muscular, loping along at a steady pace. Despite the chill, he is dressed in nothing but shorts and a white vest, the word 'Pioneer' emblazoned on his front. He weaves up the avenue, gliding over potholes and cobbles. Bystanders might recognise the man – Ted Corbitt is a familiar sight, running up and around his local neighbourhood – but few will understand the significance of what is happening. This is the first AAU-sanctioned 'ultramarathon' of the modern era – 30 miles, looping five times around the Bronx – and it marks the beginning of an endurance running revival in the United States.

Theodore 'Ted' Corbitt has been described as the 'father of American distance running'.[23] Born in 1919, on a cotton farm in South Carolina, he moved with his family to Ohio, where he was educated at the University of Cincinnati. A college education was highly unusual for an African American in the pre-war era, and he faced persistent discrimination throughout his involvement in collegiate athletics. This included being barred from track meets because white athletes refused to compete against him.[24] He enlisted in the early 1940s and after a long period of training found himself aboard a troopship in the Caroline Islands, readying for the invasion of Japan. The war ended – just in time – and he narrowly managed to avoid the anticipated slaughter.[25]

He moved to New York in late 1946, brimming with enthusiasm for his post-war life. This involved marriage, work as a physical therapist and evening study for a postgraduate degree. Keen to remain active, he joined the New York Pioneer Club (NYPC) in 1947. Athletics was still deeply segregated in the United States and even in New York most clubs refused membership to African American and Jewish athletes. The NYPC had been founded in 1936 with the ethos of open membership (although women were still excluded). Corbitt embraced a new training regime, with long runs to work as part of his commute, and an innate talent for distance running began to emerge. In his marathon debut, at Boston in 1951, he managed 15th place. A year later, he competed in the 1952 Helsinki Olympics, with an admittedly below par performance, which saw him take 44th place – almost 20 minutes slower than his marathon best at the Shanahan Marathon four years later (2:26:44). There were only a small number of marathons in the United States in the 1950s, and Corbitt competed in almost all of them. He consistently managed a top ten or top twenty finish. But while he was undoubtedly talented at the marathon distance, it would be the unexpected revival of ultra-distance running and the modern concept of ultramarathon running that would cement his legacy as an athlete.

In 1958, the American distance runner and Olympian Browning Ross had returned home from competition in Britain to Philadelphia, to establish the Middle Atlantic Road Runners Club (MARRC).[26] Inspired by Ernest Neville, he had joined the Road Running Club while in the UK and hoped to start a similar movement in the United States. MARRC quickly evolved into a national organisation – the Road Runners Club of America (RRCA) – with six regional chapters opening up across the country. Corbitt became an important part of this endurance revival. While initially cautious of adopting a time-consuming administrative role, he relented and became the first president of the New York Road Runners Club (NYRRC).

With training meets at Macombs Dam Park, in the Bronx, the club grew rapidly to a membership of around 250. These converts to road running began to adopt committee positions and campaign for the expansion of road running distance events. They were successful. In February and March 1959, two AAU-approved road events were organised by the RRC in New York: the Cherry Tree Marathon (destined to evolve into the New York Marathon) and a 30 mile ultramarathon. There were only four competitors in this watershed ultra-distance race – and Corbitt won easily in a time of 3 hours 4 minutes and 13 seconds – but ever so slowly interest would grow in what was becoming perceived as a new category of athletics: the 'ultramarathon'.

Ultrarunning had of course been taking place for over a century by this point, but the glory days of pedestrianism were a distant memory. For this generation of runners – accustomed only to the marathon distance – this must have felt like an evolutionary leap. Corbitt has sometimes been credited with coining the term 'ultramarathon'. While this is not entirely true – the word itself can be found in newspaper coverage from at least as early as the 1920s[27] – Corbitt undoubtedly popularised both the discipline and the term. There were to be only a handful of ultramarathons in the United States during the 1960s – the marathon remained the pre-eminent test for endurance runners – but almost all these ultramarathons were organised by the New York Road Runners Club. In 1965, for example, there were five ultra-distance events in the United States, four of which were in New York, varying in distance between 32 and 45 miles. The number of competitors was tiny – usually in single figures – but the Bronx had become the beating heart of a new American ultramarathon culture.

While he himself would be dominant on this new ultra-distance scene in the United States, Corbitt also became the international face of American ultrarunning. Partly because of a unique historical legacy – partly also because of the work done by Neville and the

RRC – London to Brighton was widely recognised as the premier international 'ultramarathon' (although the term was not used in Britain at the time). Accordingly, Browning Ross came forward in 1961 with a proposal for Corbitt: the RRCA would cover the cost of travel if Corbitt would agree to represent the United States at London to Brighton.

Corbitt prepared for the race through the early part of 1962, before flying out to London for the competition. He was under no illusions about the scale of the challenge: he had not yet competed at the 50 mile distance, nor against ultra-distance athletes of this calibre. He destroyed himself on the course – an all-out effort to compete at the front of the pack – before eventually racing into Brighton for fourth place, in a time of 5 hours 53 minutes and 27 seconds.[28] It was an impressive result for a London to Brighton and 50 mile debut. He would return regularly to the UK over the next decade to compete on this iconic course and in longer 100 mile track races. Corbitt would never crack a first-place finish at London to Brighton – although he appeared a total of five times over the course of his career – and in 1969 he managed his best and final performance: having just turned fifty years of age, he came second in a time of 5 hours 38 minutes and 11 seconds.

Corbitt was essentially fusing the culture of contemporary road marathon running with an experimentative push beyond the standard marathon distance. Within this small and emergent world of the ultramarathon, there was no interest in off-road running. Cross-country running itself was still relatively unformed in 1950s America. The National Collegiate Athletic Association (NCAA), which would become a dominant force in American cross country, had only been established in 1938, and it was not until 1957 that it would launch the divisional national championships that have become such an important feature of American athletics.

Trail racing was still almost entirely absent from the American sporting lexicon. The Dipsea and Mount Wilson races continued to take place in California – and Mount Marathon in Alaska – but these were essentially local/regional races that had little cachet or recognition in the national sport of athletics. It is this context that makes Pikes Peak, in Colorado, such a fascinating and influential race. It was the first place where trail running – or mountain running – would truly begin to grow in way that would influence the wider sport.

Ascent-only racing had already taken place on Pikes Peak during the 1930s, but the race had folded shortly before the war (see Chapter 3). It was not until 1956, two decades later, that Arne Suominen (1900–1972) would step forward to revive the Pikes Peak challenge, this time as an authentic up-and-down trail race. Suominen had a great deal of endurance experience. As a young man he had briefly been the lead runner in the transcontinental race of 1928, pulling out from pole position only due to injury (see Chapter 4). A medical doctor by trade, he shared widespread public concern with the apparent declining health of the nation. Smoking, in particular, troubled him, and in the early 1950s he penned several polemical newspaper letters on the subject. Then, in 1956, he issued a challenge: he (and other interested non-smokers) would race any smoker to the summit of Pikes Peak and back down. They would even allow the smokers a 15-minute break for a cigarette at the top.[29] His challenge ruffled more than a few feathers. Almost 50 per cent of Americans smoked at the time – a majority of them men[30] – and Suominen was widely derided in newspaper coverage as a 'smoking-hater'.[31] A 22-year-old smoker and college student, Ron Bierstedt, came forward and claimed to have summitted many of Colorado's fourteeners[32] without any detriment from tobacco consumption. Challenge accepted – the race was on.

Sponsored by KRDO radio-TV, in Colorado Springs, there was intense local interest, and a date was set for 10 August. The planned route began at the railway depot in Manitou Springs, went straight up the rocky zig-zagging Barr Trail to the summit and then back down. It was 24 miles with almost 2,500 metres of climbing (the route would be extended to the standard marathon distance in 1976). Twelve non-smokers lined up against three smokers, including Lou Wille, winner of the 1936 ascent race (at which time he had been a non-smoker). Off they went, under a hot and relentless sun, slogging up the trail. The clanking of the nearby funicular railway could be heard echoing out over the swaying ponderosa pine trees. Huffing and puffing, Wille made it to the top first – clearly a master of the ascent despite his tobacco habit – but he was forced to stop because of an injured knee.[33] It was red-haired, 28-year-old gym owner Monte Wolford – fitness enthusiast and champion body builder – who turned first for the dive back down to Manitou Springs. He finished first in 5 hours 39 minutes and 58 seconds – the earliest known time for the up-and-down of Pikes Peak. Only four runners finished, including Suominen – all of them non-smokers.

The race immediately gathered enough local support to allow it to continue in subsequent years. In 1957, it was still billed as a 'smokers versus non-smokers' contest (and once again won by Wolford), although gradually this unique feature of the race would be forgotten. Recognised as a significant test of endurance and athletic prowess, it was beginning to attract a rising calibre of athlete, including, in 1958, an Olympic cyclist from New Mexico. In general, however, participants were not drawn from the realm of competitive and national US athletics. There existed no official AAU validation or support for the race, which meant that it sat outside of elite running circles and the wider athletic fraternity. Rather, it was a motley collection of local fitness enthusiasts, runners, hikers, cyclists and mountaineers that were drawn to the race. This would prove to be significant. While Pikes Peak is the third oldest marathon in the United States – following Boston and Yonkers – it was never part of mainstream marathon culture.

And then, in 1959, something extraordinary happened – what is now known to be the first *official* completion of an American marathon by a female athlete, Arlene Pieper (1931–2021). In August of that year, Pieper had been planning to open a gym in Fort Worth, Texas. This would be her second venture, building on an already successful gym that she ran with her husband in their home of Colorado Springs. The gyms – or 'health studios' as they were known ('gyms' were exclusively male spaces) – catered specifically for women, with personalised training plans for 'health' and 'weight loss'.[34] Pieper was setting up on the ground floor of America's emergent fitness boom, with a canny eye on the growing female market. Pieper's entry to Pikes Peak was part of a local marketing strategy to help promote the gym. There was some predictably dismissive newspaper coverage of the seeming novelty of a woman running Pikes Peak: 'Included in the entries is a girl, name not known here', wrote the Pennsylvania paper *New Castle News*.[35] Decades later, Pieper would recount her memories of the race:

> That day there was 12 of us at the starting line. There was another lady, my daughter, myself, and I was 29. And the others were men. It was a beautiful day. Couldn't have asked for a better day. Sunshiny, I had my short shorts on that we used to wear back then and a white blouse, tied in a knot — that's how we did things back in the '50s. And my tennis shoes from the dime store, and off I went.[36]

She was well prepared. While entry to the race was partly about promoting her fitness studio, Pieper had nonetheless spent two years training in anticipation. This involved laps around the local track – while her three young children played and tumbled around in the central isle – and a hike every Sunday up to Barr Camp for altitude training. On race day, she hiked hard to the summit, accompanied by her 9-year-old daughter, Kathy, often at times overtaking men, many of whom were struggling with the altitude. Turning at the summit for the descent (where she would leave her daughter), she skipped back down for a total finish time of 9 hours and 16 minutes. The *Colorado Springs Gazette* barely registered the achievement – no mention at all of this barrier-breaking achievement by a woman – and the paper instead focused on the undeniable novelty of Pieper's daughter, describing how the crowd 'almost raised the sky with its cheers for the little girl'.[37] A decade later, young Kathy (by then a Fresno college student) could be found testing specialised clothing for the moon landings in an arduous trek across Death Valley.[38] Clearly her endurance upbringing had not been entirely forgotten. Arlene Pieper would not reprise her participation in the Pikes Peak race, nor would she gain contemporaneous recognition. It was not until the early 2000s that she would gain recognition as the first woman to officially complete a US marathon.

Pikes Peak itself continued to grow modestly, with a roster of anywhere up to around forty competitors by the end of the 1960s – and yet for these first two decades it remained essentially a unique and exotic challenge, rather than being recognised as part of any wider sporting culture. Pikes Peak foreshadowed the sport of American trail running that would eventually develop in the 1970s and 1980s.

Across the Atlantic, something similar was already taking place. Perhaps due to the older and more established origins of fell running, Britain had been quicker off the mark to combine recreational running with mountain craft. As in America, British mountain running would be shaped by the unique experiences of a post-war generation. This included not just a growing interest in athletics and outdoor recreation, but also changing attitudes to gender and social class. The parallels are fascinating. Something similar was taking place at the same time in the United States and Britain – and for British fell runners, this would involve an important connection to the already established roots of this rather idiosyncratic sport.

26 June 1960 – the hottest day of the year. A fit and healthy-looking 77-year-old man stands under a sweltering midday sun, watching four runners at they descend the grassy slope of Dale Head, down to the rubble-strewn gap of Honister Pass. Even here in the Lake District, this unassuming man would most likely be passed without recognition. But to a dedicated few, Bob Graham is instantly recognisable – particularly today, as an attempt is made on his almost three-decade-old record (see Chapter 5).

Three of the runners are making the attempt together – Alan Heaton, his brother Kenneth, and Stan Bradshaw – and the fourth has the unenviable role of sole pacer and water carrier. Only 32-year-old Alan Heaton is eventually successful, racing down into Keswick on a quiet Sunday morning with a finishing time of 22 hours and 48 minutes, almost an hour quicker than Graham's 1932 record. 'I'm not the least upset the record's gone – it's lasted much too long. This young fellow has put up a wonderful performance', remarked a philosophical and generous Bob Graham upon hearing the news.[39] It was only a warm-up for Heaton: he would be back to 'lower' the record further, adding an additional eighteen summits to the 24-hour record in 1965.

Fell running was undergoing a transition in the 1950s and early 1960s. Almost a century old, the sport had been characterised by two distinct worlds: on the one hand, working-class locals in the professional guides races, on the other, endurance mountaineers and long-distance hikers. This was changing in the 1950s. A new generation of athletes – many of whom were cross-country runners attached to running clubs and athletics associations – were drawn to the fells and hills of northern England. They would begin to combine skills and abilities that had previously been somewhat distinct: speed and distance, athletic prowess and technicality, power and mountain craft. There was also an important change to the social admixture of fell running. It was becoming more geographically and culturally dispersed: no longer just locals or expedition-focused mountaineers, but a more jumbled mix of those from the large towns and suburbs of northern England. The post-war lower-middle and technical classes were especially well represented.

Alan Heaton (1928–2019) was emblematic of this change. A small and quiet man, raised in the Lancashire town of Accrington, Heaton worked as a clerk for a Preston-based bus company, Ribble Motor Services. In the mid-1950s, while in his late twenties, he joined Clayton-le-Moors Harriers, a prominent cross-country athletics club (which would in time become one of the earliest athletics clubs to specialise in fell running). Heaton already had a passion for hill walking and cycling, so soon found himself among a small group of club members regularly making the short trip northwards to the Lake District. He was joined by others with a similar set of interests; fellow club member Stanley Bradshaw, another talented cross-country runner and heir to a family tripe business; Fred Bagley, an aeronautical engineer and member of Preston Harriers; Eric 'Beardie' Beard, a wandering soul from Yorkshire, former tram conductor, labourer and salesman, now an instructor in the small outdoor recreation industry; Fred Rogerson, owner of a Cumbrian building firm and the grandson of a champion guides racer. Between them they represented the 'golden triangle' of fell running in northern England – Cumbria, Lancashire and Yorkshire – and a post-war generation that had the time and ability to pursue new forms of outdoor leisure.

The Lake District Mountain Trial (LDMT) emerged at the beginning of this generational shift. First held in 1952, the LDMT was organised by a Cumbrian branch of the Youth Hostels Association (YHA). The YHA had witnessed a massive post-war surge of membership – up to 200,000 members by 1950 – and it was continuing to play a key role in the development of the outdoor movement.[40] For hikers and climbers – and an emergent generation of fell runners – youth hostels provided affordable accommodation and a base of operations during regular weekend or holiday excursions. The first LDMT was planned as a one-off celebration by the local YHA branch, with 21 participants (including a solicitor and a well-heeled schoolmaster) scrambling up the 16 mile route from Langdale over Bowell, Esk Pike, Scafell Pike and Great Gable.[41] The route was rough, steep and rocky, with 2,000 metres of climbing. The winner, Roland Moore, raced into the finish at the Dungeon Ghyll Hotel in 3 hours and 45 minutes, where he promptly shared the prize winnings – a barrel of cider – with the other competitors and race officials.[42] The LDMT was unlike the guides races that had dominated fell racing up until this moment: it combined speed with self-sufficiency and navigation over longer distances. It was a combination that would not be without debate: 'harriers versus mountaineers', speed or mountain craft. The desirable balance of these qualities would continue to be a point of contention.

Only two years later, another newly launched race would play a critical role in shaping this dawning era of fell running: the Yorkshire Three Peaks Race. First held in 1954, navigation was less of an issue on this well-trodden route, which summited three fells in the Yorkshire Dales (Pen-y-Ghent, Whernside and Ingleborough) – but the distance was something else entirely. There were only around a dozen fell races across the whole of the UK in the mid-1950s. Most were a few miles in distance – the longest was Ben Nevis at 10 miles. In contrast, the Yorkshire Three Peaks was 23 miles, with

1,600 metres of ascent, on an occasionally steep but mostly runnable route, demanding both speed and endurance. The 1954 race was organised by Fred Bagley of Preston Harriers – a race that he won, in 3 hours and 48 mins, with Stan Bradshaw battling for second – but responsibility for the event was then taken over by Clayton-le-Moors Harriers. An official organising committee was eventually established in 1963 for the Three Peaks Race, with representation from a selection of running clubs in northern England – some of whom were now developing a reputation as 'fell running' clubs. These clubs would become the core institutional component of this new amateur fell running culture. Much like mainstream athletics, fell running was growing and diversifying, and in 1970 the creation of the Fell Runners Association (FRA) would provide institutional ballast and longevity for this distinctive sport (see Chapter 8). And yet there was a notable absence: women.

The second edition of the LDMT, in 1953, had been dedicated to the coronation of Queen Elizabeth. In a nod to the ascension of a female monarch, the organisers decided to include a women's race. Once again in Langdale, the women's race was on a shortened course of around 10 miles, over Rosset Gill, Esk Pike and Bowfell, before heading back down the Band. There were four starters, with the race winner, Jane Allesbrook, accompanied by her two dogs, crossing the line in 2 hours and 14 minutes. The race was held again the following year – with three starting, but only one finishing – but was then discontinued. There was a brief revival in 1968, again with three starters, but sadly none were to finish. Other fell races were gradually appearing over the course of the late 1950s and 1960s, but none were open to women. Fell racing would largely mirror mainstream athletics, with races only gradually opening up for women towards the end of the 1970s. Women were seen as athletically incapable – and also lacking in endurance, navigation skills and mountain craft. This social conservatism extended north of the border, into Scotland, despite the extraordinary story of Kathleen Connochie at the 1955 Ben Nevis race.

The Ben Nevis race had been revived and relaunched in 1951. It quickly developed a stature that was significant enough to attract the best fell runners from across northern England. Together, the LDMT, Three Peaks and Ben Nevis formed the definitive triptych of amateur fell running during the 1950s and 1960s: these were the three races that mattered.

Kathleen Connochie was a 16-year-old schoolgirl who had been deeply associated with the race for most of her childhood. Her father was the race medical director, and their close family friend, one-eyed Duncan MacIntyre (known as 'Duncan the Butcher' – a butcher by trade, he had lost his eye in a game of shinty), had been a regular competitor in earlier iterations of the race. Connochie recalled how MacIntyre's encouragement was crucial for her entry to compete in the race:

> We were all sitting in the house one evening just about three weeks before the race itself and talk was as ever about the arrangements. For no apparent reason, Duncan said to me: 'Do you think you could run the Ben race yourself?' I said 'I don't see why not!' Duncan said he'd train me and it started from there.[43]

Training in secret together on the peat tracks around Fort William, and in the forests between Torlundy and Leanachan, Connochie registered for the race, but was told only hours before by the SAAA that she was barred from competition. MacIntyre resigned from the race in furious protest. The Ben Nevis race committee themselves raised an outcry at the SAAA ruling, with one official angrily stating: 'It is a disgrace. We would not have let Kathleen run if we had not been absolutely certain that she could do the course. We know the Ben … and we know our Kathleen.'[44]

Local anger proved to be at least partially effective. SAAA officials allowed Connochie to compete – although, shamefully, on the condition that MacIntyre accompany her and that she start two minutes behind the male competitors (several of whom she inevitably overtook). The race was won that day, with a 1 hour and 50 minute course record, by Eddie Campbell – a giant of Scottish mountain running who would compete at Ben Nevis forty-four times – but it was Connochie who made headlines. There was a splash across Scottish newspapers ('She beat the Ben Nevis ban') and, incredibly, a story in Britain's most widely read tabloid, *News of the World*.

The race to the finish was a moment of triumph and vindication for Connochie:

> I felt really fresh and we had had a great time coming down the hill. At one stage, Duncan disappeared to go and wash himself having fallen in a bog. I know there was consternation in the field when it was announced that we had been separated. Then we passed the SAAA official on the way down and that gave Duncan and I a lot of pleasure. But really I had to feel sorry for Eddie on the day. There he was, the only man breaking two hours and no-one was interested. I still have the washbag I was given as a prize. It's a treasured possession.[45]

Connochie's finish established a new female record for the full ascent and descent, in 3 hours and 2 minutes – she was in 25th place, out of 27 runners, although was not included in the official list of finishers. Her remarkable story was to spark a flourishing of growth at Ben Nevis. The number of competitors doubled the following year, with continued exponential growth, and yet while a temporary exception had been made for Connochie, a red-faced SAAA continued in subsequent years to enforce a ban on female competition – as did the rest of British athletics. It would not be until 1981 that women would first officially compete at Ben Nevis.

Before these restrictions were eventually lifted, women would often need to seek alternative forms of competition. In an echo of the early Dipsea women's hike (see Chapter 3), it would be so-called challenge hikes – on both sides of the Atlantic in the 1960s – that would provide a unique space for female endurance athletics.

There is a perfect symmetry between the oldest ultramarathons in Britain and the United States. Launched only a year apart – in 1962 and 1963 – the Fellsman and JFK 50 Mile were conceived as gruelling hikes that tested both grit and character. Either fully or partly off-road, each roughly 50 miles or more in distance, they were part of a wider social movement that sought to embed physical fitness in nations that were seen to be 'going soft'. They also both maintained a strong connection to the armed forces. The Fellsman was organised by the scouting movement – a quasi-military organisation that had emerged from the martial and patriotic impulses of Edwardian Britain

Plate 1 Grasmere Sports, *c.* 1920–1950.

Plate 2 Emma Reimann, winner of the Dipsea women's hike, 1921.

Plate 3 Harvey Haggard running in the Mount Baker Marathon, 1913

Plate 4 Eddie Gardner, at the 1928 transcontinental race, running into Oklahoma with John Gober.

Plate 5 Bob Graham (centre) and pacers at Dunmail Raise, midway through his successful 24-hour Lakeland round, 1932.

Plate 6 Arlene Pieper at the Pikes Peak Marathon, 1959.

Plate 7 Ted Corbitt at London to Brighton, 1964.

Plate 8 Rick Trujillo and Joss Naylor at the Pikes Peak Marathon, 1975.

Plate 9 Mo Livemore running Western States, 1981.

Plate 10 Gary Cantrell (Lazarus Lake) running the Vol State 500k, 1989.

Plate 11 Helene Diamantides and Martin Stone at the Dragon's Back Race finish, 1992.

Plate 12 Scott Jurek at the Badwater finish, 2006.

Plate 13 Kyle Skaggs at the Hardrock 100, 2008, as featured on the cover of *UltraRunning Magazine*.

Plate 14 Anton Krupicka during his Sagebrush & Summits run/bike/climb tour, 2021.

Plate 15 Jasmin Paris and daughter at the Montane Spine Race finish, 2019.

Plate 16 Courtney Dauwalter at the UTMB Mont-Blanc finish, 2023.

– and in the early years it attracted dozens of serving soldiers and airmen. The JFK 50 was more explicitly linked to the armed forces, with a special award – the Kennedy Cup – for the highest placed military team. Unlike London to Brighton, or the RRCA ultramarathons in New York, these races were not confined to a small group of competitive athletes. The goal was not an ever-receding push to shave seconds and minutes from split times: for most competitors, just crossing the finish line was victory enough.

This spirit of inclusivity would allow these two events to blossom: by 1972, the JFK 50 had over 1,000 participants and the Fellsman around 400. By way of contrast, there were only 41 finishers at London to Brighton that year and only 18 finishers at the AAU 50 mile championship race in Rocklin (see Chapter 7). The 'closed' world of male, inter-club athletic rivalry was always going to be small and exclusive, and yet, by way of contrast, these challenge hikes were able to reach a more socially diverse group of fitness and outdoor enthusiasts. It was a deeply felt ethos that continues to animate the sport of mountain, ultra and trail running.

The first Fellsman, in 1962, was a very British affair. Small groups gathered on a dark and cloudy morning in the village of Grassington, tucked away in the pastoral heart of the Yorkshire Dales. Squalls of rain were sweeping in to batter the already wet and muddy hillsides. Fifty-four hikers set off in teams of six – all young men and teenage boys, Rover Scouts for the most part – dressed in sturdy walking boots and carrying canvas rucksacks, weighed down by metal canteens, sandwiches and woolly jumpers. This event had been organised by Don Thompson and an adult scouting group (the Brigantes Rover Crew). Thompson himself was a champion racewalker – fresh from winning gold in the 50 km race at the 1960 Rome Olympics – and a former runner (retired due to injury) with a second-place finish at the 1954 London to Brighton. The race itself was not an especially unusual format. Throughout the 1950s there had been a rise in these long-distance hiking challenges. The Fellsman was notable because it was to go further and over more difficult terrain. Running from Grassington to Ingleton (a route that would be reversed in future editions), it stretched somewhere between around 55 and 60 miles (estimates varied, and the route would often change slightly), with over 3,000 metres of ascent. Much of it crossed open and trackless land, so navigation ability was key, and bog-hopping a requisite skill. Only fifteen finished that first event. There were two joint winners – David Howe and Martin Roulson – who arrived in a little over 23 hours, taking home an Iron Age axe head as trophy.

The event was considered a great success. The following year, in 1963, there were 200 entries. No longer just a select group of Scouts, the starting line began to include an eclectic mix of servicemen from the RAF and the British Army, along with others from a range of different backgrounds and professions. The *Daily Mail*, one of Britain's most widely read national newspapers, in 1970, was to describe the Fellsman as Britain's great 'social leveller': 'covering 53 miles of hard, rugged Yorkshire country, solicitors and accountants will rub shoulders with labourers and bottle-washers. And bank managers and company directors will find the blisters just as painful as do bus drivers and stockbrokers.'[46]

It was also becoming more competitive. Fell runners – who even by the mid-1960s only had a smattering of races to compete in – were searching out new forms of regular competition. Alan Heaton first stepped up for the Fellsman in 1965 (he would win a total of ten times). He brought a level of prestige to the event, and in subsequent years some of the best long-distance fell runners would begin to test themselves against the route. This would include female finishers. The AAA did not permit women to compete in marathon events until 1975, yet a full seven years earlier, in 1968, Hazel Costello became the first woman to attempt the Fellsman – and so the first woman in Britain to officially complete a modern ultra-distance race. Female competitors to follow in the 1970s would include Jean Dawes and Anne-Marie Grindley (the first and second women to complete the Bob Graham Round) and Ann Sayer (the first woman in Britain to qualify as a Centurion and to set a women's record on Lands' End to John O'Groats). This was extraordinary. At a time when women were excluded from British road marathons – and shorter distance fell running – women were excelling at self-navigating ultra-distance racing over technical hill terrain.

The JFK 50 Mile race was sparked by a much larger craze that swept across America in 1963: the 'Kennedy March'. Concerned with the declining health and fitness of American youth, President-elect Kennedy had written an article for *Sports Illustrated* in 1960, entitled 'The soft American'. A keen sportsman himself, Kennedy argued: 'The television set, the movies and the myriad conveniences and distractions of modern life all lure our young people away from the strenuous physical activity that is the basis of fitness in youth and in later life.'[47] This set the tenor for Kennedy's approach to sport and fitness during his presidency. Various initiatives followed, including, in late 1962, a request that his marine commandant, General David M. Shoup, investigate the ability of servicemen to meet a requirement that had originally been established by Theodore Roosevelt: to complete a 50 mile hike within 20 hours. This challenge was initially tackled by a small number of servicemen in early 1963. Only a few days later, on 9 February, Attorney General Robert F. Kennedy – with typical Kennedy panache – completed the hike, in slacks and leather oxford shoes, as a way to demonstrate the vitality of the administration. Americans across the country were inspired and began themselves to take up the challenge – and so was born the Kennedy March.

Hikes were organised across the nation (and even internationally, especially in West Germany), such as a 400-strong contingent of schoolchildren in Marin County, including 8-year-old Judy Aylwin, on 11 February. Dressed in jeans and Bermuda shorts, 97 of them crossed the line within the 20-hour mark (young Judy made it to mile 42).[48] President Kennedy had made a call to fitness – and young Americans were answering.

In Maryland, running coach and champion track athlete Buzz Sawyer decided to hold a small 'Kennedy march' event on 30 March. It was a private challenge for his young athletes at Cumberland Valley Athletic Club (CVAC). Eleven participated – ten high school students and Sawyer himself. The route was an unusual mix of road and trail, around 51 miles in distance: starting at Boonsboro Junior High School, it ran along Route 40 to the Appalachian Trail, through to Harpers Ferry, and then along the C&O Canal path to

Downsville and Hagerstown. Four of them finished, including Sawyer, in 13 hours and 10 minutes. There were no plans to reprise the hike – it had been considered a one-off challenge – but the following year Sawyer's young athletes asked to run it again. It remained a private event for CVAC members – now a 'memorial hike' following the assassination of President Kennedy – but in 1965 it was opened to the public. Numbers began to grow modestly, up to 153 by 1969, with a roster of participants that was gradually shifting away from high school track athletes to adult recreational athletes. The first woman, 18-year-old Donna Aycoth, crossed the line in 1968, coming third overall (in an impressive 10:41:15) and paving the way for a gradual rise of female competition over the next decade. The finishing times also dropped: 10:39 for the victor in 1965, down to 8:32 in 1969. And then in 1971 – with a record 589 competitors – cross-country coach Baxter Berryhill crossed the line in 8:32:04.

It was in 1972 – the ten-year anniversary of the 'Kennedy March' – that the field more than doubled to almost 1,200 competitors. The record also dropped substantially: 28-year-old Park Barner, from Pennsylvania, made it across the line in 6:29:27. Barner typified a shift that had taken place for the JFK 50. While it was still an open 'hike' that attracted competitors with a range of athletic abilities, Barner was an aspiring marathon runner who – following Ted Corbitt's suggestion – had gravitated to ultra-distance running. A former track and field high school star, he brought a new level of speed and training intensity to the JFK 50. Barner would become a dominant figure in the emergent ultrarunning scene of the 1970s, including international competition at London to Brighton (with a 12th place finish in 1972). More importantly, he was illustrative of the way in which track and cross-country athletes in the United States were starting to 'move up' in distance.

The divergent paths taken by the Fellsman and JFK 50 highlight interesting variations between Britain and the United States. The Fellsman was becoming associated with fell running – slower, yet more technical and largely self-supported – while the JFK 50 remained linked to mainstream athletics, with a focus on overall speed. Despite these differences – and rising levels of competition – both would continue to connect with the ever-expanding number of recreational runners that were continuing to emerge in the late 1960s and 1970s.

The immediate post-war decades had brought with them an immense change to the social and cultural fabric of North America and Britain. Suburbanisation and rising living standards were accompanying a widespread concern with health – partially linked to Cold War anxieties – and a desire to encourage public involvement in sport and physical activity. While gender and class divisions would persist for decades, a new recreational running culture was at least beginning to reconceive athleticism in more inclusive and democratised terms. This would largely be rooted in mainstream jogging culture – the so-called 'running boom' of the 1960s and 1970s – but on the periphery there was a desire to experiment with alternative running practices, from fell and mountain running to challenge hikes and the newly conceived ultramarathon. Like seeds scattered to the wind, these new recreational disciplines were taking root – at first fragile and small, but on the cusp of sudden growth.

Chapter 7

Gold rush

It is a relatively cool summer across the Sierra Nevada in 1978 – a prelude to Hurricane Norman and the coldest winter on record later that year. Even so, the midday sun is too warm for Pat Smythe. Shedding her woollen sweater – now damp and heavy with perspiration – she runs through Robinson Flat in shorts and T-shirt. Moving at a steady trot with her temporary running companion Phil Lenihan, a marathoner and marketing manager at *Runners World*, she continues on from the high country, down into the western foothills and fractured maze of winding ravines. Beneath the dappled shade of fir and pine, they are deep in the remnants of mining country, heat radiating up from the red-brown dust as they move through a ghostly and overgrown expanse of abandoned camps, old mining equipment and scarred canyon sides: Miller's Defeat, Deadwood, Devil's Basin, El Dorado – names that evoke the hard-scrabble romance of a forgotten era.

Or perhaps not entirely forgotten. An old miner appears, as if from a dream. 'I've heard about you. I've got something for you' – he passes a small gold nugget to Smythe.[1] Clutching this unexpected talisman, she continues with her companion as darkness falls. The steep climb to Michigan Bluff, along the ridgeline to Foresthill – once a bustling hub of trade and a staging post for prospectors – and then down along the winding valley sides, to the American River, flowing out towards the urban sprawl of Sacramento Valley. Fording in pre-dawn light – weary but determined – Smythe and Lenihan continue along easier trails and undulating hills. As they finally arrive in the city of Auburn, Smyth and Lenihan hold hands to sprint the final quarter of a mile to Auburn High School. Crossing the finish line together, it has taken them 29 hours and 34 minutes to traverse the Sierra Nevada from Olympic Valley.[2] In doing so, Pat Smythe enters history as the first woman to finish the Western States Endurance Run (WSER).

The 1978 WSER was a watershed moment. While an official race had been held for the first time in 1977 – with only 14 starters, alongside the larger Tevis Cup equestrian contest – the 1978 edition was on a different date, held as a standalone race, with 63 starters. It continued to grow quickly, doubling every year until a lottery system was introduced in 1980, and began to have a formative impact on American trail and ultra running. The statistics are breathtaking. In 1972, there were only six ultra-distance events in the United States, climbing to a modest twenty-three events in 1978 and then exploding to 209 events in 1982: a 900 per cent rise in just four years. In contrast, ultrarunning remained a marginal activity in Britain, with only twenty-two events in 1982 – a number that would hardly grow until as late as the 2000s – although shorter distance fell running and challenge hikes would continue to flourish (see Chapter 6).

These figures are important. They illustrate how Western States would permanently change the course of American off-road endurance running. It helped to create an ultrarunning boom that was unique to the United States – although this brand of American ultrarunning would eventually be exported around the world. And yet Western States itself did not appear out of thin air. Only fifteen minutes down the road from Auburn, the first seeds of ultrarunning in California had been planted almost a decade before.

Sunset Oaks Country Club was in some respects an unusual location for new American endurance running records. Located in the small city of Rocklin – an old granite mining settlement on the outskirts of Sacramento – the club had an extensive golf course, but otherwise few facilities that made it an obvious site for athletic competition. Looked at another way, it was also the perfect place.

For years, Sacramento had been an important regional hub for the Pacific AAU. Until the mid-1960s, this cautious administrative body had focused on the more popular and familiar disciplines of sub-marathon cross-country and track. The West Coast in general also had a thriving National Collegiate Athletics Association (NCAA) scene – the organisation responsible for intercollegiate competition – with famed iconoclastic runners, such as Steve Prefontaine, whose charisma and celebrity would turbocharge public interest in competitive athletics. Collegiate clubs – from Portland to Los Angeles – regularly travelled to Sacramento for annual championship running meets. When searching for a way to promote ultrarunning on the West Coast, it made sense for the Pacific AAU to scout a location in the Sacramento area. A quiet, well-lit and scenic loop around the local country club must have seemed ideal.

Distance running was still overlooked in 1960s America. While numbers at Boston were growing, even the marathon was neglected by the AAU. The marathon was perceived to appeal to those from a lower social class (i.e., it was still associated with inner-city communities) and seemed to offer little in the way of dramatic spectacle for impatient spectators. The NCAA entirely ignored marathon running. And yet, leading an internal rebellion within this bureaucratic and elitist athletic culture, the New York Road Runners Club (NYRRC) was continuing to push long-distance running.[3]

As part of this revolt, Ted Corbitt had been cajoling ultra-distance running forward in New York, making canny use of his status as a long-distance icon and his ability to energetically organise and launch new events. And yet, despite Corbitt's success, ultramarathon races remained rare in the mid-1960s – and were non-existent on the West Coast. For the most part, ultramarathon races were one-off events, rather than annual affairs over a defined or established course. The few events that did exist were organised by the NYRRC, mostly as qualification races, designed with the aim of selecting runners to represent America at London to Brighton, which remained the most important international space for competition. At the urging of Aldo Scandurra, the chairman of the AAU National Long Distance Running Committee, the first of these qualification races had taken place on Staten Island in 1966. It was billed as the AAU 50 mile National Championship. There were only four finishers, with Corbitt finishing second, losing out to Irish American Jim McDonagh (immediately dubbed 'Shufflin' Mac' by the *New York Times*, due to his fast and efficient running cadence[4]). That was it – only four potential athletes – the best that America could muster in the mid-1960s for international ultra-distance competition.

Keen to expand beyond this limited pool of runners, the AAU decided the following year to sponsor a West Coast edition. Rocklin was chosen as the site of the 1967 regional championship, with a matched regional event in Poughkeepsie, New York. The Rocklin event was a 50 mile course on a tarmac loop around the country club. It took place that season alongside other distance running championship events (e.g., 10,000 metres).[5] Another 50 mile championship qualifier was held a year later – in 1968, again in Rocklin – this time won by All American cross-country, boxing and track star Skip Houk, from Reno, with a new American 50 mile record of 5 hours 58 minutes and 15.6 seconds.[6] Competitors at these championship qualifiers were all track and field athletes. They were fast, deeply embedded in the emergent science of athletics training – and they were part of a small group interested in pushing competitive distance beyond the marathon.

The record only stood for two years. In 1970 – once again in Rocklin – another 50 mile championship was held. Unlike in previous years, this was not just a regional championship, but a national qualifier for London to Brighton – it was the *only* championship ultramarathon in America that year. For the first time, the East Coast ultra elite would travel to compete against their West Coast rivals. It also pitted the old guard against the young guns. Corbitt was now in his fifties, Jim McDonagh in his late forties, and they were facing off against the likes of Skip Houk, Darryl Beardell, Rob Deines and Jose Cortez – a new breed of Californian collegiate athlete that were decades younger (Cortez was only eighteen). Anticipation was high for an historic and record-breaking race. Writing in a letter to John Chodes, Corbitt was to say: 'If I had not been aware of the force that the West Coast had become, it would have been like walking into a big ambush. I figured that I could break the American 50 mile record and [still only] finish as high as 10th place.'[7]

As expected, the race was fierce. Houk and Beardell led for most of it, with Corbitt, McDonagh and Deines trailing behind. At mile 40, with two loops to go, Deines made his move and stepped on the gas. At mile 44, this ratty, long-haired and bespectacled runner – an athletic embodiment of the beatnik generation – pushed out in front of Houk and took the lead. Then, with leaden legs and only two miles to go, he began to falter. Houk was gaining – now only 30 yards behind. With a surge of adrenaline, Deines mustered one last effort. He crossed the line in 5 hours 15 minutes and 20 seconds, with Houk breathing down his neck, only 2.8 seconds behind.[8] Six runners ran under the American 50 mile record that day, including Corbitt (in sixth place).[9] There were 26 finishers in total. Elite American ultrarunning had suddenly stepped up a competitive notch.

Almost unremarked at the time, one of the finishers that day was Natalie Cullimore, a cyclist from Mill Valley. While the AAU did not yet officially sanction female competition at this distance (or indeed in the marathon), there had been a gradual relaxation since the 1968 Boston Marathon. This meant that women were occasionally permitted to compete unofficially. Cullimore did so – the only woman on the starting line – and finished 18th overall, in a time of 7 hours 35 minutes and 57 seconds. It was a women's world record for the 50 mile distance, though unofficial and largely unacknowledged at the time. It was an astonishing achievement, especially considering that women were still banned from even official marathon competition.

Incredibly, Rocklin was not yet done with American record breaking. Since the 1940s, a festival had been organised across Sacramento to celebrate local pride in the cultivation of the camellia flower. Various activities at this jamboree included boating contests, pageants and parades. In 1971, the organisers decided to add a foot race to the festivities – and not just any foot race, but an AAU-sanctioned 100 mile race. This was the first such AAU event since the 1907 dual between Albert Corey and Sidney Hatch. Seventeen runners lined up on 13 March to run forty 2.5 mile loops on a sidewalk around the country club. A handful of the Californian elite were back: Darryl Beardell, Jose Cortez and Natalie Cullimore (once again the only woman). Cortez and Beardell ran together for 25 miles, until the latter dropped out with breathing issues. Cortez continued alone, hallucinating over the last 10 to 15 miles, but clocking in with a finish of 12 hours 54 minutes and 30 seconds.[10] It was a new American record, besting the 1969 record set by Corbitt at a London track event in 1969. Cullimore crossed the line a few hours later, in 16 hours and 11 minutes – another (unofficial) world record to add to her endurance resumé.

With these two regional pillars of American ultrarunning now firmly established – East Coast and West Coast – the annual ultramarathon calendar began to creep up in the early to mid-1970s: the Lake Montebello 37 mile run in Maryland, organised by Baltimore Road Runners;[11] the Lake Waramaug 50 mile and 100 km races in Connecticut, hosted by the Bethel Bananas Track Club;[12] the C&O Canal 100km, along the Potomac, from Washington Monument to Harper's Ferry;[13] the Lake Merced 100k m in San Francisco; a 72 mile race around Lake Tahoe.[14] They were all on paved paths or road – usually with a single or low double-digit number of finishers – and they slotted in alongside a smattering of track events and the annual AAU championship races. It was a tiny, but committed and competitive, community of American ultrarunners.

These new races were channelling and changing the direction that ultrarunning was beginning to take. Dwindling in number were the grinding loops around city blocks or the local park – a mainstay of 1960s East Coast ultrarunning. Instead, race organisers were out to find areas of natural beauty and a more logical, continuous race line, whether that be around a lake or along a riverside towpath. It made sense. Why run for hours on end in the same place?

It all began in 1955, when accomplished high country rider Wendell Robie sought to demonstrate the possibility of riding on horseback, from Lake Tahoe to Auburn, over an historic mining trail that had been rediscovered in the 1930s. He did so successfully – and was soon joined by others to make this an annual tradition. So was born the Tevis Cup. In time it would become the most prestigious endurance riding event in the United States. There was inevitable speculation about whether such a journey would be possible on foot. In 1972, twenty soldiers travelled from Fort Riley, in Kansas, to hike the route alongside the Tevis Cup riders. Accompanied by Jim Larimer as guide – Robie's grandson-in-law – seven of the soldiers made it to the finish, in 46 hours and 49 minutes[15] (Larimer would return to compete in the 1979 WSER, finishing in 26 hours and 29 minutes). It had been proved possible – and that might have been the end of it.

Then, in 1974, a new chapter was written in the annals of trail and ultra running history. Gordy Ainsleigh, a 'longhaired, long-bearded mountain man' and two-time finisher of the Tevis Cup,[16] found himself without a horse for the upcoming 1974 edition of the endurance ride. Encouraged by Dru Barner – an accomplished rider and confidante of Robie – Ainsleigh decided to make an attempt on foot. Already an established runner, with a sub-3-hour marathon time and having completed a 50 mile run in 1973 (as part of another riding event), Ainsleigh believed he could finish on foot under the 24-hour time limit. He was right. In the early morning light, he crossed the finishing line at McCann Stadium in Auburn – performing somersaults and handstands before the crowd of riding enthusiasts – having covered the (at the time) 89 mile distance in 23 hours and 42 minutes.[17]

Over the next two years, hikers began to backpack across the Western States trail. There were also attempts to replicate Ainsleigh's achievement. Ron Kelley ran alongside the Tevis Cup in 1975 (withdrawing at No Hands Bridge), as did Ken 'Cowman' Shirk in 1976, finishing 30 minutes over the 24-hour cut-off for the riding event. In 1977, Robie decided there was sufficient interest to organise a formal running race alongside the annual riding event.

Arranged at the last minute, there were fourteen starters, largely from the local area and recruited via word of mouth. Most were inexperienced, with little or no background in ultrarunning. Peter Mattei and Ralph Paffenbarger were exceptions, having raced at the Pacific AAU championships in Rocklin, as was Andy Gonzales, who only the month before had (rather bizarrely) completed a solo 50 mile run in Sacramento as training to qualify for the 1 mile event at the Moscow Olympics.[18] Dave Niederhaus, a Vietnam veteran from Indiana, also had some experience – although nothing like this – having finished 18th the previous year at the JFK 50. John Cappis had cut his teeth at Pikes Peak, but had no ultra experience, and Ken Shirk had of course completed his solo run the year before (a year in which he also ran through Tahoe City naked, wearing only horns, as part of the bicentennial celebrations[19]). Mike Catlin was a young physiology graduate student, with a bedrock of running experience, but nothing over this distance. Apart from Cowman – the horned spirit of the trail – all of the runners were embarking on the unknown, including the first female aspirant at WSER, Tracy Fifer.

The runners camped out in sleeping bags the night before. At that moment in California, eager moviegoers were queuing around the block to watch a science fiction movie, *Star Wars*, that had been released only a month before. The small band of Western States competitors were similarly gazing up at the night sky, wondering about their own place in the heavens, as Mike Catlin remembers:

> We laid there the night before drinking beer, wondering what we were getting ourselves into. It was pitch dark and the stars were in full bloom. We talked. We were both a little anxious and nervous. Basically, we did not know what we were doing.[20]

The following morning, almost all the runners went out too fast and by Robinson Flat (at mile 30) six of them dropped, including military hopeful Niederhaus. Dr Bob Lind – the famed Western States medical director – dutifully assessed the physical state of runners at predetermined checkpoints. The heat mounted to over 100 degrees – Gonzales' choice of Speedo swimming shorts now seemed sensible – and by Michigan Bluff only the three most experienced ultrarunners remained: Gonzales, Mattei and Paffenbarger. Struggling with dehydration and a general lack of aid stations, they continued, with only Gonzales managing to maintain a steady pace to the end. He crossed the line in 22 hours and 57 minutes.

Mattei and Paffenbarger were timed out, but continued to the finish, running together, in 28 hours and 36 minutes. It was crazy and by contemporary standards poorly organised – nobody knew what they were doing – but it was a success that would not be forgotten by those there to witness it.

Inspired by the 1977 race, a small group of riders involved with the Tevis Cup – the so-called Gang of Four – Mo Livemore, Shannon Weil, Phil Gardner and Curt Sproul – came together to organise this new running race as a standalone event. Livemore and Weil were young women in their twenties, and they would serve together as co-race directors for the first years of the race, between 1978 and 1981. They were a force of nature, combining vision, passion and organisation. Growing the race involved extensive planning, logistics, marketing and branding, in the form of distinctive typography and imagery that captured the American West heritage of the trail. John Trent, a Western States board director and race historian, reflects on the extraordinary story of Livemore and Weil:

> This is the late 1970s, I don't know if there were any other female race directors in the running space … They're young women in their mid to late twenties, and it is their job to make this thing a success. They took it incredibly seriously. Mo Livemore's wheelhouse is getting volunteers, the details, inspiring people. She got all of her friends to go out and practice aid stationing. They would literally go out and practice aid stations, because nobody knew what an aid station was. Because that is how detail-oriented Mo was … and in this day and age we all know about branding and marketing, and Shannon understood it like no other … from the very beginning there was a certain look and feel to everything that was associated with Western States.[21]

Under the guidance of Livemore and Weil, Western States ballooned from 63 starters in 1978 to 143 in 1979 and 251 in 1980. A lottery was introduced from 1980 to limit numbers due to the narrowness of the trail, but the athletic background of the runners remained consistent. There were those who had cut their teeth at Pacific AAU ultras; some were from out of state, with experience at a small selection of East Coast events; and roughly half the field in these early years had no competitive background in ultrarunning at all. For many, it would be the beginning of an ultra career that would span decades. The number of female competitors also crept up, hovering somewhere between 10 and 15 per cent. To give credit to *UltraRunning Magazine*, launched in 1981, their first full coverage of Western States focused entirely on female competitors. Writing about 1981 race winner (and 8th overall), Norwegian-heritage Bjorg Austrheim-Smith, in 18 hours and 46 minutes, Ruth Anderson wrote:

> Women are now training for this race very much like the men. Many of Bjorg's 120 miles a week were spent on the trails between Squaw Valley and Auburn. She also included weight training and ballet in her schedule. Her marvellous condition at the awards banquet was testimony to how well she survived the gruelling event. It's hard to believe that she has been running for less than 4 years, and has a 2½ year old child, which must have taken a bit of time from her training.[22]

Perhaps because of this more serious attempt to develop course-specific training – and a growing awareness of what ultrarunning involved – the percentage of successful finishers also grew: from only 18.8 per cent in 1977 to usually around 50–70 per cent in subsequent years.

It was an experience that would be seared into the sinews of these early WSER competitors. Just as evangelical Pentecostalism had rippled out from California at the beginning of the twentieth century, these runners were scattered like burning embers across the continent – and where they landed, the gospel of trail and ultra running would grow. Was Western States the first trail 100 mile race? Perhaps; it depends how you define 'running' and 'racing', although it is certainly the oldest. Regardless, across the Atlantic, a year before Ainsleigh's famed run on the Western States trail, experimentation had already taken place with 100 mile off-road 'racing' along one of Britain's newest national trails, the South Downs Way.

The annual London to Brighton race was still the pre-eminent British ultra in the 1970s, but it was mostly confined to a small group of hyper-competitive road runners. There were 41 finishers in 1972 – fewer than almost any fell race – and all these finishers were men. At the beginning of the 1970s – much like in the United States

– ultra-distance running had yet to make the transition away from road and track to something else.

This changed in 1972. Three keen hikers in Surrey – Chris Steer and Alan and Barbara Blatchford – decided that a new organisation was needed to support long-distance walking. Between them they founded the Long Distance Walkers Association (LDWA). The aim of the organisation was to hold organised social walks – typically around 30 miles in distance – and longer 'challenge' events. The flagship annual event was a 100 mile, supported, self-navigation hike that would take place every year in a different part of the UK. There was undoubtedly an appetite for the LDWA. Their membership roster skyrocketed: from 355 in 1972 to 4,078 by 1980.[23] The creation of the LDWA was also well timed: the late 1960s/early 1970s saw the opening of Britain's first long-distance national trails.

The inaugural 100 mile 'challenge' event – the Downsman – took place on the South Downs Way, in June 1973, only weeks before it was officially unveiled as Britain's third long-distance national trail. It was the first such trail in the south of England, and it followed the opening in northern England of the Pennine Way, in 1965, and the Cleveland Way, in 1969. It was a rolling course, with over 4,000 metres of ascent, on well-marked bridleways that snaked up and down undulating chalk hills, with the green and wrinkled Sussex Weald to the north, the grey swell of the English Channel to the south. This was the heart of ancient England – Roman ruins, Saxon beacons and Norman castles – living inspiration for the mythology and manuscripts of J. R. R. Tolkien.

Beneath the city walls of Winchester, on a sweltering June morning, 115 men and 8 women gathered together in anticipation. With the blast of a whistle, they were off. There were thirteen aid stations, stocked full of Mars Bars and also liquid nutrition, in the form of Complan (a powdered milk drink) and Glucodin (a glucose mix). It was a 'challenge event' – mostly for those just hoping to finish – but it was also described by the organisers as a race, with a competitive spirit among the front-runners. Leading the pack were David Rosen, from London, and Pete Dawes, a noted fell runner from Ambleside.

Racing together for the first half, they were only 1 minute apart as they crossed the 50 mile mark, in a little over 9 hours. Further back, participants were dropping in the unrelenting heat (there would only be a 54% per cent finish rate that first year).[24] Dawes began to tire during the second half and the gap between them grew ever larger. Rosen finally finished in a time of 22 hours and 20 minutes, with Dawes an hour behind. The first woman, Dianne Pegg, finished in 34 hours and 30 minutes.

The event became known as 'The Hundred'. Following the race, Alan Blatchford was to tell the *Surrey Advertiser*: 'Although there have been many races of the same distance on the road, I believe that the Downsman Hundred is the first event of this distance to be held over a cross country course.'[25]

It moved every year to a different part of the UK – Northumbria, the Peak District, Dartmoor, Cumbria, Snowdonia – and the number of challengers increased: up to 265 by 1980. It remained technically a hiking event, but at the time it was the only 100 mile off-road 'race' in the UK, and naturally it attracted a small number of competitive athletes. Many of the top finishers could also be found at British road ultras, including London to Brighton. As with Dawes, a niche group of fell runners would travel for competition to The Hundred, including Alan Heaton, Roger Baumeister (who in 1979 was the first to complete a double Bob Graham Round) and a young Martin Stone (future advocate and custodian of long-distance fell running). The winner of the inaugural event, David Rosen, lowered the Downsman course record to 16 hours and 13 minutes in 1980. He was among eight runners that year to finish in under 20 hours.

This was the beginning of modern trail and ultra running in Britain. Trail running did not yet formally exist in the UK, but in the 1970s and early 1980s, the LDWA provided a gateway through which a new generation would discover the joy of long-distance running over marked trails. Many of these athletes would become staple participants at the earliest ultra-distance trail races in Britain. In time, some would begin to look across the Atlantic for inspiration – and even travel to the United States for competition – much in the same way that fell runners were already beginning to do during the mid-1970s.

Meditating hippies, a Chinese Taoist master and a Cumbrian sheep farmer. Sometimes history surpasses even the wildest embellishments of fiction.

Located at the foot of the Barr Trail, Manitou Springs, the Stillpoint Foundation – a retreat and rustic lodging – was in 1975 run by legendary sage, Gia-Fu-Feng, a friend and mentor to Jack Kerouac and Alan Watts. As the 'spiritual master' of the Pikes Peak Marathon, he had some words of wisdom for their newest, temporary house guest: 'Accept what is in front of you without wanting the situation to be other than it is.'[26] Perhaps Joss Naylor remembered those words as he slogged up the trail, his heart hammering against the unfamiliar altitude. A dose of mindfulness and humility was no doubt welcome.

He was being overtaken – again, and again. As Naylor approached the summit in 18th place, barely alive and crusted with salt, Rick Trujillo, race leader and famed local mountain runner, burnt past him to begin the rocky descent. Two friends were waiting for Naylor with a bottle of lime Acolade – a British version of Gatorade – which he slowly poured into his shattered body. Revived, he turned and began to bound ever downward – another mantra kicking in, this time perhaps a familiar fragment of fell running lore: 'brakes off, brain off'. As others began to tire, Naylor found his stride, rising to eighth place. Spotting two runners through the trees, he quickened, leaving them behind, and then down into Manitou Springs.[27] Finding himself lost, Naylor was directed by a passing policeman towards the finish. He crossed the line in sixth place, in 4 hours and 7 minutes. Despite finishing 36 minutes behind race winner Trujillo, he was 7 minutes quicker on the descent – a partial salvaging of fell running pride. In a telephone interview with BBC London later that day, 39-year-old Naylor summed it all up in a laconic Cumbrian drawl: 'I was sixth, pretty good for an old man, and could you ring the wife and tell her I had a good run and I would be home Tuesday night nine o'clockish?'[28]

Buzz Burrell was running the race 'bandit' (i.e., without registering) that year and remembers Naylor's visit to Colorado:

> I thought that was an excellent result because it's got a lot of elevation. People were aware that he was this British athlete who was coming over. I suppose that there wasn't much in the way of transatlantic exchange at the time, I guess, in the seventies, but he got reported in the local paper. And that really caught my eye because it opened me up to the rich history in the UK, and all of a sudden people are going, wow, look at that.[29]

In the mid-1970s, Naylor – 'Iron Joss' as he would become known to the fell running faithful – was at the height of his powers. His trip to Colorado slotted into a particularly eventful summer. Only two months before, he had resumed his dual with Alan Heaton to better the Lakeland 24-hour record. Naylor had beaten Heaton's 1965 attempt in 1971 (with 61 peaks), then bettered his own record with a second attempt in 1972 (with 62 peaks). Heaton retaliated and came close to surpassing Naylor's record later that year, with 63 peaks, but failed in a little over the 24-hour time limit. Then, in June of 1975, Naylor ran in heat-wave conditions to summit 72 peaks, in 23 hours and 11 minutes – reckoned at the time to be 100 miles and 11,500 metres of ascent over rough and often pathless Lakeland terrain.[30] It was a record that would stand for more than a decade.

A month later he was slumming it with Taoists at Pikes Peak, and then, on arriving home, off within days to Switzerland as part of a British contingent at Sierra-Zinal for the first edition of the International Mountain Cup (CIME). No doubt exhausted from his 24-hour record and the Pikes Peak Marathon, he finished a creditable but disappointing 29th out of 469 finishers. Even so, Britain took the international team prize that year, with first, third and fourth place finishes by the other GB team members.

Fell running was trying to go global. As Naylor said at the time: 'I want to make fell running an international sport. There are so many good athletes that have dedicated themselves to running hills. They should be able to compete more.'[31] Having been reliant on community donations for his international tour, Naylor, like other fell runners, was ultimately unable to make that dream a reality. There were no serious sponsorship opportunities available for fell or mountain running – it was too small, with little to nothing in the way of interest from commercial sponsors or the bureaucratic institution of British athletics.

Joss Naylor represented a particular strand of the fell running community. The late 1960s and early 1970s had seen a surge of interest in the sport, with particular appeal to amateur athletes across the towns and cities of northern England. In contrast to these 'outcomers', Naylor owned a Lake District farm, in the remote valley of Wasdale, at the base of Scafell Pike. Chasing sheep up and down the steep fell sides, his training was lifelong and written into the tapestry of everyday life. He took up running in 1960, and, with the likes of Heaton, helped to raise the profile of fell running. Longer and more rugged races began to emerge: the 23 mile Ennerdale (2,200 metres of ascent), in 1968; the 31.5 mile Manx Mountain Marathon (2,400 metres), in 1970; the 21 mile Wasdale (2,700 metres), in 1972. While he often found himself bested at the shorter and more traditional 'up and down' fell races, Naylor excelled at this new wave of endurance events – he regularly won and set records at all of them. He was also one of the few fell runners interested in running ultra distances.

While fell runners have often been sceptical of a perceived 'Americanisation' of the sport, the concept of 'ultrarunning' had already seeped into the language. The earliest issues of *The Fellrunner* magazine can be found discussing 'ultra-distance' running. And yet, ultra-distance fell racing itself did not really exist. For those wanting to run further and test the limits of endurance, solo efforts and self-determined adventures were usually the only outlet. It was a niche discipline within a niche sport – confined to a handful of runners – and Joss Naylor was the undisputed master.

Almost singly, he continued to pioneer ultra-distance fell running. This included record times on established routes: the Welsh 3000s (1973), Lakeland 24-hour (1975), Pennine Way (1976) and Coast to Coast (1976). As his speed faded with age, 'Old Man Joss' began to devise entirely new challenges, including the 105 mile Lakes, Meres and Waters (1983), and, in 1986 at the age of fifty, a full circuit of 214 Wainwright fell tops, in a little over 7 days – a record that would stand for almost three decades, until it was bested by Steve Birkinshaw in 2014 (in another much later moment of transatlantic exchange, American John Kelly would set the current record in 2022, in 5 days and 12 hours).

Joss Naylor is perhaps the most famous and revered athlete in fell running history. Following his death in 2024, the fell running community turned out in their hundreds, dressed in multi-hued club vests, to create a guard of honour for his internment at St Olaf's, England's smallest parish church, in his beloved Wasdale Head. This dramatic final ceremony – for a man often referred to as 'King of the Fells' – was akin to the burial of a monarch. Naylor's fame had been cemented over decades through his extraordinary ability to claim almost every ultra-distance off-road record in Britain. Yet his dream to make fell running a global sport was never truly realised and his ability to travel internationally was markedly limited. One can only wonder: what might he have achieved on something like the Appalachian Trail?

May 1978. A sodden and rapidly cooling evening in the Smoky Mountains, made famous only a few years before by Jon Voight and Burt Reynolds in *Deliverance*, a film notorious for violent scenes of rape and murder in backwoods Georgia. Today, wisps of fog cling to spruce and fir, as a young man, alone, in stout boots and with a light backpack, treads quickly through this haunted and ethereal landscape. John Avery is approaching the end of a long day on the Appalachian Trail. Hungry and tired – with taught nerves – he marches towards the haven of a waiting support van. Suddenly, a terrifying snuffling emanates from the shrouded foliage and two shaggy black boars shamble out of the gloom. These wily, non-native animals are the descendants of European hogs, escapees from a ranch in the early 1900s. Heart hammering, with indrawn breath, Avery stands still – but they move off. And then, for a short time, they follow alongside the trail. This is just one of many encounters that Avery has along his journey. Two months later, he becomes the first competitive runner to set a record on the Appalachian Trail, in 65 days 11 hours and 15 minutes.[32]

Unbeknownst to Avery, in the 1970s there was a surge of interest in record breaking on the long-distance trails of the United States. Ultra-distance racing remained a niche and overlooked sport – WSER had only recently been launched – but media interest in record breaking was acute. The expansive canvas of long-distance trails also provided competitors with a degree freedom to play around with style and format. Rather than simply trying to finish under record time, *how* one completes an epic journey was seen by some to matter just as much. Warren Doyle typified this free-form and experimental approach to the long-distance trails of America. Now most famous for having completed the full Appalachian Trail through-hike nine times, he set a record on the route in 1973, in a little over 66 days. Typifying his anarchic spirit, he remarked: 'There are fewer rules and regulations out there, and what regulations there are, you can disobey them if you feel they don't apply to you.'[33] Doyle was continuing a subculture of through-hiking that had thrived since the time of Appleby, on the Long Trail, and Shaffer and Gatewood, on the Appalachian Trail – that is, as a self-sufficient journey of discovery. And yet, as ultra-distance trail running began to grow in the late 1970s, it was inevitable that runners would begin to target these long-distance routes in a more experimental and competitive way.

Avery was the first. While not directly connected to the ultrarunning scene of the 1970s, he was a modestly competitive marathon runner who would eventually achieve his goal of a sub-3-hour finish at the Boston Marathon (in 1981). His 1978 Appalachian Trail record – which would remain unbeaten for over a decade – only managed to surpass Doyle by a single day. It was a testament to the uncertain debate and blurred line between 'hiking versus running'. Cadence aside, with the use of a support van and lightweight gear, Avery was trying something new: moving fast and light in a supported fashion.

There were other records set during the 1970s and early 1980s – such as on the John Muir and Pacific Crest trails – but most of these records were modest and often overlooked. While newspapers, magazines and broadcasters would not really recognise the unique challenge of these long-distance trails, which were arduous and without glamour, there was a degree of media interest in more notorious and novel endurance attempts.

Max Telford – the 'Super Marathon Man'[34] – was a master at stoking public interest in feats of extreme running. A native Scot, he moved to New Zealand in his twenties, where he began training with Arthur Lydiard, a coach made famous for the recreational 'jogging' movement, as well as the science of base training and periodisation.[35] After failing to qualify for the Mexico Olympics in 1968, Telford decided to focus on ultra-distance running – and so began a string of carefully self-promoted 'record' attempts. Each was dutifully documented for submission to the *Guinness Book of Records*, a popular but often unreliable (and sometimes farcical) tome of record keeping. His initial efforts involved a 24-hour running attempt (reaching 114 miles, well short of the world record) and then two record-breaking (if uncompetitive) runs between Auckland and Wellington.[36]

Then, in 1972, he announced his intention to beat the transcontinental record across the United States. This was a route that had already received some attention in the 1960s – obviously it was a reprise of the celebrated Pyle races – with successful record attempts made by South African Don Shepherd, in 1964, and then, in 1969, by British athletics champion (and famed advocate of barefoot running) Bruce Tulloh, in 64 days.[37] Despite widespread promotion to excited American newspapers, Telford never completed the transcontinental run. It did, however, highlight the direction that he was taking: big and daring runs, capable of cutting through into the wider public consciousness.

Telford was an outstanding runner, but it seemed unlikely that he would ever match the more established and competitive athletic records of the day (such as the 100 mile or 24-hour record). Instead, he turned to colourful and inspiring spectacles of endurance. This involved, in June 1976, the first attempt to set a competitive record on the double Grand Canyon crossing (Rim to Rim to Rim). He managed in a time of 8 hours and 34 minutes, before then travelling to California to attempt a double crossing of Death Valley. He had set the one-way record in Death Valley only the winter before, crossing the 111 mile distance in 19 hours, but was told by locals that the 'real challenge' was to attempt a double crossing in summer heat. On 1 July 1976, he started running from Shoshone in a 125 degree furnace. His wife Doris was supporting him in a converted van, with spare shoes kept in the fridge to keep them cool and, at one point – reprising an old Death Valley tradition – cracking an egg on the superheated tarmac to watch it fry. He made it to Scotty's Castle – a distance of 120 miles – and then turned to make his way to back to the start, finishing the 240 mile attempt in a record time of 73 hours. Newspapers were fascinated by his lurid accounts of running through Death Valley. As he told the *Miami News*, with a familiar bent for the dramatic, 'There's only one word for that place: hell.'[38]

Telford was back the following year, in 1977, with another famed run across the breadth of Canada, this time sponsored and covered by the Canadian Broadcasting Corporation. Telford had initially applied to race across the Soviet Union, but when permission was denied, he settled for the 5,180 mile stretch from Anchorage to Halifax – which he finished in 106 days.[39] Breathless media coverage discussed his ambition to be the 'greatest runner of all time'.[40] He would continue to nurture a carefully curated profile, with unrealised plans to run across the Great Wall of China, speaking tours in Hawaii, and a commercial film, *Into the Valley of Death*. In many respects he was a peculiarity: simultaneously the most famous pop-culture ultrarunner of the 1970s, but also a runner who in pure athletic terms was 'good' rather than 'great'. There might understandably have been a feeling of *schadenfreude* among Telford's ultrarunning contemporaries when he toed the line at Western States, in 1981, and finished only in 31st position, with a time of 22 hours 26 minutes. Depending on the lens through which we choose to view Telford, his career might be seen in two different ways: he was either a charismatic source of inspiration and a natural storyteller, or an energetic self-promoter and gifted media operator. Perhaps it is simply impossible to make such a distinction.

American ultrarunning would continue to be shaped by the success of Western States. This was truly a pivotal moment. While off-road and ultra-distance running cultures would simmer away in Britain – and fell running would continue to thrive – there was nothing comparable to the extraordinary energy that exploded out from the dusty trails of northern California. Rather than just a tiny group of eccentrics pushing beyond the standard marathon distance, ultrarunning was growing to become a real community and an established sport. Set against the booming optimism of 1980s America, there would be a crackling sense of excitement and enthusiasm. But fundamental questions would remain. Would this new sport align itself with the values and culture of mainstream athletics – or would it push back against them?

Chapter 8

Countercultural misfits

It was a masterclass in strategy – a grinding game of move and countermove. There were 22 runners at the start, contemplative and nervous, on a muggy Sunday afternoon, with bruised clouds gathering overhead. The dirty cinder track at Farnham Park was a leafy oasis – encircled by the bisecting criss-cross of highway and interstate – located only a few miles from the bustling chaos of downtown Philadelphia. This would be home for the next six days. Don Choi and Ray Krolewicz led from the start. Their battle, in June 1983, would be one of mental endurance and mathematical precision.

Choi, a Chinese American athlete, had become a prolific and dominant competitor in the sudden and unexpected revival of six-day racing. His daily grind as a mailman, up and down the steep steps of San Francisco Bay, provided a ready-made training regime – perfect for multi-day efforts. Krolewicz, a Bostonian teacher, now living in South Carolina, had erupted onto the ultrarunning scene only a few years before. He was the new golden boy – a 100 mile and 24-hour track expert – crushing his East Coast contemporaries on a fantastically regular basis. After this soul-destroying effort in New Jersey, both Choi and Krolewicz would travel, only three weeks later, to New York for another six-day race. There were other familiar names and faces, everyone cracking jokes as they crunched around the never-ending cinder loop: Park Barner, slowing down in his forties, only a few years from retirement; Malcolm Campbell, a fresh-faced pioneer and leading light in British ultrarunning; Gary

Cantrell, from Tennessee, race director and running media columnist. Each runner was matched by their own volunteer lap counter: an army of administrators, clustered together with pen and paper.

By the end of the first day, the runners were filthy, many wearing homemade shoe guards to keep out the cinders. Choi was leading, with 113 miles to Krolewicz's 107. They were engulfed in torrential rain on the second day, with many competitors wisely choosing to huddle together in the main tent during the worst of the downpour – snatching whatever sleep they could – or, as with Krolewicz and Choi, sneaking in extra mileage: lone figures through the haze of rain. The athletes were a pitiful sight by the end of the third day – bandaged, sodden and blackened – as they continued to limp ever onward, like refugees fleeing conflict. Choi and Krolewicz were matching one another, mile for mile, in a predictable pattern: one would rest, the other would take the lead, only to be overtaken by the fresher set of legs, and so on.

By the fourth day, Choi's metronomic relentlessness was beginning to push through: he had logged mileage in 95 out of 96 hours. But as the fifth day blurred into a sixth, even he was succumbing to fatigue. He retreated to the tent for some concentrated rest, allowing Krolewicz to take the lead. Choi returned, clocking in some fast miles, but then once again retreated with exhaustion. As midnight struck – marking only 12 hours to go – Krolewicz led by almost five miles. In the early dawn light, they continued to shamble onward, the end now in sight. A revived Choi quickened, taking, and then extending, his lead. And just like that, the Edward Payson Weston Six-day Race was over, Choi finishing with a personal best of 460 miles, Krolewicz with 451.[1] It was a new 'modern American record' – although still some way short of Weston himself, who, in 1879, had managed 550 miles in the Astley Belt series (see Chapter 1). This would not be the end: a new generation of runners were laying down their mark, hungry to surpass the old records of pedestrianism.

As trail and ultra running boomed in the United States, there was a rush to experience everything all at once: new races, new routes, new styles of running, new products. It was a tremendous burst of energy and growth that would rapidly shift the Anglophone centre of the sport away from Britain, and to the United States.

Almost all of those embracing this emergent discipline were graduates of the 1970s marathon boom. The jogging movement – of which the marathon was perceived to be the pinnacle achievement – had been most pronounced in the United States.[2] It was accompanied at times by a pervasive sense of moral superiority and righteousness, exemplified best in a 1976 *Runner's World* article, which declared that runners 'are part of an elite' and inherently superior to their non-running neighbours.[3] Given this focus on self-improvement and personal character – and as the marathon became more commonplace (there were more than 10,000 participants in the 1979 New York Marathon) – it was inevitable that a small number of overachievers would search for their next challenge *beyond* the marathon.

A post-race survey, conducted in 1983, found that almost two thirds of ultra-distance finishers were attracted to the sport precisely because they wanted to 'cover a distance that only a select few can'; the prestige and challenge of a marathon was no longer sufficient. It was not just a sport, but also a form of *social distinction*, appealing to those who were already socially privileged: 83 per cent of these respondents were college/university educated, working in a variety of professional roles, including business (32%), medicine (18%), education (14%), the arts (13%) and law (9%).[4] Tellingly, there were few female respondents – ultrarunning remained mostly a male sport – and while there would be a series of trailblazing female athletes over the next decade, in 1983 only 9.5 per cent of ultra-distance race finishers in the United States were women.[5]

This focus on mental discipline and personal achievement was in stark contrast to wider fitness trends. The surging popularity of 1980s gym culture prioritised *outcome* – in the form of outward bodily aesthetics – over *process*. As one gym equipment manufacturer was to retort: 'To hell with the heart and lungs and all this marathon running stuff – I want to look better, not like somebody who just got out of a prisoner-of-war camp.'[6] Ripped, flexing bodies were more frequently on display, not least by film stars and cultural icons. President Reagan was himself to encourage this new age of muscle-minded heroism, notoriously rolling up his sleeves and pumping iron for the cameras. Such displays were often connected to ideas of American power, militarism and the vigour of individualism and capitalism.[7]

Ultra-distance running both reflected and subverted these social themes. There were noted values of heroism and self-sufficiency within the sport, but these were tempered by a countervailing sense of community, connection and solidarity. Outcome was important – particularly the satisfaction of overcoming a seemingly insurmountable challenge – but it was matched by an equal emphasis on process: the consistency and discipline of training, the camaraderie of shared experience, and the emotional journey contained within any extended endurance attempt. Only 11 per cent of ultra-distance runners were involved in the sport to improve their personal aesthetics and self-image – and only 2 per cent as a way to demonstrate that they were 'better' than their peers.[8] As with the marathon culture of the past decade, then, ultrarunning combined a complicated set of values concerning individual distinction, personal growth, the experience itself and the fellowship of belonging to a select group.[9]

It was indeed a 'select' group, with estimates of only around 3,000 participants in the American ultrarunning scene during the early part of the decade. Much like a kink subculture or secret society, members of this niche community were geographically scattered, but they were bound together by the connective glue of specialist running media. Being an 'ultrarunner' was a mark of communal and individual identity – a way to define oneself – with 'ultrarunning' T-shirts selling out via mail order. And as the community continued to flourish, there were fundamental questions about what this growth should look like. Who would organise the sport – and where? Which disciplines would or should dominate – track, trail or road? Should the sport be focused on elite athletes, or should it be built up around the needs of everyday recreational runners? Should ultrarunning be governed – if so, by whom and for what purpose? How should it be financed? Who should wield power and influence? Would the sport be ruined by commercialisation, or would sponsorship enhance event management and the experience of runners? What are *our* core values?

British fell runners were themselves grappling with a similar set of questions. While ultrarunning in Britain was still mostly a minor adjunct to mainstream track and road athletics – with barely hundreds of participants – fell running was thriving and developing a strong sense of communal identity. The parallels with ultrarunning in the United States are striking: to be a fell runner *meant something*; it was a distinct way of life that was built up around a tightly knit community.[10] As the sport continued to expand – both to other parts of the United Kingdom and with increasing international and commercial links – the trick would be to manage this growth while also maintaining the golden thread of fell running heritage and tradition.

These were deep and existential questions – with subtle differences between British fell runners and American ultrarunners – but with one common set of values shining through: that this should be an egalitarian sport, rooted in grassroots community, and balanced between the needs of both recreational and elite runners.

As ultrarunning emerged blinking and bloody into the neon light of Reagan's America, a deep fissure was becoming apparent within the sport. This divide was partly geographical – East Coast versus West Coast – but it was also based on running discipline – trail versus track. The Northeast, particularly New York and Pennsylvania, continued with a focus on track and road racing: 24-hour and six-day races were endowed with outsized media prominence during the 1980s – despite the low numbers participating in them – partly because they were seen as suitable formats to break established records. There was a reverence for the old records of pedestrianism – and a desire to surpass them. Trail races, meanwhile, were few and far between in the Northeast, partly due to local difficulties in securing permits for organised events on public land. This would be a persistent problem, not always helped by the ongoing resistance of groups like the GMC and AMC, which could be hostile to racing in the mountains of the Northeast.[11] In striking contrast, the Southwest was becoming a national hub for trail running, especially in California and Arizona, with dozens of small races.

This grand continental and cultural divide became a persistent source of speculation and occasional regret. It seemed unfortunate that the best ultrarunners in America were not to compete against one another. This was more often about specialism (trail versus track) rather than geography. Sandra Kiddy, Marcy Schwam and Sue Ellen Trap – a blazing American trio who between them would set new records across every established ultramarathon distance in the 1980s – would largely be absent from Western States (only Schwam would compete at WSER, and only once). Rather, they focused their efforts on international track and road competition. Away from the elite field, recreational runners were beginning to make the annual pilgrimage to Olympic Valley – although WSER would remain dominated by Californians. The first non-Californian win finally came in 1986, with Mary Hammes, from Fort Worth, Texas.[12] There were also flashes of Eastern promise. Dan Brennan, race director and media commentator, reflected on this continental divide in 1983, when recollecting his experience at Western States:

> I had ventured westward for an eastern assessment of this legendary western athletic event. Really, how tough could this trail be, and how tough are these Californian mountain runners who seem to limit their entire athletic lives to this one course, this one, all-consuming event? I also had it in mind to represent the east favourably, to show these mountain folks that the Appalachians can prepare us for any course they can offer. Though I failed miserably in this latter goal, fortunately Virginia's David Horton came through and cracked the top 10. As for the course and the Californians... Yes, my eastern friends, they really are as tough as the best we've ever come up with.[13]

Track races would come and go throughout the 1980s – almost any location was as good as another, assuming the facilities and travel connections were suitable. Trail races, meanwhile, were beginning to take on a hallowed aspect, inextricably rooted in place and landscape. Strung like pearls across the continent, there were four principal 100 mile trail events by the mid-1980s: Western States (California, 1974), Wasatch Front (Utah, 1980), Leadville (Colorado,

1983) and Old Dominion (Virginia, 1979). These race routes might occasionally change very slightly, but they followed a logical and contiguous line, each traversing a landscape that possessed an inherent sense of history, climate and local character. As a mythology began to quickly build up around each of them, participants were becoming pilgrims, tracing the steps and memories of their forebears over sacred ground.

Each of these races would receive extensive media coverage – in mainstream newspapers and broadcasters, but also in specialist running media – and between them they would (rightly or wrongly) cement the idea of the 100 mile trail race as the *pinnacle format* within the sport. This was despite the fact that Wasatch Front and Old Dominion would only have modest entry numbers (typically less than 100). They also served to concentrate local trail talent – essentially acting as de facto regional championships – and each would become magnets for those wanting to travel for exploration and competition. In 1985, Fred Pilon, co-editor of *UltraRunning Magazine*, proposed a competitive series that would see participants attempt to run all four races in a single calendar year. The 'Grand Slam of Ultrarunning' was officially launched in 1986, with the cumulative time for each registered participant added together, and a sculpted eagle trophy presented to the winner at Wasatch Front, the final race of the series.[14] The Vermont 100 (Vermont, 1989) was eventually added to the series, providing representation from the Northeast, and by the end of the decade Angeles Crest (California, 1986) was viewed as an unofficial addition to the series. Famed runner and mountaineer Marshall Ulrich was the first to complete all six in one year, in 1989 (with a top ten finish in five of them – he finished 30th at the more competitive WSER).

There were also shorter distance events that achieved or maintained national prominence. The annual JFK 50 (already described in the early 1980s as 'more ritual than race'[15]), Pikes Peak and Dipsea races each continued to attract hundreds of competitors. These shorter, but historically popular, races acted as gateway events for runners to the more expansive world of trail and ultra running. The most important new entry to the calendar was the American River

50 Mile Endurance Run, first held in 1980. A fast and relatively flat route, running on non-technical trails alongside Folsom Lake, it was designed as a season-opener, in early April, and as a warm-up for Western States. It quickly became one of the largest events in the United States. There were other shorter races across the country, some of which swelled in size, such as the Ice Age Trail 50 in Wisconsin. Running along a section of the 1,200 mile Ice Age trail – a broken and wet landscape of glacial-formed kettles, potholes, eskers and kames – the race was launched in 1981 and quickly built up to a regular starting line of hundreds. It too acted as something of a regional qualifier for Western States. With a rough, mist-obscured course, it had a unique character that would continue to showcase the geographical diversity of trail running.

These large and prominent races dominated the American ultrarunning media landscape in the 1980s, but they were also exceptional and did not reflect the annual racing experience for most recreational runners. More common were smaller, low-key races that drew in runners from across their home state. In 1986, there were 170 different events advertised across the United States. The vast majority of these had fewer than twenty participants – some were as low as single digit entries, with only one or two finishers. They had a minimal entry fee, or even no entry fee at all, and were organised with a shoestring budget – often losing money – all for the love of the sport. Each would reflect the diverse landscape and heritage of different states and regions across the United States.

Gary Cantrell – or Lazarus Lake as he would later become known – was a one-man enigma: athlete, writer, accountant, sports fanatic, all tossed together and seasoned with the mind of an organisational genius. Having earned his athletic spurs in the running boom of the 1970s, this 24-year-old marathon runner and accounting student, in the athletic backwater of Tennessee, found himself drawn to the suddenly visible sport of ultrarunning. At the time, he could be found out training with a small group, the Horse Mountain Runners, logging daily 10 mile runs and a fortnightly 30 mile effort around the fields and wrinkled hills of Bedford County. It was a farming and pastoral landscape, rolling eastward into the vast green-orange forests and sandstone bluffs of the Cumberland Plateau and Appalachian Mountains. There were no ultra-distance races in the Southeast of the United States at the time – so Cantrell decided to create one. Named after the first Grand National Tennessee Walking Horse – famed equine symbol of local pride – the Strolling Jim 40 mile race was first held in May 1979. Typifying the approach that Cantrell would take to ultrarunning – mind over body, landscape merged with heritage – he described the upcoming first edition of the race to *The Tennessean*:

> The course is mostly hills and I believe for a runner to finish the race it will be less what's in the legs and more of what's in the mind. It's about 90 percent mental, although anyone attempting a course like this should have done a lot of base training at long distances. Runners will have to run with the course rather than at it.[16]

There were twenty competitors in this first edition – including Cantrell – all from Tennessee and neighbouring Southern states. It was the beginning of an ultrarunning community in the American South. Over the next decade, the number and variety of races would grow – including, in 1986, a small and (at the time) mostly overlooked race known as the Barkley Marathons (see Chapter 9) – and Cantrell would become an advocate not just for the wider sport but also for the region. His regular 'From the South' column for *UltraRunning Magazine* became a mainstay in the ultrarunning media ecosphere.

Cantrell was one of a handful of race directors who were beginning to organise new races in different regions of the United States. Almost all of these new race directors were athletes themselves – including some who were competing at the highest levels of the sport. This grassroots, self-driven approach to race organisation proved to be significant. An entire book could be filled with the stories of these events and those behind them, but a few notable examples provide a sense of what was taking place.

Originally from Pasadena, Ken Young (1941–2018) ran his first ultra in 1970 at the historic AAU 50 mile championship in Rocklin. He came a creditable 11th, in a race that saw six men break the American record that day (see Chapter 7). Following a PhD in Physics from the University of Chicago, he spent time at the National Centre for Atmospheric Research, in Boulder, where he went running around the Front Range with Pike's Peak legend Rick Trujillo. Every inch the data scientist – with thick-rimmed glasses and a wiry body that over the years would become adorned with Japanese-themed tattoos – Young began spending up to 40 hours a week collating and organising running and race statistics. He would later try to explain his personal character and obsession in an interview: 'The world is full of so much chaos, and I'm a born planner, an organizer. I try to make sense out of things and look for an underlying structure.'[17]

Following a move to the University of Arizona, he began exploring the extensive trail network around Tucson and soon looked to apply his competitive nature to this convenient backcountry. Starting in 1977, Young established what would become known as the Tucson Trail Runs (TTR). Obsessive and competitive, Young would hunt out and invite the fastest runners to compete. His race calendar quickly grew: Bear Canyon Loop, Mount Lemmon Ascent, Winter Bear Canyon, Cowhead Saddle, Esperero Canyon Loop, Mica Mountain Marathon and so on.[18] There was a race every month. Usually relatively short – around 15 miles or so – they were nonetheless tough and beefy, with significant elevation gain. They also reflected Young's approach to trail running: total self-reliance. There were no entry fees, and usually no support; just a group of runners, setting off together and racing hard. He was also to experiment with unusual trail running formats, including the Multiple Wrightson Massacre: a 10 mile ascent and descent of Mount Wrightson (2,882 metres), up and down as many times as possible between dawn and dusk.

John Cappis (1942–), based in New Mexico – although originally from the high-altitude mining town of Telluride, in Colorado – had been among the small group of competitors at the first organised Western States (1977), followed by a third place finish the following year. Towards the end of the 1970s, he could often be found training alone, running hard on local New Mexico trails: from the ponderosa forests and mesa formations of Bandelier, through to the rugged and rocky elevations of the Caballo and Pajarito Mountains. Inspired by Ken Young in neighbouring Arizona, Cappis launched his own event series in 1982. Initially there were four: South Baldy Ridge, Lake Peak to Sante Fe Baldy, Capulin Canyon (all in New Mexico) and, in his childhood home, Telluride Get High. The race series – which became known as 'MTN RNR' (i.e., 'mountain runner', after his personalised plate number) – would eventually grow to an annual calendar of twenty events, mostly sub-marathon, or just inching into ultra-distance.[19] Again, the spirit was one of self-reliance and low-key organisation. In time, Cappis would produce a newsletter for the run series, with memorable words at the front of every issue:

> Camaraderie and enjoyment of the mountains are the main reasons these runs are held... There will be no aid stations and you will be on your own to get back. Trail briefings will be given before each run. Listen carefully, the life you save may be your own![20]

This ethos would continue to be reflected through American mountain, ultra and trail running: minimalism and self-reliance, buoyed by camaraderie and community. Unlike the TTR race series, MTN RNR events were designed as a 'run' rather than a 'race'. The emphasis was not on competition, but the provision of an accessible (if intense) introduction to mountain running.

It was a remarkable blossoming of trail running that took place over the space of a few short years. California would see the most substantial growth: dozens of tiny races popped up across the state. Some would succeed and become regular features in the calendar – others did not, like the short-lived Donner Trail 100, or the attempt by Dave Niederhaus (another 1977 WSER competitor) to establish the Holy Jim 100. In the same way that the fell running calendar had exploded in Britain during the 1970s, by the early 1980s the United States was witnessing a sudden and entirely unprecedented surge in organised trail running.

In September 1983, as he entered the final hour and passed the 150 mile mark, on a circular track in Maine, Bernd Heinrich was given a clear message by his crew: the American 24-hour record is in sight, but you need to push – you need to push *hard*. With a surge of adrenaline, Henrich increased his pace. Caught up in the excitement, event staff raced onto the track to accompany Heinrich for the final few laps.[21] As the clock elapsed, his mark was 156 miles and 1,388 yards. It was seemingly a new American record. Or was it? Early next year, he received a letter from The Athletics Congress (TAC). His record had been rejected by the TAC Records Committee in a 6-1 vote. The reason: anonymous witnesses claimed that Heinrich had been 'paced' during the event.[22]. According to TAC rules this made the record ineligible.

The American ultrarunning community was left stunned. A bureaucratic organisation, with little connection to the heritage of ultrarunning, had denied one of their own. The dissenting vote had been from Ken Young, the only ultrarunner to sit on the committee. An upset and confused Heinrich protested that he had no control over the actions of spectators or other runners, he was simply running his own race.[23] Burning with resentment, he turned out in May for the Sri Chimnoy 24-hour race in Ottawa, setting a blistering 100 mile American record of 12:27:01 (a record that would stand for two decades). The furore continued until finally, later that year, TAC reversed their decision and Heinrich was officially awarded the 24-hour American record.

The controversy highlighted a dilemma that existed in both the United States and Britain: who should advocate for and administer the sport? American and British runners and race organisers were mostly sceptical of bureaucratic institutions, preferring instead a grassroots and anarchic approach, but there were undeniable external pressures: permitting and access, financial restrictions for elite athletes, qualification for international competition, race insurance and official record certification. There were still also unresolved issues relating to professional versus amateur running. A complete separation from mainstream athletics was not always possible, nor even desirable. Some form of institutional architecture would be required.

This dilemma had long been present in British fell running. By the early 1970s, historic professional races – such as Grasmere and Kilnsey – had dwindled in size to just a handful of competitors. Amateur fell running, meanwhile, had grown to dominate the racing calendar. This division was channelled through a new organisational framework. In 1970, two competing organisations were created to represent amateur and professional fell running: the Fell Runners Association (FRA) and the Northern Sports Promoters Association (NSPA). The FRA immediately began negotiations with the AAA to officially recognise and administer amateur fell races within the framework of English and Welsh athletics (Scottish hill running was administered by different national organisations). In 1982, the FRA was eventually given delegated responsibility on the condition that it enforce established AAA rules. The smaller NSPA, which was replaced in 1982 by the British Open Fell Runners' Association (BOFRA), sought to protect those few who still competed on the professional circuit. So far, so good – but then a bitter feud began to develop.

The Cumbrian branch of the AAA began to actively blacklist anyone who had competed in a professional event, *or who had ever* competed against another professional. Given the artificial crossover between the supposedly professional and amateur sides of the sport, this created huge problems. Shamefully, this blacklisting would even extend to junior runners that had participated in a prize-giving school competition. Race organisers often turned a blind eye, but anonymous complaints would at times be lodged by those seeking to eliminate competition before the race had even started. The AAA had long allowed reinstatement to the amateur scene – a humiliating process of 'letter begging' – but the fell running community was aghast at this division within their sport.

The controversy came to a head in 1986 when the AAA instructed Ambleside Athletic Club not to accept the membership fee of Guy Russell. His supposed crime: breaching AAA rules by competing in two events alongside professional runners. A rebellion erupted and the 'Russell case' rapidly became a cause célèbre within the small fell running world. The FRA sought – and was initially declined – a meeting with the AAA. The FRA were bombarded with letters from outraged members. In defiance of AAA rules, the Blisco Dash organisers loudly and proudly allowed Russell and another 'professional' to compete. A petition was circulated in which runners from fifteen different clubs – and including four FRA committee members

– declared their own supposed amateur ineligibility. They were daring the AAA to engage in mass expulsions. Selwyn Wright – who was himself briefly banned by the AAA during the protest and had since been appointed as FRA Secretary – captured the prevailing mood in a newsletter to members:

> It's a shame that we have to go to these lengths for the AAA to recognise our seriousness. The issue is quite straightforward and has nothing to do with money. Fell runners simply will not have outsiders telling us where we can run and where we can't.[24]

A meeting eventually took place between the AAA and FRA on 7 August. A tentative resolution was agreed: rule changes would soften the overly punitive definition of 'professionalism' and, in return, BOFRA events should be listed in the FRA annual calendar.[25] Negotiations would continue for a time on this second point – BOFRA was uncertain about being placed under nominal FRA governance – but an agreement was finally reached in 1992. All British fell running would now be considered 'open': *anyone* would be able to compete in *any* fell race.

The mid-1980s was a defining time for fell running. The entire sport was bucking against the enforced and arbitrary rules of an external bureaucratic organisation, but there were also deeper roots to this wayward and independent spirit. As Selwyn Wright famously remarked: 'To run up a fell is the simplest thing. Let's not make it complicated.'[26] This attitude partly stemmed from important regional and class dimensions. Fell running had become increasingly diverse since the 1950s and 1960s, drawing in athletes from towns and cities across the UK (remarkably, Cambridge University itself had a fell running club by the mid-1980s[27]), but it was still firmly attached to the working-class agricultural communities of Cumbria. This class division was most striking in the organisational culture of the sport. While fell running champions would often come from manual working backgrounds – such as Bill Teasdale, Joss Naylor, Kenny Stuart and Billy Bland – the committee positions of the FRA were typically filled with university-educated professionals and those working within managerial roles. This diversity was a source of great strength, but there were inevitable tensions. The organising and administrative impulses of a managerial middle class would at times rub up against tough manual workers who just wanted to get out and run hard.

Amid these simmering concerns, FRA Chairman Hugh Symonds felt compelled to address them directly. Writing to the FRA membership, in 1985, he raised a number of points that were seemingly linked to the increasingly organised growth of the sport: mandatory event insurance, standardised race rules, commercial sponsorship, and links to international mountain running:

> Take a number of runners and a bonny hill or a rough mountain and you can have a race. It sounds simple but are we in the FRA making things more complicated? ... [Are we] furthering the bureaucratic interests of the committee or acting in the interests of the membership? There have been big fears that these subtle changes may be the beginning of a big change in fell running as we know it.[28]

Ultimately these fears would be misplaced – the sport was evolving rather than undergoing radical transformation – but the custodians of fell running would continue to tread a cautious line between change and tradition.

Curiously, a similar debate was taking place in the United States. Mainstream American athletics was in a state of transition during the 1970s and 1980s. In a radical shake-up, a federal ruling – through the 1978 Amateur Sports Act – legislated to remove responsibility for athletics from the AAU. A new spin-off organisation was created – The Athletics Congress (TAC) – which was then succeeded in 1992 by USA Track and Field (USATF). The debate was a little irrelevant for trail and ultra running – there were few sponsorship opportunities anyway – but the turmoil happened to occur in parallel with post-Western States expansion. Institutional chaos, and a general sense of disenchantment with mainstream athletics, would lead many new race organisers to remain unaffiliated from TAC. Unlike with British fell running, there would be no singular or overarching governing body. Rather, a constellation of organisations would adopt overlapping administrative and advocacy roles within the sport. There were three key issues that needed addressing: record certification, elite sponsorship and international competition.

Record certification was less of a concern for trail running – such records were linked to specific courses rather than a fixed distance or time – although there was some speculation and debate about course measurement (WSER made several changes to achieve a full 100 mile course and John Cappis famously rolled a measuring wheel up Pikes Peak as it sought full marathon status[29]). However, for those wanting to target track and road records, the integrity of these attempts mattered a great deal. The National Running Data Center (NRDC) had been established in 1973, by Ken Young, with the aim of collecting and preserving long-distance running records. In December 1983, an arrangement was reached through which NRDC would collect and verify records, with times then being approved by the new TAC Records Committee. The aim was to have a standardised process of record keeping for the whole of American athletics, from the 100 metre sprint through to the six-day race. The change brought with it additional layers of bureaucracy and other potential hurdles. Race organisers would need to apply for validation in advance and athletes would need to abide by certain restrictions.

The professional versus amateur situation was still also unresolved – with implications for elite sponsorship and prize winnings. Professional athletes were required to place their earnings in a trust fund, so as to be eligible for record attempts and amateur competition. Ultra and trail running largely lacked prize and sponsorship money – which made this a non-issue – until Jim King, Bjorg Austrheim-Smith and Jim Howard (all WSER champions) established the Western Endurance Racers Association (WERA), in 1984, to lobby for the interests of elite runners. Their complaint was largely around the lack of financial support and an annual calendar that saw important races clash with one another.[30] In June of that year, Western States secured $12,500 in prize money from their sponsor, Levi Strauss. This was a huge and unprecedented sum of money – vastly dwarfing anything in the sport either at the time or even today. It was carefully administered by TAC and given to athletes through a system of 'expense claims' for 'training purposes' – a fudge that would prevent the amateur status of WSER competitors from being brought into question. This proved to be a short-lived problem. While Levis Strauss remained the sponsor, prize money was discontinued the following year.

TAC would also begin to play a role in tendering out bids for existing races to become an official 'USA Championship Race' – with stringent conditions around course certification, prize money, trust funds, officiating, and travel expenses.[31] All of a sudden, TAC was now involved with the elite side of the sport in a meaningful way. It was a shock, then, when the first meeting of the TAC Records Committee rejected Heinrich's 24-hour American record. The controversy was eventually resolved, but reputational damage had been done. There was a sense among the ultrarunning community that mainstream athletics and marathon road running had been 'ruined' – and now the 'pen pushers' were coming for trail and ultra running.[32] Regardless, TAC would continue to administer the only universally accepted system for ultra-distance records in the United States.

In a further layering of institutional confusion, in June 1984 it was announced that the International Association of Ultrarunners (IAU) had been established at an inaugural meeting in Austria. Founding members of this new organisation were from the UK, USA, West Germany, Austria and France. The stated aims of the IAU were to foster international cooperation, organise international competitive events, and (somewhat controversially) to have 'the *final* say as to the status of *all* claimed world and national records for all distances above the marathon'.[33] Immediate backlash commenced. Not only would the IAU arguably be drawn into conflict with national governing bodies that already claimed the verification of athletic records – such as TAC and the AAA – but athletes in the United States raised objections to the idea of a membership-based organisation. The creation of the IAU was coming soon after the TAC–Heinrich controversy and administrative athletic bodies were not held in high regard.

Concerned letters were published in running media, including one which captured the resistance among some to creeping institutionalisation:

> Come on, folks, aren't we getting a little too organized and professionalised a bit too quickly? Pretty soon, just as people feel pressured to join TAC in order to qualify for some races, the same will be true of the IAU. And then we shall have to be concerned with who is eligible to compete, and the organization geared toward fostering 'communication and cooperation, regardless of ethnic or national considerations' will be deciding who can or cannot compete on the basis of other extraneous reasons.[34]

It is difficult to know just how widely shared these concerns were – most recreational runners were perhaps uninterested with the elite side of the sport – but the IAU felt compelled to issue a series of clarifications: it would *not* be membership-based, but rather a looser organisation tasked with helping to coordinate international competition.[35] National governing bodies would also still have ultimate responsibility for record verification. Gary Cantrell – the newly appointed North American President of the IAU – entered the fray to make a strong case for the principles of self-organisation: 'If we fail to organize ourselves only two things can happen – we will muddle along until some scandal ruins our sport, or someone else will organize us to suit their own purposes.'[36]

The controversy was something of a red herring. The IAU was only really interested in a very narrow slice of ultra-distance athletics – international elite track competition – and it would have little impact on the grassroots and trail side of the sport. The first IAU-supported event took place in Belgium, in 1987 – the 100 km World Championship. It was then reprised in Spain, in 1988, this time also supported by the governing body of world athletics, the International Amateur Athletic Federation (IAAF). The IAU retained responsibility for inviting elite athletes and providing partial if limited financial support to these competitors. It was the beginning of *formal* international competition – rather than de facto international championships (such as London to Brighton) – and the IAU would continue to help coordinate this aspect of the sport. This growing arena of international competition would, however, remain confined to the track. Despite some of the best American trail runners participating in these IAU championship events – including Jim King (in 1987) and Ann Trason (in 1988) – there seemed to be little interest in international trail competition. It would take exactly two decades for the IAU Trail World Championship to be finally established (in 2007).

Sally Edwards was an unstoppable whirlwind of energy, bursting onto the American athletics scene with a flurry of activity. As a sponsored triathlete, she clinched silver and bronze at the 1981 and 1982 Ironman Championships, punctuated with first and second place at the 1980 and 1981 editions of Western States.[37] A published book on triathlon training came soon after – the first of twenty-five self-authored books – along with qualification for the first women's Olympic marathon trials. She also found time to establish both the American River 50 (1980) and the California International Marathon (1983). It was the beginning of a lengthy career that would see Edwards found no less than six different commercial sports companies.

It was against this backdrop that Edwards launched a withering attack on the 'dying' sport of ultra-distance running. In a lengthy essay, she lambasted race organisers. According to Edwards, they lacked an enterprising spirit that was necessary to adequately support elite athletes and, by extension, the wider sport:

> There is a cure for the death of ultramarathoning and the cure is not an easy pill to swallow. There will always be the few participants who will challenge the barriers of human performance for no greater reward than meeting the challenge. Yet, the satisfaction gained from the challenge simply does not pay the rent or buy groceries. Neither does it promote the sport. Ultramarathoning needs to grow and one of the best ways is by providing athletes with incentives, race promoters with adequate budgets, the media with invitations, and sponsors with visibility.[38]

Edwards represented one side of an existential debate that was taking place in both Britain and the United States: what are the values of the sport and *who* exactly should be celebrated? Are elite athletes worthy of monetised acclaim, or does every competitor deserve equal recognition? Edwards – who was more successfully making the very same argument in the world of triathlon[39] – had a clear view on this final point:

> Many race directors even call their races 'runs,' not races. A classic example is the 1983 Western States 100. When *Sacramento Magazine* asked the race directors which athlete to feature in a major article on the race, they recommended Stanford Brown because he exemplified the spirit of the race by finishing in 29 hours and 59 minutes – the last finisher. Last year's champions Jim King and Bjorg Austrheim-Smith have little chance of either athletic sponsorship or due credit for their accomplishments, because they remain obscure.[40]

Edwards was a rare voice in ultrarunning – largely representing the views of a small group of elite athletes – while prevailing opinion elsewhere in the sport tended to lean towards the egalitarianism of 'recreational' running. The response to the Edwards essay was overwhelming.

A deluge of letters flooded *UltraRunning Magazine* – too many for them all to be printed in any one edition – along with more lengthy responses by Gary Cantrell and Curt Sproul (the Western States race director). Sproul, while supporting elite athletes and a general expansion of the sport, defended the current approach by the Western States board: 'I am reluctant to fiddle with a successful formula in the hope of securing a relatively insignificant amount of money for a very small number of the sport's participants.'[41] Similarly, Cantrell acknowledged the natural human tendency to place race winners on a pedestal, but suggested that this urge in ultrarunning was balanced out against more inclusive aspects of the sport:

> We have a very pleasant situation right now. The sport is growing, but in a manageable way. The friendly communal spirit of ultrarunning is surviving and the quality of our events has been maintained or improved as the number of events has grown. Our sport is one of the very few in which any man or woman has the opportunity to join, as a full member, an athletic community. There are no mediocre ultramarathoners, only great ones.[42]

The issue was not just one of elite versus recreational running; bubbling underneath were anxieties about a widespread commercialisation of the sport. Jokes were shared about the unwelcome prospect of 'Stu Mittleman running shorts' and 'Marcy Schwamsuits'.

In truth, creeping commercialisation and sponsorship were already taking place – just slowly. Western States resisted prize money for a time – refusing an offer from Nike in 1982 to sponsor the event with a prize purse – but only two years later a similar if short-lived arrangement was adopted with Levi Strauss. The classic Lake Tahoe race was now the 'Pepsi of Reno Lake Tahoe Run'. The first edition of Leadville would be bannered by both Pepsi and Nike. Meaningful athlete sponsorship was not yet a reality – hence the critique by Edwards – but some were able to claim modest sponsorship deals. However, while Austrheim-Smith (Nike) and Heinrich (Ocean Spray) no doubt appreciated free running shoes and an unlimited supply of cranberry juice, this hardly provided a living. The era of professional ultrarunning was still decades away.

Fell runners expressed similar concerns, although the scale of feared commercialisation was perhaps quaint by American standards. The fells themselves – steep, technical, remote and often wet – would always place a limit on mass expansion, media interest and monetisation. However, in something of an echo of the 'Edwards furore', discontent began to brew when a sponsored fell race with a significant prize purse was launched, in 1985.[43] The sponsor in question was a local bathroom supplier – hardly a multinational apparel or drinks company – but, even so, resistance was fierce: 'Amateur fell running is blatantly on the same slippery slope as road running and track with sportsmanship and fun taking second place to overt competition and the avid collecting of sponsors.'[44] So grumbled one of several letters to the FRA, including those who complained about rising entry fees and all the associated 'gubbins': 'Fell runners do not expect fancy facilities; they should not have to pay fancy fees.'[45] While nobody truly expected the mass commercialisation of fell running, Selwyn Wright raised concerns that ordinary runners would in time be expected to subsidise prestigious international mountain running teams and events – and that this would threaten the ethos of a sport where 'everybody, whether champion or duffer, is in the same race and the same pub afterwards'.[46]

Were anxieties about commercialisation misplaced? Not entirely. Fell runners were perhaps more concerned with protecting the spirit of the sport, rather than genuinely fearing widespread commercialisation, which seemed unlikely. It was a little different in the United States. Ultrarunning and triathlon were in identical positions during the 1980s – they were niche and grassroots – but this was also the point of divergence. For better or worse, triathlon embraced the argument made by Edwards: it would grow into a multibillion-dollar industry, but with radically different 'pricing levels' in the sport and a sharper separation between elite and recreational athletes. Ultrarunners resisted this direction of travel: they traded away sponsorship and professionalisation – for a time at least – but in so doing were able to retain values more closely associated with 'amateurism' and the notion of grassroots sport and community. This placed limits on public exposure and growth, ensuring that American ultrarunning and British fell running would remain distinct and unique subcultures, both on the fringes of mainstream athletics culture.

The peripherality of off-road endurance running would not last. Over the next decade, mountain, ultra and trail running would become more closely associated with the rise of mountain and adventure sports. And as the next chapter argues, this would represent a decisive shift from *marathon* culture to *mountain* culture.

Chapter 9

Soul sport

A camera pans across the crumbling and misty facade of Conwy Castle, nestled on the shoreline of North Wales, before a revolving close-up around the cast-bronze trophy of a curled, slumbering dragon. With a flair for the dramatic, the documentary producers billow smoke around this coveted prize. All the while, a guttural droning sound reverberates in the background, conjuring visions of a remote and mythologised mountain kingdom.

The Channel 4 documentary for the 1992 Dragon's Back Race – watched by viewers in more than sixty countries – would be the first such programme to cover ultra-distance mountain running in the UK. A stage race, over five days, the 220 mile route snaked down the mountainous backbone of Wales. For safety, most competitors would run in pairs, reliant on their own navigation, and sleeping each night in a temporary event campsite. The race founder, Ian Waddell, a former paratrooper, was able to generate publicity to attract the sponsorship of a major petroleum company. Former comrades in the British Parachute Regiment would provide safety and support, imparting a sense of order and martial gravitas. It was an adventure-style foot race, inspired by the Marathon des Sables (first held in 1986), but otherwise utterly unprecedented. Nobody had ever before attempted to organise a mountain race of this magnitude.

The race attracted an elite field – 55 in total – including some of the most prolific international ultrarunners of the time. Rune Larsson, from Sweden, three-time winner of Spartathlon, would run the race solo. Stefan Schlett – fresh from having just finished the 3,000 mile Trans America Footrace – would pair with fellow German Stefan Fecher. There was an American duo – Adrian Crane and Tom Possert – veterans of Western States, Angeles Crest, Badwater and the Barkley Marathons. They were joined by some of the best long-distance mountain runners in the UK. Despite the strong international showing, victory would balance precariously between two British teams: Adrian Belton/Mark McDermott versus Helene Diamantides/Martin Stone. All four were fell running stalwarts, who between them held many of the most prestigious long-distance mountain records in Britain.

The first day saw competitors leave Conwy Castle in early morning sunshine, surrounded by a police escort, before rising into the thick mist of the Carneddau range. On notoriously steep and rocky terrain, the runners took different routes, with many finding themselves lost during the 2,000 foot climb up the pyramidal buttress of Tryfan. Alone, Larsson faltered, his cries for help echoing out over the bleak moonscape. Several times he climbed back down, searching for a more viable route upward. Like many from the international contingent, he would continue to struggle over this wild and unfamiliar landscape.[1] The 36 mile day ended in a virtual tie: Diamantides/Stone leading by two minutes over Belton/McDermott.

The next four days – each 46 miles – would run on ever more forgiving terrain: rough hills in the Moelwynd and Rhinogd, gradually giving way to open country, forest tracks and paved road, before the sting of the Black Mountains. Belton/McDermott were able to sneak ahead on the second day – taking a 4-minute lead – only for Diamantides/Stone to push hard for a 20-minute lead by the end of the third day. The fourth day began in drizzle, Belton/McDermott burning ahead from the start, with a bold and aggressive pace over a long road section – it was a deliberate attempt to break the struggling Diamantides/Stone. Their strategy worked, bridging the gap, before then inching them ahead for a 5-minute lead.

The final day would prove to be decisive. Belton began to suffer from shin splints – switching to a frustrating hobble as they fell into second place – only to regain a 15-minute lead after a disastrous navigational error by Diamantides/Stone. Drawing on a burst of determination and willpower, Diamantides pushed her weary partner forward, cajoling him faster and faster over the bleak and trackless hills. Passing through a checkpoint, one of the parachute troopers was to remark: 'She came through here with steam coming out of her ears.'[2] It was enough. Diamantides and Stone are the first team to thread their way up the thirteenth-century ramparts of Carreg Cennen, perched in black, brooding silence over the empty Carmarthenshire countryside. Tearful and emotional, Stone embraces Diamantides. He lies on the ground, out of view, as she remains standing to be interviewed by an expectant camera crew that are thrilled with the novelty of a woman winning this male-dominated, military-supported event.

The race marked an important moment in ultra-distance mountain and trail running. The sport was maturing – and it was also changing. While the Dragon's Back race would only happen once – before a revamp and relaunch in 2012 – it tapped into the zeitgeist of 1990s endurance mountain running. The modern, post-Western States sport was now almost two decades old. There was a desire for new challenges – longer, harder, rougher – particularly among veterans looking for something fresher and a little different. This evolution – characterised at the time in *UltraRunning Magazine* as a 'never-ending search for new and exciting ultra challenges' – was occurring alongside the wider media-driven phenomenon of 'lifestyle' and 'extreme' sport. Like dirtbag climbers in Yosemite and Chamonix – or ski bums in search of pristine powder – off-road endurance runners were embracing a lifestyle that was built up around their running. For those who had been at the heart of ultrarunning for more than a decade, the sport was everything – from friendships and family, to travel, clothing and food – *it defined who they were*.

The running community was also getting larger, with much of this growth explained by increased female participation. A rise in global aviation was enabling more frequent international competition at 'prestige' races and a rise in so-called 'adventure running' – including to 'destination' locations, such as the Himalayas and Africa

– where exploration would be emphasised in place of competition. Having long been neglected by mainstream athletics brands, the sport was also becoming associated with the wider outdoor sports industry. Established companies – such as North Face and Patagonia – were to find a receptive market among a growing community of trail and mountain runners. This commodification and commercialisation would develop to become important features of the sport (see Chapter 10).

The sport was growing and changing throughout the 1990s and into the early 2000s: more professional, commercial and global, but also increasingly diverse, with a richer array of running styles and experiences, and a stronger sense of shared cultural identity. As would prove to be decisive for the sport, these changes were part of a broader cultural pivot in the Western world towards ideas of 'adventure' and 'lifestyle'.

'If you want to understand America, you must know extreme sports' – so intoned an excited cover story by U.S. News and World Report, in June 1997.[3] Throughout the decade, there had been a sense that the sporting world of America was in upheaval. If one were to believe excited media pundits, an entire generation of young people had turned towards peripheral, counterculture sports. The list was extensive: from skateboarding to BASE jumping, and indoor climbing to SCUBA diving, to a whole collection of the weird and the wonderful. It was a profound cultural turn.

Writers and academics struggled to find a language to describe what was happening. Were these activities best described as extreme, or alternative? As fun, or deadly serious? As lifestyle, or as sport? Similarly, the media was fascinated but often confused.[4] Coverage in the early to mid-1990s would initially depict these new leisure pursuits as strongly associated with suburban Gen-Xers – the MTV generation – who supposedly possessed fleeting attention spans and a nihilistic approach to life. This perception was only strengthened by the launch of ESPN's X-Games, in 1995 – which focused on the adrenaline-pumping, pop-punk rush of skateboarding, snowboarding and BMX – and the surge to global fame of renowned skater Tony

Hawks, who would, in a 2002 poll of young people, be declared America's 'coolest' athlete.[5]

Towards the end of the decade media depictions were also beginning to shift. Lifestyle sports that were connected to the outdoors – climbing, diving, kitesurfing, snowboarding and so forth – were becoming more favourably covered by flagship media outlets, ranging from glossy articles to cinematic documentary programming and filmmaking. They were framed as 'adventurous activities' that were now pitched with commercial fervour to (predominantly) middle-class and middle-aged white men. This new narrative emphasised the American nature of alternative outdoor sport. In an echo of past presidents – from Theodore Roosevelt to John F. Kennedy – adventure activities were seen to exemplify American ideals of masculinity, innovation, rugged individualism and the pursuit of new frontiers.[6] It chimed with a pervasive sense of optimism and possibility.[7] The Soviet Union had broken apart in 1991 – American and Western liberal capitalism was ascendent – and a world of hedonistic adventure seemingly lay ahead.

While these sports were of course in many ways radically different from one another – for example, board sports share little technical or physical overlap with bouldering or skydiving – they often possessed similar values and an overlapping sense of style. This was in sharp contrast to mainstream sport. These new adventure sports were expressive and individualistic, rather than a spectacle for the crowd; grassroots, rather than professional; non-aggressive, rather than violently competitive; spiritual and self-actualising, rather than regulated or institutionalised. Unlike rule-bound stadium sports, they sought to reclaim spaces – from the city block to the mountainside – in ways that were creative and intuitive. Following rapid growth and commercialisation, it was no coincidence that many of these new sporting subcultures would begin to share identical apparel brands – from Converse and Vans, to Rip Curl and North Face.

Mountain sports themselves were hitting the mainstream during the 1990s. The indoor climbing movement in particular was rapidly propelled by televised competition and the emergence of climbing superstars, many of whom had come up through the countercultural climbing scene of Yosemite.[8] The pioneering free climber Lynne Hill – who made a celebrated appearance before an audience of millions on *Late Night with David Letterman* – would later describe this Californian climbing scene as 'a ragged occupying army, annoying park rangers by eluding camp fees, overstaying their welcome, and comporting themselves like gypsies'. The idea of the 'dirtbag' – someone passionately dedicated to their 'soul sport' at the expense of domestic life – was suddenly popularised beyond climbing. There was an explosion of interest in fun, accessible and safe ways to encounter the mountains: from *via ferrata* and canyoning, to snowshoeing and cross-country skiing. Meanwhile, popular culture was awash with literary and cinematic exploits – both real and fictional – of daring mountaineering expeditions in the Alps and the Himalayas. Niche climbing brands that had specialised in pioneering technical equipment and apparel in the 1970s and 1980s – North Face, Patagonia and Black Diamond (the latter two both founded by legendary Yosemite climber Yvon Chouinard) – were encountering unprecedented success that would see their market expand beyond climbers to a wider collection of more casual outdoor enthusiasts.[9]

Mountain, ultra and trail running was a small but distinctive part of this broader cultural shift. The centre of gravity for the sport had historically been located at the outer edge of mainstream track and road athletics – it had in the past been more *marathon culture* than *mountain culture*. Yet this was changing. In 1982, 38 per cent of ultra-distance race finishes in the United States were in a trail event (and roughly half of these in only four races). By 1992, this figure was 80 per cent – across more than fifty different trail/mountain events – climbing to 87 per cent by the end of the decade. Ultrarunning was growing, but in doing so it was also becoming more clearly a mountain sport. As ultra-distance trail running drifted decisively into the orbit of mountain culture, it too would be shaped by this new constellation of beliefs and values: exploration, hedonism, adventure – and for some, a search for the 'extreme'.

It was pitched as the 'postgraduate' of ultras. Devised by Gordon Hardman, the plan was for an event in the San Juan mountains of Colorado that would be tougher than anything else in the calendar. John Cappis was brought in to map a potential course, with help from old hands that included Rick Trujillo and David Horton. Starting in the mining settlement of Silverton – recently devastated by the closure of Sunnyside Mine – the course would loop for 99 miles, through the towns of Telluride, Ouray and a series of abandoned mining settlements. Climbing and descending a total of 30,000 feet – with an average elevation of 11,000 feet – it would cross an area with more land mass at this elevation that anywhere else in the lower continental United States. The race organisers declared that it would be a 'salute to the toughness and perseverance of the hardrock miners who initially developed the area'. The Hardrock 100 was born – and, on 10 July 1992, only one question was on the lips of those at the starting line: 'Can it be done?'

The course was marked – and re-marked following the curious and destructive attention of elk and marmots – but skilled navigation would prove to be vital. Shell-shocked competitors came away with war stories about sheer drops, collapsing scree slopes, rotten cornices and a 40 mph snowstorm. Asked why she had dropped out at mile 90, one competitor was to remark with acerbic bluntness: 'Because I didn't want to die'. After the race, another was to find himself 'babbling incoherently for two days'.[10] Forty-two experienced runners started – all among the very best – but only 18 finished. David Horton triumphed, in 32:34. At the age of 42, he had now been at the top of the sport – perhaps the singularly most dominant competitor in ultra-distance trail running – since his first run at Old Dominion, in 1980. The median age of finishers at the 1992 Hardrock also happened to be just under 42 years.[11] It was an age profile that reflected deeper trends.

In the 1990s, the modern sport was finally 'coming of age' – both literally and metaphorically. For over a decade, ultrarunning had been an upstart branch of athletics. Runners and competitors in the early years – those who rode in on the boom of 1970s marathon running – had needed to build up around them a new ultra-distance athletic culture. In the 1980s, they were young firebrands – many in their twenties and thirties – rediscovering the 'lost' heritage of pedestrianism and looking to interwar running legends, like Arthur Newton and Johnny Salo. Yet this 'first generation' had also been ageing alongside their sport. Horton, Trujillo and Cappis – all of whom entered the sport in their twenties – were now in their forties and fifties.

In 1982, the average age of race competitors in North America was 37 years – the average age of race *winners* was 33. By 1992, this had risen, respectively, to 43 and 38 years – a figure that would then remain relatively constant into the early 2000s. New entrants continued to bring youth and speed, but there were fewer of them – both the proportion and *actual number* of competitors in their twenties dropped, despite an overall growth in the number of participants across the sport. Meanwhile, veterans of the previous decade were keen to seek fresh challenges – such as the Hardrock 100 – where experience and skill mattered perhaps more than pure athleticism. Even in long-standing 'runnable' events, where speed and power could remain decisive, early pioneers of the modern sport were at times still able to continue their dominance. Tim Twietmeyer's impressive string of five victories at Western States – which finally ended with a second-place finish to Scott Jurek in 1999 (see Chapter 10) – was to take place as he approached nearly two decades in the sport.

This growing maturity was significant. Unlike many other sports, it was possible to have tremendous longevity. Rather than appearing on the scene in a blazing flash – only to then abruptly disappear – athletes were able to continue for decades. As ultrarunners were finding, experience might at times offset the raw physicality of youth.

Paradoxically, the ageing profile of the sport would promote both stability and change. Continuing involvement by older participants would ensure the transmission of values and beliefs to the next generation – and the generation after that. The ethics forged during the heated debates of the 1980s – that this should be a grassroots and egalitarian sport – would be preserved rather than forgotten. Yet many of these older athletes were also seeking new challenges, just as they were settling down into the relative financial comfort and responsibilities of middle age. Combined with a general rise in prosperity and living standards across North America and Europe, this would provide the opportunity for a small few to take their aspirations to new and unfamiliar parts of the world – or perhaps even to unfamiliar corners of their own backyard.

Where was Mark? That was the question everyone was asking, huddled around the park gate, as dawn broke on the third day. With only 30 minutes left before the cut-off time, a bleary Mark Williams stumbled out from his tent, having overslept through three alarms. Tapping the gate, he disappeared into the gloomy woods of Tennessee – and into the unknown. He was the first person to ever attempt a fifth loop of the Barkley Marathons. In March 1995, the race had only been running for a decade – yet it was already legendary and increasingly viewed as 'impossible'.

Williams was himself an unlikely figure to make the attempt. A 29-year-old computer programmer from Oxfordshire, in Britain, he had taken up fell running and orienteering while at university. Even by the mid-1990s, there were hardly any off-road ultra-distance races in the UK, where there was still a preference for shorter (if rougher) racing over trackless terrain. Williams was drawn to what little there was, including his first entry to the 95 mile West Highland Way, in 1991. He also looked abroad, taking long fast-packing trips in the Alps and, from 1993, became a regular participant at Spartathlon. He hadn't won anything at this distance or even found himself on the podium. He was talented, but seemingly not exceptional – meat for the grinder of the Barkley.

By the mid-1990s, the Barkley Marathons had already entered ultrarunning folklore. First held in 1986, the original course ran for three loops around Frozen Head State Park in Tennessee, for a total of 55 miles and 27,000 feet of climbing. The race founder and director, Gary Cantrell/Lazarus Lake (see Chapter 8), had designed the course to provide an elusive challenge: 'The point of the Barkley is challenge.

And if you know you can finish, then what's the challenge? There are no guarantees at Barkley.'[12]

The course was unbeaten for two years, until 1988, when North Carolinian Ed Furtaw managed to finish the full 55 miles in a time of 32:14. Tom Possert also finished the course that year – in a stunningly fast time of 24:47 – but after having accidently skipped a small part of the course his 'win' was disqualified. After this double blow against the Barkley, an additional 'long' course was now added by Cantrell: five loops, equating to around 100 miles, with a 50-hour cut-off (extended in later editions to 60 hours). From 1989, competitors would aim to complete the 'short' course and then continue (if they could) to make an attempt on the full five loops. As the years passed, nobody was coming even close – not a single runner had yet ventured beyond the original three loops.

The legend of the Barkley was born from this obvious difficulty, but also from Cantrell's evocative annual race reports and increasingly mythologised 'survivor' stories from the runners themselves. Famed German racewalker Ulrich Kamm would achieve his first and only race DNF in the 1990 Barkley – and subsequently avoid steep terrain for a whole year afterward due to the battering his body had taken.[13] Cantrell's 1993 account of the course was typical of his 'promotion' to prospective runners:

> A gut-wrenching, man-eater of a course, spartan aid stations, negligible course markings, mud, rocks, blowdowns, briers, and a nasty habit of breaking runners up like so much kindling wood ... the Barkley is to the lunatics what a flame is to a moth.[14]

An aura of invincibility was beginning to grow around the full 100 mile course. In 1994, David Horton ran a blisteringly fast three loops in 23:49:50 – the fastest time (and still the record) for what was now being called a 'fun run' – but, shivering and grim-faced, he declined to continue. Cantrell was to gleefully report that 'Gumby Horton' could be heard moaning and crying in the shower, 'I can't believe it hurts so bad.'[15]

So, a year later, there was widespread astonishment when Mark Williams became the first runner to continue beyond a 'fun run'.

He started and finished Loop 4 – crawled into his tent at 4 a.m. for a two-hour sleep – and, eventually woken by an insistent alarm, stumbled into Loop 5. His fourth circuit had taken him 13 hours and 35 minutes. For this final lap he had only around 12 hours and 30 minutes remaining on the clock. Time was impossibly tight – but it was warm, and a new day was breaking. Rested and revived, Williams began to make good progress. Without drama or despair, he pushed through and appeared at the gate later that evening. Tapping the park gate that marked the race finish, in a time of 59:28:48, Williams looked strong and ecstatic – a delightful grin splashed across his face. 'Was it as easy as it looked?' they asked. His response, with a touch of British understatement: 'It wasn't actually easy, loop five got a bit difficult.'[16] The edge of the impossible had be found. Cantrell would continue to modify the course – making it tantalisingly ever more challenging – and it would not be until 2001 that the Barkley would see another finisher (two finishers in fact: David Horton, back for vengeance, and Blake Wood).

Why was (and is) the Barkley so alluring? After all, the race was low key, with no more than 40 starters, and often in terrible weather. By the mid-1990s it had begun to attract a smattering of international runners – from Britain, Germany, Poland, Switzerland, Russia, Lithuania and Ukraine – which was still largely a rarity on the American racing circuit. What drew these runners to travel across the world to a hidden corner of Tennessee?

Even in this mostly pre-Internet age, the international ultrarunning community was connected through sports publications, word of mouth and international institutions (such as the IAU). The Barkley had begun to develop a certain mystique among this community. Year after year, runners were trying – and always failing – to defeat this unique course. The sense of impossibility was intoxicating. There was also undoubtedly a fascination with the format: the grinding repetition of race loops, an ever-changing course, unmanned checkpoints (marked solely by a hidden book, from which runners were required to tear a page as proof of their progress) and a non-standard entry process (involving a short essay that prospective entrants were required to write – entry decisions would then be made by Cantrell, 'based entirely on a whim'). While lacking the glamour of California, or the majesty of the San Juans, the landscape itself also proved fascinating. The race crossed rough and unforgiving terrain – razor-sharp briars, dense woods and iron-hard hills – skirting the edge of Brushy Mountain State prison (in 1996, two lost runners were stopped by prison guards and made to lie on the floor at gunpoint).[17] The Barkley had it all – a mix of mythology, elaborate war stories, an ominous landscape, and perhaps an innate human desire to seek the limits of the possible.

The number of finishers would slowly tick up over the next two decades – with only 17 runners having finished by 2023. American runner Beverley Anderson-Abbs became the first woman to complete three full loops in 2012, but female completion remained frustratingly distant and perhaps impossible. That was until 2024, when Jasmin Paris became the first woman to complete all five loops. Her shambling and exhausted sprint to the finish – with success hanging in the balance until the very last moment – saw Paris complete the final loop with only 99 seconds remaining on the clock. The finishing photograph of Paris – collapsed, pale and gaunt by the park gate – would rapidly enter ultrarunning folklore as one of the most iconic images in the sport.

Barkley, Hardrock and Dragon's Back all shared one thing in common: they were an irresistible lure to a new generation of globe-trotting mountain and ultra athletes. They joined a growing collection of 'prestige' races, including Marathon des Sable and Spartathlon, both of which had been running since the early to mid-1980s. While international competition would still remain rare throughout the 1990s – with only 2–4 per cent of American race finishes coming from an international contingent – a small group of athletes were beginning to explore the potential to take their running to new destinations.

This was not entirely new. Throughout the 1980s there had been a handful of attempts to put together 'running holidays' in more exotic locations. As early as 1978, the Midnight Sun Marathon had been launched in Canada. This pioneering, all-inclusive event involved a five-day visit to Baffin Island, with a number of races (10 km, 32 km, 42 km and 84 km) for participants of different abilities – all in the Arctic Circle, beneath the ever-present summer sun. Despite the obvious costs involved, it was a success, continuing in some form through to the early 2000s. And yet, events of this kind were rare during the 1980s; trail and ultra running remained a mostly local and regional sport.

Meanwhile, the cost of air travel was beginning to plummet. The average cost of a domestic flight in the United States was around $600 in 1981 (adjusted for inflation) – this had dropped to a little over $400 by 1995.[18] International tourism (estimated by arrival numbers) roughly doubled in size between 1980 and 1995 (from 250 million to 500 million) – including particularly pronounced growth to more 'exotic' destinations for Western tourists, in Asia, Africa and Latin America.[19] The birth of the Internet and the explosion of the travel guide industry fuelled both knowledge and an interest in parts of the world that had typically been out of reach to casual tourists from North America and Europe. Runners and outdoor enthusiasts – many of whom were part of a salaried middle class – inevitably embraced and linked this culture of international travel and exploration to their recreational athleticism.

Two things became commonplace in the 1990s. Runners were beginning to write long-form, essay-style accounts of running in remote locations. These articles were published in running magazines – and they emphasised travel, experience and lifestyle over a traditional focus on competition. Alongside this, a specialised tourism industry was beginning to target runners as a new and viable market. It was a niche activity within a niche sport – but it was growing. Eric Clifton, one of the most dominant athletes across American ultrarunning in the 1990s, was among the first to write a report that captured this spirit of travel and adventure. His report captures a visit to Big Lake, in Northwest Alaska, for the Iditasport 125 km foot race (and concurrent snowshoe race). Rather than discussing the back and forth of competition on race day, the expansive article dwells on place, the joy of travel, the richness of personal experience and a sense of jeopardy:

> I approached this race as an adventure, and no true adventure exists without risks ... Even though this was a competition, the real competitors were not fellow runners, but the whistling wind blowing ice crystals in your face and through your clothes; the white soft surface you flounder and fall in; the short icy hill you slip on and slide back to the bottom; the lack of food, shelter, or aid of any kind in the remote location between checkpoints; and always present, the numbing cold hovering constantly, patiently, waiting to bite.[20]

Nestled within this lengthy piece could be found a sponsored advert by Force 10 Expeditions – a travel company based in California – for a 'Himalayan Run and Trek' 100 mile stage race in India. Rather than elite competition, this was a non-competitive experience for runners of 'all ability levels' – with 'stunning' views of Tibet and Bhutan. Testimonials from elite runners, including Marshall Ulrich and Norm Klein (race director for Western States), added to the prestige of this rather pricey running holiday. The frequency of these articles would increase over the next few years – alongside the growth of this tourism industry – with lengthy reports that began to discuss trips to the Andes, Patagonia, the Himalayas and elsewhere.

In 2001, *UltraRunning Magazine* introduced a dedicated monthly section entitled 'Adventure Run'. Alongside trip reports to exotic destinations, such as the Inca Trail and the volcanic plains of Iceland, were accounts of running closer to home – from the Wonderland Trail to the Grand Canyon. A new space was opening up. The predominant focus of running media throughout the 1980s had been on competition; racing and record attempts provided the primary structure within which the sport was organised. But this was changing as the sport geared more towards the idea of *lifestyle*. In the late 1980s, for example, a typical issue of *UltraRunning Magazine* would dedicate around 65 per cent of its content to race reports and the upcoming racing calendar. The remaining 35 per cent would comprise service-based content (training, gear, nutrition etc.), general running news (access issues, governance etc.) and reflections on the sport by regular columnists. By the early 2000s, race content had dropped to less than 50 per cent – sometimes as low as 35 per cent – while general lifestyle articles (including adventure running) now comprised around 20 per cent of content.

This longer, richer content was almost always the leading feature. In the 2002 November issue, for example, the magazine dedicated around a third of content to adventure running and athletic/mountain culture in the Pacific Northwest. This all amounted to a distinct philosophical shift. Ultrarunning was becoming more expansive. Racing would of course always remain important; however, building on the life-affirming and recreational ethos of the sport, the parameters of meaningful challenge were expanding. This might involve travel and exploration – including to foreign destinations for a lucky few – but it also began to encompass other forms of creative and self-determined adventure a little closer to home.

Fred Vance had been interested in the idea of a new adventure run in the Sawatch Range from as early as 1991. A chance encounter with local mountaineer, Jim Nolan, sparked a fascination with the 14,000 foot mountains of Colorado ('the fourteeners' – of which there are fifty-four). Nolan had climbed all of them. Vance could not understand why existing ultra-distance races avoided these majestic summits. Reflecting years later, he remarked: 'I couldn't stop looking at those Collegiate Peaks 14ers and wondering why we were running on a dirt road in the Arkansas River Valley.'[21] Accordingly, Vance began to work with Nolan to devise a 100 mile route that would link together as many fourteeners as possible. A move to California scuppered plans for the proposed point-to-point route, but a few years later, at a meeting held just before the 1998 Hardrock 100, Vance discussed with Blake Wood and Charlie Thorn the prospect of reviving the idea. Setting up a steering group – which now also included Nolan, Jon MacManus and Gordon Hardman – they devised a route that ran from Mount Shavano to Mount Massive, a roughly 90 mile route that linked together fourteen fourteeners. The objective: to summit as many of these fourteen summits as possible within a 60-hour time limit.[22] The name of the route: Nolan's 14.

Wood, Hardman and Vance made the first attempt in August 1999. Volunteers were roped in to offer support, although these unofficial 'aid stations' were little more than a tarp strung between trees and boiled water for a packet of soup. Weatherwise, the timing could not have been worse. Climbing the first peak, Wood and Hardman pulled ahead together – leaving Vance trailing at a slower pace – but they were to encounter a rough storm through the first night. After descending from Mount Yale (the fifth summit), they were unable to find the planned aid station (which was further down the access trail). They continued to Mount Harvard in a snowstorm – falling six hours behind schedule – only to find that the next aid station had already packed up and left. Now entirely without food, they wisely called it a day and headed down a jeep road to hitch a lift home. They had made it over seven summits, in a time of 36 hours. Meanwhile, Vance struggled along in a semi-conscious state, also making it to Mount Harvard, in around 48 hours, before similarly making the sensible decision to finish.

They were back the following August, this time more organised and better prepared. The 'race' now started at the Leadville Fish Hatchery and ran in the opposite direction. Jon MacManus coordinated efforts, with shortwave radios used to communicate between aid station volunteers and the runners themselves. There were six starters this year, with Wood making it to Mount Princeton – despite spending an hour clinging precariously to a pine tree during a lightning storm – and setting a new record for eleven peaks within the 60-hour time limit.[23] It was the following year, in 2001, that the full route was finally completed. Twelve runners – including the first woman (Ginny LaForme) – began the attempt. Mike Tilden, from Salt Lake City, made it to Mount Shavano first, racing down to the finish just over an hour before the 60-hour cut-off. Wood followed with minutes to spare – becoming the second successful finisher – with Jim Nelson and John Robinson also completing all fourteen summits but arriving after the 60-hour mark. LaForme – a rock climber by background – managed eleven summits. Interest continued to grow in this race/not-a-race event, but Wilderness Act restrictions limited the number of participants to only fifteen. In

2003, the Forest Service learned about the event and warned Vance that the event was in breach of wilderness restrictions – and so ended organised group attempts.

It had never really been a race anyway. Nolan's 14 was a personal challenge – an adventure – that just happened to be done alongside others. 'I didn't know we were racing', exclaimed Wood,[24] when asked about his 'second place' finish in 2001. Nolan's 14 would be attempted again and again over the next two decades – in different styles (supported and unsupported) – but always with the same ethos: to have an adventure.

This new style of adventure running was just on the cusp of sustained growth – and it would soon become more organised.

In the late 1990s, Buzz Burrell and Peter Bakwin had been busy targeting records on iconic routes that included the John Muir Trail and the 500 mile Colorado Trail. They were successful on both of those occasions – or at least they *thought* they were: there was no definitive database or archive of record-breaking times or route information. With this in mind, they coined the term 'fastest known time', and Bakwin began to log times, records and other route-related information on his personal website. As Burrell remarked about the terminology and spirit of the endeavour:

> We needed a term that paid homage to the people who came before. We didn't know what the fastest time was, and so the term was born. By saying 'fastest-known time,' you're leaving the door open for some great athlete who was off the radar and did it in the pre-Internet era.[25]

Over the next decade, interest in FKTs would gradually rise, and by 2009 interest had risen sufficiently for Bakwin to create an interactive bulletin board that would cover hundreds of routes in North America and internationally. For prospective record breakers, the bulletin board provided both important information and a way to interact with an otherwise scattered and niche community. By 2017, the bulletin board evolved into a dedicated and professional website, with an accompanying podcast hosted by Burrell.

A new era of American trail running was gradually being born in the 1990s – one where creativity and self-determined routes would become a feature alongside traditional competition and racing. And yet a new era was also dawning in another important way – the depth and quality of female athletes.

The 1970s had witnessed a push by women for inclusion in long-distance athletics. Following the Switzer affair, at the 1967 Boston Marathon, there had been a sustained decade of campaigning to advocate for female participation in marathon competition. Compared to Britain, the United States was racing ahead in respect to female participation. In 1981, almost 11 per cent of finishers at the Boston Marathon were women, compared with only 2.5 per cent in the first London Marathon (also held that year). These proportions would creep up, but traditional ideas of femininity would persist, especially around the need to protect 'fragile' female bodies, a focus on running for weight loss, and female athletic apparel that was marketed with aesthetics emphasised over utility. Female performance was deprioritised and overlooked in running magazines; the focus was on traditional gender roles anchored in female beauty, motherhood and lifestyle.[26]

Similar trends were to some extent evident in off-road and ultra-distance running. In 1983, only 9.5 per cent of American ultra-distance race finishers were women. Meanwhile, female participation in British fell and ultra-distance events was as low as 1–2 per cent. This mirrored participation trends in mainstream athletics. There were celebrated stories of women breaking through in the sport – from Sandra Kiddy (USA) and Eleanor Adams (UK) on the track, through to Bjorg Austrheim-Smith (USA) and Wendy Dodds (UK) in off-road running – but female athletes faced continued gender barriers. *UltraRunning Magazine* made a deliberate and early decision to raise the profile of female athletes, but with relatively low female participation rates in the sport, women received scant coverage and there was little attention to gender-specific issues (such as the female body, training, etc.). In the space of an entire decade – from 1980 to 1989 – there were only three articles directly addressing female performance or the wider culture of female involvement in the sport. As Austrheim-Smith recounted, after winning at Western

States in 1981, while she received a rare sponsorship deal from Nike, the running shoes and apparel provided were for men, not women: 'I am built like a woman, I have curves, and so they did not make clothes for women. It was a great problem, both clothes and shoes didn't do it for women.'[27]

The state of British fell running was even more dire. Casual sexism was at times scattered throughout the pages of *Fellrunner* magazine. Adult women were frequently referred to as 'girls' and 'housewives' (one could be both, it seemed). There were jokes about the supposed 'distraction' that women posed to male athletes, not to mention a more pervasive downplaying of female athleticism. The first official women's fell race – which occurred separately and before the men's race – took place at Pendle in April 1977. Twenty women competed, followed by almost two hundred men. The race report – which ended with a dismissive 'Congratulations Girls!' – captured the macho environment that women were required to navigate:

> The winner received the Tiger Lily Cup. Afterwards she said that she had found the race relatively easy and she would like to run in more fell races. The winning time was faster than the last hundred in the men's race, so watch out fellas or you may find yourselves holding the tracksuits and carrying the drinks as I am sure ladies fell racing is here to stay.[28]

While seemingly a throwaway line – 'holding the tracksuits' and 'drinks' – the report highlighted deeper gender dynamics on both sides of the Atlantic. There was not just a condescension directed at female athletic ability – 'good for a woman' – but also an expectation that women would play a supporting role in relation to male ambition. Women might find the time to train and run for pleasure – around school, work and home obligations – but, on race day, women would be expected to care for young children, act as crew chief, staff aid stations, and provide for the finishing table of baked goods.

Change would occur – slowly – not just due to the determination of women to run and compete, but also through the supporting and outspoken role of men. Successful female athletes were either young enough to lack caring responsibilities, or they were part of a marital team whereby support flowed in both directions (as with the support that Jean Dawes received from her husband, Pete, to complete the first women's sub-24-hour Bob Graham Round in 1977). There were also men in the sport willing to speak up directly about the treatment of women. Gary Cantrell was a rare voice, addressing the situation directly, in a 1984 magazine column:

> Let's remember the ladies next time we run. Let's treat them as equals and enjoy their companionship, along with everyone else. Above all, let's try to avoid telling them that they have done well 'for a woman'. They might respond that we did well, 'for a wimp'.[29]

Female participation in mainstream athletics continued to rise over the course of the decade and this would filter through into mountain, ultra and trail running. By 1990, female entrants had risen to 18 per cent at the Boston Marathon and 9 per cent at the London Marathon. This upward trend was mirrored in ultra-distance and off-road running: 16 per cent of American ultra-distance and roughly 8 per cent of British fell and ultrarunners were women by the beginning of the 1990s. It was on this tide of rising female performance that two breakout athletes would emerge to dominate the ultra-distance and off-road scenes over the course of the decade: Helene Diamantides (UK) and Ann Trason (USA).

Diamantides (1964–) was born in North Yorkshire, but spent much of her childhood in Greece, where as a teenager she excelled at the pentathlon and cross country. Returning to Britain for teacher training, in the mid-1980s, she became involved in mountaineering, before joining the fell running club at Durham University. Fell racing success followed almost immediately, but Diamantides found herself drawn to more arduous mountain running adventures. A BGR (Bob Graham Round) was an inevitability – and in 1987 she finished the round in a little over 22 hours – but already her ambitions were stretching far beyond the borders of northern England.

Later that year, Diamantides and Alison Wright travelled to Nepal, together setting the overall record on the historic Everest Base Camp to Kathmandu 'postal route' – 188 miles and 13,000 metres of ascent

– in 3 days and 10 hours. The following year, Diamantides returned to the BGR, running solo and unsupported – the first woman to do so – to set a new overall female record of 20 hours and 17 minutes. Not yet done with the British rounds, in the summer of 1989 Diamantides capped the decade by becoming the first person (along with Adrian Belton) to complete all three classic British rounds in one calendar year (BGR, Paddy Buckley and Ramsay). Despite the male-dominated culture of British fell running, she was named by the FRA as 'Long Distance Runner of the Year'.[30] It was a remarkable flurry of achievement that would see Diamantides propelled onto the international stage over the course of the next decade.

Ann Trason (1960–) had a similar background and pedigree: a talented teenage athlete, ranked second at the 2 mile distance, and earning All American status with a 35:11 best for the 10,000 metres. At the age of twenty, she dabbled in the small but growing ultra scene at the 1982 American River 50, dropping out due to poor pacing and nutrition. Returning to the race four years later – for only her second attempt at an ultra-distance race – she set the American female record. Further victories would soon follow, but so too would failure. Trason dropped out during her first two attempts at Western States, in 1987 and 1988. Her first successful attempt at WSER, in 1989, witnessed a fierce battle among the top three women, with Trason setting a new course record and finishing 10th overall. It would be the first of fourteen victories at Western States – a record that is unlikely ever to be broken – and a driven career that would include 200 mile training weeks.

For the next two decades, Trason would win almost every race that she entered, on track, road or trail. There would be notable races missing from her résumé – she would never race at the Hardrock 100 – but her performance was almost always unmatched. In 1994, only weeks following her sixth victory at Western States, Trason famously raced against visiting Tarahumara runners at the Leadville 100, taking second place overall and the only American (male or female) to feature in the top five. While her fame would be forever burned into the trails of California, Trason would occasionally venture further afield for international competition on the track and the road, including with a 100 km world record (set twice in Europe – in 1988 and 1995) and, in 1996, a course record at the Comrades Marathon.

By the time Trason retired from the elite side of the sport, in 2003, a quarter of American finishers in ultra-distance racing were women (compared to 36 per cent at the Boston Marathon). It was a gradual, upward trend that would only continue. It is unlikely that Trason or Diamantides actually attracted *new* female participants to the sport – their visibility to an external public was limited – but they provided inspiration to women *within* the sport and were achieving something that had long been doubted: viable female competition against the best male athletes. In 1992, both would secure victories against men in competitive off-road ultra-distance races, Trason at the Quicksilver 50 mile in California, and Diamantides at the Dragon's Back. And then, in 1994 and 1995, Trason achieved something remarkable at Western States.

Western States remained the most competitive ultra-distance event in the world and was therefore the perfect barometer of endurance talent. In 1994, to widespread astonishment, Trason finished second overall, less than an hour back from Tim Twietmeyer. She returned in 1995, sparking with ambition. It would have been a memorable year anyway – 876 inches of snow had fallen over Emigrant Pass during the winter months and a designated team of 'snow patrol' volunteers were recruited to provide aid to injured or struggling runners, including one helicopter rescue from the high country. Twietmeyer, Trason and several visiting Tarahumara runners battled it out at the front. Descending into the canyons, the snow disappeared, and the heat rose to an oppressive 107 degrees. Twietmeyer sustained his position, as Trason fell behind the leading Tarahumara, Gabriel Bautista, before just managing to catch him at the Rucky Chucky raft crossing (which was swollen with snow melt). Trason continued to push hard for the last 20 miles, inching ahead of Bautista, and closing on Twietmeyer. In a feature-length article the following year, Trason, with a touch of laughter, recounted the memory: 'I'd never beaten him, because he would die before I beat him, but it's like, I caught him, and it scared him, and then he ran as hard as he could. And it was like, this is good, I like this.'[31] Sprinting for the last two miles, Trason had narrowed the gap, but not quite enough. Twietmeyer crossed the line first, with Trason breathing down his neck, only 5 minutes behind. It was the closest that a woman had ever come – or still has – to overall victory at the most competitive ultra-distance trail race in the United States. Norman Klein, the race director, would later that year describe Trason as 'the greatest runner in the world today'.[32] And yet – despite a 1996 *Runner's World* article describing her as the most accomplished female runner in America – she remained largely unknown and unrecognised beyond the small endurance running community, with little more than a modest sponsorship deal from Nike and a recently founded nutrition company, GU, which was working with Trason to pioneer gel-based nutrition (the founder of GU lived down the road from Trason, in Berkeley).

Diamantides and Trason would race against one another twice. Their first duel occurred at the Comrades Marathon, in 1996, where Trason's pure athletic ability propelled her to victory and a course record on this runnable road course. Two years later, Diamantides travelled without fanfare to compete at Western States, but in deliberate search for competition:

> I simply went out to the U.S. as it was an unofficial championship of sorts for ultra mountain runners. It's where the competition would be, and therefore where you went, if you wanted to see how good you were. There were not enough women at that time to race against in Europe really.[33]

There was indeed a small but growing international presence at Western States, but the race remained almost entirely dominated by American athletes. Diamantides herself was an unknown quantity, lacking familiarity with the conditions and course, and largely overlooked by an American athletic community that had little familiarity with British fell running. Trason arrived with an unmatched Western States résumé: ten consecutive wins and a three-time finish on the overall podium. They would have to contend with another dark horse – a young French ski mountaineer and sky runner, 27-year-old Corrine Favre, who would later achieve distinction with victories at the Pikes Peak Marathon and in multiple prestigious French races, including Templiers and Le Grand Raid. It was the greatest concentration of international female trail and ultra talent that had yet been witnessed on the same competitive stage.

Favre burnt ahead from the start. To widespread astonishment, she was running the steep climb up the Escarpment. Cresting out, she was in fifth place overall, and a minute ahead of Trason. Diamantides was close behind, in third place, but very gradually dropping back. Favre's lead continued to grow as she pushed harder and harder, chased by a confident and controlled Trason. At Michigan Bluff, Favre was now fourth overall, with a 4-minute lead over Trason, and Diamantides around 50 minutes further back. Favre exploded past a startled Twietmeyer on the climb out of Volcano Canyon. As she arrived at Foresthill – 62 miles into the race – she had inched into second overall place, only 6 minutes behind race leader Dave Scott. Pounding down the long descent to the river crossing, Favre's aggressive pace would begin to falter. Holding true to Western States folklore – 'the race begins at Foresthill' – Trason passed Favre on the 16 mile Cal Street descent. Tired and with fading spirits, a disastrous wrong turn saw Favre drop into eighth position, followed by a decision to withdraw from the race, only six miles from the finish. Diamantides was an hour behind at Foresthill, unable to match the leg speed and experience of Trason, but continued with typical resilience to finish in 14th overall place, a little over two hours behind Trason (who finished fourth, with Twietmeyer clinching his fifth WSER victory). Despite missing the drama at the front of the race, Diamantides had secured the fastest time for a non-Californian woman at Western States.

It was the forerunner for something that was only just emerging and that would take at least another decade to come to fruition: a growing field of international female competition.

The 1990s had brought about a widespread interest in extreme and lifestyle sports. These changes were complex and were often linked to a new cultural politics that emphasised individual distinction and self-fulfilment. As it transitioned from *marathon culture* to *mountain culture*, MUT running was bound up with this complexity. It remained an alternative subculture – preserving values of independence and grassroots camaraderie – but it was also becoming aligned with an increasingly commercialised and privileged outdoor industry. The very structures of late-modern consumer capitalism prioritise individual consumption and experience, rather than collective activity or group agency – and yet MUT running would continue to hold this seeming paradox together. The decade was full of incredible examples of personal success that pushed the limits of human achievement in the mountains and on the trails – from Helene Diamantides and Martin Stone, to Ann Trason and David Horton – but these individual achievements were made possible by underpinning community support and teams of volunteers. Barkley, Western States, Hardrock, Dragon's Back – each of these were independent, non-commercial and volunteer-led races. And yet MUT running was on the cusp of a new period of growth that would bring with it something that had long been resisted – professionalisation and commercialisation.

Chapter 10

Marble in a groove

The footage is grainy, the handheld camera a little unsteady, but the Apollonian cheekbones, olive skin and tousled black curls are unmistakeable. Scott Jurek flashes a tired but compelling smile at the camera, sitting back in his camping chair, before a logo-studded backdrop for the post-race interview. Jurek has just taken his second win at the Badwater Ultramarathon, in July 2006, on a 135 mile route from Death Valley through to Mount Whitney. Tarmac-melting temperatures had risen on course to more than 125 degrees. Unbeknownst to him, only an eight-hour drive away, in San Francisco, something similarly intense is taking place.

Google executives are busy negotiating the acquisition of a new video-sharing start-up, YouTube, which only six months before had been officially launched to the public. Videos are limited to around 30 seconds, but by the time Jurek finds himself slogging through the dusty village of Stovepipe Wells, and up toward the cooler heights of Mount Witney, there are 65,000 uploads each day to this new digital phenomenon. Jurek's triumphant Badwater finish will soon become one of these uploads – and one of the earliest ultrarunning videos to be stored on this content-sharing platform. Over the next couple of years, it will be watched by almost a quarter of a million viewers, a number that dwarfs the core ultrarunning community. In the summer of 2006, digital self-publishing and social media are only just beginning to take off. Another brash start-up, Twitter, will be launched only four days after Jurek's Badwater finish. Two months later, in September, a hitherto closed networking website for college students, Facebook, opens to the general public. A new digital world is unveiling itself. No activity or aspect of human life – including the sport of mountain, ultra and trail running – will remain untouched by this technological and social revolution.

While correlation does not always imply causation, there is a remarkable parallel if one places a graph of social media use alongside the growth of ultra-distance running. Globally, between 2006 and 2016, the number of active runners, with an ultra-distance finish that year, rises exponentially: from 70,000 to 321,000. It is the steepest and most sustained rise in the modern sport – and it was occurring during a unique moment of digitally driven, civilisational change.

Digital technologies brought with them widespread social and cultural upheaval that remains yet to be fully unpacked. Techno evangelists were quick to highlight the immense communicative power of social media platforms and their ability to engender novel forms of creativity, citizenship and connection.[1] More darkly, there would in time be a growing awareness of digital addiction, information silos, misinformation and the profoundly negative impact of social media use on self-esteem.[2] This digital tumult was accompanied by the parallel rise of 'wellbeing culture' – an increasing concern with mental health, sleep, diet, fitness and personal 'me time' – and the 'experience economy' – memorable activities that supposedly promote personal growth (from quirky holidays and interactive performances, to adventure days and spiritual retreats) – along with a partial turn *away* from traditional ideas of material success (such as career advancement or financial gain).[3] As future ultrarunning champion Courtney Dauwalter would remark following her third victory at the 2024 Hardrock – in an attempt to find words that captured the significance of the sport – ultrarunning is essentially a 'tool for making memories'.[4] Dauwalter was reflecting on the embodied fragments of running moments, but with some irony the disembodied Internet has also become a space for projecting and cultivating memories that would otherwise have remained private. There are two sides to the digital revolution: an aspirational urge to pursue and display lives full of transformational richness – to be *visibly seen* as the lead character in *our own story* – along with the periodic need to somehow disconnect from the froth and chaos of the digital world.

While difficult to definitively prove – after all, correlation does not *always* imply causation – it is hard not to locate a discernible change to lifestyle sport and recreation within this wider cultural shift. In the United States, between 2006 and 2016, the fastest growing physical sport and recreation activities were adventure racing, triathlon, trail running, kayaking and yoga.[5] All contain a complicated mix of aspiration and disconnection. That is, they are each an enriching challenge and experience – photo-friendly and a notch in the ledger of a life well lived – but also a way to quieten the mind and 'reconnect' with oneself or with the natural world. Similarly, recreational running was itself encountering another period of growth, with marathon running almost doubling worldwide between 2006 and 2016, largely due to increasing female involvement (reaching numerical parity with men in 2018), but also following the rise in popularity of online charity fundraising.[6] Overall, we have become more interested in adventurous activities, healthy lifestyles and outdoor recreation – and these wider social changes have undoubtedly created underlying conditions for the growth of MUT running.

However, there were also important changes within MUT running itself. In the late 1990s, the sport entered a virtuous cycle of commercialisation and growth: growing market size would encourage brand interest – subsequently driving commodification and consumer visibility – which would in turn encourage market expansion, and so on. This commercialisation and growth began first in the United States, but it would be globalised and supercharged by the social media revolution and essentially begin to export a version of American trail and ultra running to the rest of the world. It was a synergistic alignment – commercialisation and digital media – at just the right moment. While MUT running would remain largely grassroots and participative, a new era of spectatorship and professionalism was beginning to dawn.

The rain is still pounding down as alarms begin to sound in the pre-dawn darkness. Thankfully, as runners begin to apprehensively drift out from their motel accommodation – or the slightly less glamorous sleeping arrangements of a parked car – the clouds are parting to reveal a blanket of stars and the rolling silhouette of conifer-covered hills. The small town of Cle Elum – a little more than 80 miles from Seattle – is the eastern-most gateway to the Mount Rainier National Park. In September 1997, it is hosting the third edition of a 50 km trail race that runs along a bucolic ridgeline, then down through narrow valleys and dripping forests of Douglas fir and hemlock spruce. These kinds of trail events are two decades old in the United States now, but they remain a niche sport, almost entirely overlooked by an outdoor industry that is interested in glamour and high-octane adventure. This is about to change.

The 112 starters set off at 4 a.m., sloshing through the dirty tracks and splattering one another with mud. Many are slowed down by the rain-soaked terrain, alternately choosing to leap, dodge or simply plough through deep puddles and hillside run-off. The race leader, a young firecracker, burns ahead without a glance backward. Wiser and more experienced heads smile knowingly – as he tires, they will no doubt reel him back in. But he doesn't – and they don't. Scott Jurek, an unknown 23-year-old, currently living in Seattle for a physical therapist internship, crosses the line in 4 hours and 31 minutes. Afterwards, race director Frank Fleetham will muse with a touch of unwitting understatement: 'Scott has a promising ultra career ahead of him.'[7]

Also racing that day is Scott McCoubrey, a talented trail and ultra runner, who himself places ninth. Personal competition aside, McCoubrey is at Cle Elum as a member of the marketing team for a small, Seattle-based hiking boot company, One Sport, which had been founded only a few years before. The founder of the company, Menno van Wyk, is also there to participate in his very first trail event. It is more than just a team building awayday for One Sport management. Not only are they the title sponsor for the event, but there is deep internal discussion about how to promote a new and innovative product that has just been brought to market: a lightweight trail running shoe, the Vitesse (French for 'speed'). The concept of a trail running shoe was not unique – Nike had launched a range of All Conditions Gear (ACG) shoes in the late 1980s and early 1990s – but trail and ultra running lacked a footwear brand dedicated to the sport. Trail runners were an afterthought for corporate giants – and even for the specialist outdoor industry – with the sport somehow slipping into the cracks between a lucrative market for running sneakers and hiking boots. Under McCoubrey's guidance, One Sport – which by 1997 is undergoing a rebrand to become Montrail – was exploring the viability of a distinct trail running market. McCoubrey and Jurek stand chatting together as they watch runners cross the finish line in Cle Elum. These two men have only just met one another, but a friendship and future business relationship is being born. Jurek will soon become one of the first sponsored athletes for the One Sport/Montrail team.

Sponsorship already existed in the elite sphere of MUT running, but it remained undeveloped and low key. An elite athlete might accept sponsorship from leading apparel and shoe manufacturers such as Nike or Adidas, or small companies in adjacent parts of the sport market like PowerBar or GU – or even regional/local running stores, such as Sacramento-based Fleet Feet – but sponsorship invariably involved little more than free gear and an opportunity for brand logos to be on display during race day. It was the lowest possible tier of sponsorship and commercial support. The most popular shoe for American trail runners in the 1980s, the Nike Lava Dome, was marketed as a lightweight hiking and approach shoe, fronted by famed mountaineer Rick Ridgeway. A decade later, Nike and Adidas would launch competing trail shoes – the Air Humara and Response Trail – but their marketing would fetishise the technology and aesthetics of the shoe. There would be no attempt to tell a story about – or connect with – the personal narrative of the athletes themselves.

It was within this commercial landscape that McCoubrey was hired by One Sport in 1995. Their new trail running shoe was unlikely to fare well in a traditional marketing battle against major footwear brands. McCoubrey instead decided to grow the brand from within the trail and ultra running community. This involved first persuading the Seattle-based outdoor store REI (Recreational Equipment Inc.), to begin stocking the Vitesse – an opening which would generate a small One Sport sales profile in the Pacific Northwest – followed by expansion to other key trail running territories. McCoubrey literally began to drive from region to region – from race to race – competing against and then recruiting a collection of the very best American ultra-distance athletes. His opening line to prospective talent was, 'If you can beat me, I'll hire you.' Scott Jurek and Kirk Apt in the Northwest – and Tim Twietmeyer and Luanne Park in northern California – would all soon become 'ambassadors' to help promote the Vitesse.

Along with free shoes and apparel, McCoubrey would use a small marketing budget to support athletes with travel and accommodation expenses. He also persuaded race directors to give free entry to One Sport/Montrail runners. Recounting this frenetic tour across the country, McCoubrey suggested that the regional nature of the sport was discouraging serious attention from the large shoe and apparel brands, and that this provided an opportunity for Montrail:

> I was the only one out there promoting to the ultrarunning community. There was nobody else showing up at those races. Everything was so regional at the time. Everybody was just racing in their own little areas. Meeting people, visiting key territories, talking with race directors, you could tell this sport could become much more of a national scene.[8]

It was a profoundly grassroots approach – cheaper, yet also more personal and authentic than glossy magazine and storefront marketing. Flying to the Vermont 100, in July 1998, he spotted another young athlete, Ian Torrence, sleeping in his car. Knocking on the window, McCoubrey introduced himself, arranged a hotel for Torrence and provided a pair of complimentary shoes. Torrence finished second the following day and immediately joined the Montrail team. Four months later, McCoubrey accompanied Torrence, Jurek and Apt down to Virginia, having persuaded race director David Horton to provide a complimentary place for each of them in the 50 mile Mountain Masochist. The race was packed full of future athletic stars. For McCoubrey, it was an opportunity to introduce Montrail to the American Southeast:

> I call David Horton, and I'm like, hey, I'm working for this brand called Montrail. I'd like to come out to your race and promote the brand, give away some free shoes ... We got to know David Horton and I met Courtney Campbell in Clifton. I then basically signed those guys on and introduced them to my rep and they would introduce them to some of the stores in the territory.[9]

Race by race, territory by territory, shoe by shoe: McCoubrey was placing Montrail at the heart of the sport. In magazines and at finish lines, emblazoned across leading athletes, the Montrail logo would rapidly become a familiar sight in every corner of the American ultrarunning scene.

As it transitioned from One Sport to Montrail, it was a Californian athlete, Ben Hian, who would become the first national face of this upstart brand. In the mid-1990s, ultrarunning was still perceived to be – in the words of *Outside Magazine* – 'middle-aged' and 'folksy'. The sport had a cultural image that was perhaps unfairly associated with the cliché of sun visors, belt bags and cargo shorts. Despite being an 'extreme' adventure activity, from a pure marketing perspective it lacked the zest and youthful cachet of climbing or snowboarding. The promotion of Hian was an attempt to change this image and to connect with a younger cohort of runners.

With a mane of blond surfer-boy hair, skull tattoos snaking down his lower body, piercings and a wildly infectious grin, he was every inch the MTV generation. His personal backstory made him doubly intriguing. A former addict – 'marijuana, LSD, speed ... lots of speed' – he spent almost two months in a rehab unit, at the age of sixteen, before turning to triathlon and then ultrarunning.[10] His brash confidence and aggressive racing style made him a fan favourite in the southern California racing scene, where he began to amass a string of repeated victories at the Angeles Crest 100 and a startlingly fast finish, in 1997, at the Rocky Racoon 100 (13:42:57). Hian was quickly thrust forward by One Sport/Montrail to become the focus of their marketing drive – with the very first direct (if modest) cash payment to an elite ultrarunner in the modern era. It was worth it. As McCoubrey would say about Hian: 'He had this visible aura.'[11] Adverts began to appear in running media with a photograph of Hian – dashing and rugged – situated above a gleaming pair of the Vitesse, with a description of his 'mohawk hair, flaming skull tattoos' and the strapline 'Run Wild'. Media appearances and a carefree braggadocio added to this mythology, including a public dismissal by Hian of the reverence for Western States ('For some runners, it's their only race of the year. I race every few weeks – and I still win') and the Leadville 100 ('If I do a 100-miler, I don't want to walk it').[12] A brief spat with Ann Trason – 'Ben who?' she was to cuttingly remark in reference to his lack of a Western States win – would add to the frisson of a semi-serious rivalry between runners in southern and northern California.

As the commercial profile of trail and ultra running gradually expanded in the late 1990s – with growing attention in the early part of the next decade from Patagonia, North Face, Brooks, New Balance and La Sportiva – brands would gravitate towards elite athletes with a narrative that combined backstory, personal character and racing style. Winning was not enough: successful sponsorship would require the projection of both image and aspiration.

New athletes would begin to rise to the forefront of the sport, each with their own distinctive story: Scott Jurek the 'zen-warrior', Karl Meltzer the outspoken 'Speedgoat', Anton Krupicka the minimalist 'hunky Jesus'. The cultural axis of the sport was pivoting away from 'middle-aged' and 'folksy' – it was instead becoming an 'edge sport', with complex personalities that combined darkness and light, obsession and pain, spiritual clarity and dreamy romanticism. As the sport further penetrated the public consciousness, the sportswriter Steve Friedman would ask: 'But what calculus of the spirit can take into account years of training, hours alone, broken bones …? Has an equation yet been written so elegant that it can encompass impossible dreams?'[13] The sport was becoming hitched to the engine of commercialism, but it was also developing a cultural image that would appeal to a new wave of athletes looking for adventure and perhaps some form of deeper meaning in their lives.

Pam Reed pauses for a moment to consider the suggestion that women might be naturally better ultra-distance athletes than their male counterparts: 'You know, I'm not so sure about that, but maybe because we have more fat on us. Or maybe because we're able to have children and mentally we can go through a lot of pain. There's definitely pain involved.' David Letterman leans back with a raised finger, dry smile, and then quips to widespread laughter: 'But you did not give birth *during* the race?' In 2003, *The Late Show* was providing an audience of millions with a rare glimpse into the hidden world of ultrarunning. A prolific ultra-distance racer – with a string of victories and podium finishes – Reed had just placed first overall in the Badwater Ultramarathon, for the second time, following a similar result in 2002. For those involved in ultrarunning there were more competitive events, but ever since Max Telford (see Chapter 7) – and further record-breaking runs by Al Arnold (1977) and Jay Birmingham (1981) – the American public remained entranced with lurid tales from Death Valley ('the hottest place on earth'). The idea that a woman could win something so extreme only added to the media scrummage. Reed had passed second-place finisher Dean Karnazes at 111 miles, and finished 30 minutes ahead, in a time of 28hrs and 26min.

Reed and Karnazes were both becoming figureheads – and gendered archetypes – at a time when public and commercial attention to the sport was continuing to build: Reed thrust forward as the 'suburban supermom', Karnazes happily cultivating his image as 'American hero'. It was a disjuncture that would lead to an ongoing rivalry – both real and confected – in the media and on the scorching roads of Badwater (Karnazes would return to beat Reed in 2004). Their narratives slotted neatly into changing cultural and social conceptions of American masculinity/fatherhood and femininity/motherhood. The fame of Karnazes hinged on his compelling origin story: a midlife crisis, juggling the demands of provider and protector, with a yearning for something *more*. With a pinch of artistic licence, in his 2005 memoir Karnazes outlined this moment of realisation:

> Something snapped on the morning of my thirtieth birthday … At that moment I realised that my life was being wasted. Disillusioned with the trappings of the corporate scene, the things that really mattered – friendship and exploration, personal expansion and a sense of meaning – had all gotten twisted around making a lot of money and buying stuff. I hungered for a place where I could explore nature and my capabilities, away from a corporate office in a corporate building in a big city with crowded supermalls and people judging me by the car I drove (which, of course, was a new Lexus).[14]

Returning home from downtown drinks that evening, he supposedly laced up a pair of old sneakers, gazed lovingly at his sleeping wife and children, and then began to run through the night. It was a powerful, if clichéd, transformation away from the stifling conformity of midlife careerism and towards self-fulfilment.

Reed would detail a different but parallel story of 'escape' from within the confines of modern American suburbia – a moving tale of anorexia, anxiety and the complexity of motherhood:

> Instead of talking about being a 'good' parent, it might be better to talk about being 'good enough.' I think a lot of people are good enough, even if they're not really good. You don't have to win. You just have to qualify. You don't have to be the best. Just don't be the worst. That seems attainable.[15]

The stories of Reed and Karnazes struck a cultural nerve. The sentiment is an old one – from the Romantics and Transcendentalists to the German philosophers Nietzche and Heidegger, through to American writers as diverse as Henry Miller and Edward Abbey – that 'modern life' somehow engenders dehumanisation and spiritual decay. Writing in 1934, the abrasive and iconoclastic Miller would famously direct his fury at the cold march of 'progress':

> The same story everywhere. If you want bread you've got to get in harness, get in lock step. Over all the earth a gray desert, a carpet of steel and cement. Production! More nuts and bolts, more barbed wire, more dog biscuits, more lawn mowers, more ball bearings, more high explosives, more tanks, more poison gas, more soap, more toothpaste, more newspapers, more education, more churches, more libraries, more museums. *Forward!*[16]

Or as Abbey reflects in his evocative call to the stark beauty of the American desert: 'We have yielded too much too easily ... the freedom of the wilderness may well be the central purpose of our national adventure.'[17] In the 2000s, this latent yearning for something else – for something *more* – was often attached to what is described as the 'politics of anti-consumerism': that is, a turn against the deadening trappings, ethical absence and environmental corrosion of mass-market consumerism, and a movement towards more authentic, life-affirming experience.[18]

Reed and Karnazes channelled this discontent. And yet, with some irony, both were also counterparts in their search for commercial sponsorship that was (and is by necessity) built upon consumption. It was a paradoxical tension that has always existed in ultra-distance running: an 'escape' from civilisation that is nonetheless perched upon the pyramidal structures of civilisational wealth and privilege.

Outside Magazine somewhat wryly derided the rivalry between Reed and Karnazes as 'Desperate Housewife Stalks Male Supermodel in Sports Death March'. Karnazes had recently appeared on the front cover of *Runner's World* – complete with red surf shorts and a rippling torso – riding high on a professional sponsorship deal with North Face and his forthcoming memoir. Meanwhile, Reed was scraping by with minimal sponsorship as a 'friend' of Red Bull – unlimited caffeinated hydration and a few travel expenses – but otherwise supporting her running career with personal financing (in 2005 she spent $25,000 on racing). As she said:

> When I won Badwater, I didn't think that much of it. But what bothers me is he gets a cover of *Runner's World*. They only did a little blurb on me. It's not him, it's our society. Dean is a really nice guy. I'm not jealous of him, but women need to get some recognition at some point. Running has politicized me.[19]

By 'recognition' what she really meant was 'sponsorship' – which meant money – of which there was an increasing amount in the sport ... just not yet, as it would transpire, for female athletes.

Themes of 'escape' and 'over-civilisation' have continued to resonate throughout the sport on both sides of the Atlantic. Richard Askwith, in 2004, published his classic travelogue account of the

British fell running scene, *Feet in the Clouds*, which quickly became a touchstone for the transformative lure of endurance mountain running. On a personal quest to find reprieve from the bustle of London, professional life, and the melancholy of middle-aged decline, Askwith recounts his fell running story. It is a journey through fell running history, culture and his personal multi-year struggle to complete the Bob Graham Round. Reflecting on the sport towards the end of this account, Askwith seeks to capture the values and sentiments of the fell running community:

> fell-runners are people who are ambitious neither for prestige nor for profit. Instead, they are motivated by a thirst for joy: the joy of being totally absorbed, as our ancestors were, in wild environments; the joy of throwing off the straightjackets of caution and civilization; the joy of finding and pushing back limits; and, occasionally, the joy of doing things that one had thought impossible.[20]

Similar ideas would be explored by the American journalist Christopher McDougall, in his 2009 book, *Born to Run*. It too would touch upon the history and culture of running – in this case American trail and ultra running – and it would also explore the scientific and spiritual benefits of barefoot running, placed in stark contrast to the 'over-designed' and 'over-marketed' shoes of the commercial running industry. The journalistic narrative follows Scott Jurek down to Mexico, in 2006, for his infamous competition against the sandal-clad Tarahumara. McDougall provided a typically romanticised description of the Tarahumara – yet one that would be strikingly influential:

> In Tarahumara Land, there was no crime, war, or theft. There was no corruption, obesity, drug addiction, greed, wife-beating, child abuse, heart disease, high blood pressure, or carbon emissions. They didn't get diabetes, or depressed, or even old: fifty-year-olds could outrun teenagers, and eighty-year-old great-grandads could hike marathon distances up mountainsides. Their cancer rates were barely detectable ... Was it a coincidence that that world's most enlightened people were also the world's most amazing runners?[21]

These books would all have an electrifying and sustained impact on the growth of MUT running. They would each help to draw new aspirants to the sport, but also provide conceptual themes that would continue to be a reference point within the origin story of so many recreational athletes, along the lines of: 'I read *Born to Run*, and then ...'. The lure of escape, minimalism and the (sometimes *ersatz*) shedding of modern life would remain animating principles within the sport and the wider outdoor movement – and yet, paradoxically, these impulses would also remain rooted in the growing commercial profile and expansion of outdoor consumerism.

'It's good we get attention for the sport [but] sometimes I wonder what kind of attention is good for the sport', Jurek was to remark on *Endurance Planet*, in 2007, one of the first podcasts to focus on endurance sport:

> At times I think that some of the Dean attention can hurt athletes like myself and other individuals ... From the standpoint of elite athletes, working their butts off, training and racing, not making any money ... it's getting a little old and it's time the media focused on the true champions of the sport.'[22]

The rise of Karnazes was dividing the American ultrarunning community: there was recognition that his media profile was inspiring new recreational athletes – with WSER race director Greg Soderlund predicting that Dean's best-selling memoir would bring new runners to the sport – but there were those who made disparaging attacks on Karnazes as 'Dean, Dean, the media machine'.[23] Jurek was quick to recognise that he was himself in a privileged position – by now he had a professional sponsorship contract – but he expressed dismay that Karnazes was dominating mainstream media coverage at the expense of race winners like Nikki Kimball and Karl Meltzer. Jurek and Kimball would both be named Ultrarunner of the Year (UROY), in 2007, by the grassroots-focused *UltraRunning Magazine* – following Meltzer and Anne Lundblad as UROY winners in 2006 – while Karnazes himself was gracing the cover of the more mainstream *Outside Magazine* and described as 'America's Greatest Runner'. It was a disjuncture that would cause understandable friction, especially given that Jurek and Kimball had both easily beaten Karnazes in every single instance of head-to-head competition. Despite these rumblings, there was increasingly more money in the sport for everyone.

Jurek's early sponsorship with Montrail had involved little more than free gear and anywhere between $6,000 and $8,000 in annual travel expenses. It was clearly not enough to support a professional athletic career. Racking up credit card debt – and often sleeping in a tent, van or sleeping bag by the finish line, with homemade race nutrition from Whole Foods – and a self-coached training plan, Jurek had emerged as the true trail running dirtbag. His lifestyle was built up around minimal living expenses and obsessive dedication to the sport. First winning Western States in 1999, where he defeated Tim Twietmeyer by only six minutes, Jurek continued to make WSER his annual focus – with an eventual series of seven consecutive wins (1999–2005) – a winning streak that was only surpassed by Ann Trason. The year of that final victory, in 2005, the post-race awards ceremony moved outside from the school cafeteria for the first time, due to an overly large crowd of spectators, runners and volunteers. Andy Jones-Wilkins – who finished in second place that year, only 13 minutes behind Jurek – pinpoints this as the moment when he realised just 'how quickly the sport was growing, even before the boom of 2010'.[24] Commercial growth within the sport would start to provide a modest living for Jurek, following a professional contract from Brooks, in 2004, that involved collaboration in both designing and then marketing the new Cascadia trail shoe. Jurek would leave his career as a physical therapist to become the sport's first full-time professional athlete – not just as a competitive runner, but also as a design collaborator and one-man marketing roadshow.

Following Montrail, other companies were beginning to express an interest in the viability of the trail and ultra running market. It was less of a commercial rush and more an experimental dip into the trail running market. Buzz Burrell – who managed the La Sportiva mountain running team following the launch of their lightweight trail running shoe, the Slingshot, in 2005 – remarked that there was a deeply conservative streak within much of the business world: 'They're there to make money … the salespeople only want what happened last year. That is all they are interested in. That guy made

6% commission selling that colorway? Then I want that.'[25] As a fusion of athletics, hiking and mountaineering, trail running lacked clear market definition, even at the most basic level of where trail shoes might be stocked and displayed: do they go in the hiking section or the running section? Nonetheless, there was a slow but steady transformation of the trail running commercial market. Writing in 2014, the author and journalist Doug Mayer would reflect on the remarkable shift that by then had taken place over the course of a decade:

> The development of more and better gear for trail runners ultimately helped feed the development of the sport ... Outdoors enthusiasts who might never have given mountain running a second thought now routinely meet the possibility whenever they walk through the doors of an Eastern Mountain Sports or thumb through the pages of a Patagonia catalog.[26]

Montrail continued to provide a model for this commercial growth. Following successful promotion of the Vitesse, Scott McCoubrey established his own running store, the Seattle Running Company (SRC), in 1999. Some of the most competitive athletes in the United States – Scott Jurek, Krissy Moehl, Brandon Sybrowsky, Hal Koerner, William Emerson – were all sponsored by Montrail and worked in the store (and at times living in the basement). The store became a hub for the local trail running community – with group runs, social events and seminars – where ordinary recreational runners were able to hang out and rub shoulders with elite athletes. Executives from Montrail and Brooks (both based in Seattle) were able to drop by and visibly witness this cultural and sporting cauldron. SRC provided a physical space where athletes, brands and a wider sporting community were brought together. It would also provide an inspiration for running stores elsewhere – from San Francisco to Salt Lake City and Colorado Springs – but most especially for Rouge Valley Runners (RVR), founded in Ashland, Oregon, by Hal Koerner, one of McCoubrey's SRC and Montrail protégés. Koerner had been victorious twice at Western States – in 2007 and 2009 – and his distinctive bronze cougar trophies would sit on display in his new running store.

Supporting his athletes with a limited Montrail marketing budget – kit, travel and occasional accommodation expenses – McCoubrey soon made another breakthrough:

> Ultimate Direction was just coming into the market too because Dana Miller, who is the marketing person for Ultimate Direction, he was the consummate winner at Wasatch at the time. They came out with the first running vest. Both of us being in the industry, we got to talking at the Outdoor Sports show. All of a sudden, I had Ultimate Direction stuff to help support the athletes for Montrail. And then to take that a step further, Jeannie Wall saw what we were doing, who was in charge of the endurance clothing line for Patagonia. And she's like, we're introducing this new clothing line and I'd like to be a part of what you're doing. And all of a sudden I had the power of Patagonia and the power of Ultimate Direction and Montrail. That tripled my offering to athletes.[27]

Critically, each of these three brands was appealing to the same commercial market, but they were not direct competitors: Montrail (shoes), Patagonia (clothing), Ultimate Direction (packs). The idea of a sponsorship portfolio would become an important dimension of professional trail and ultra running. This would begin to include nutrition, technology, accessories and (occasionally) non-endemic sponsors. From the mid-2000s, elite athletes would also begin to realise that they could capitalise on their success by offering professional coaching services to a growing market of recreational runners. This combined model of coaching and sponsorship – along with event management – would become the monetising foundation of professional trail and ultra running. It was a trifecta that would slowly become a mainstay for competitive athletes looking to make a living within the sport.

Karl Meltzer would be early and adept at putting together a working portfolio of sponsorship. With a childhood spent in the outdoors, in New Hampshire, right alongside the Appalachian Trail, Meltzer moved to Utah, in 1989, to become a 'ski bum' – tending bar and escaping to the slopes at every available opportunity – during which time he also began to run in the snowless summer months. Soon realising that he possessed a talent for endurance over rough mountain terrain, he began to save money over the winter for running adventures and racing during the quiet off-season: 'That money would last me the better part of the summer', he recounted, 'I can live pretty cheap.'[28] Meltzer would begin to notch up a series of impressive victories and podium spots, beginning with a first-place finish, in 1998, at the Wasatch Front 100. Known as the 'Speedgoat' (a trail name he acquired following competition at the 1993 Pikes Peak), Meltzer's public image – beer in hand, direct and outspoken, with a penchant for golfing and the Grateful Dead – was matched by his seemingly unstoppable and unflappable pace over steep and rugged terrain. A course record at Hardrock in 2001, beating the likes of Kirk Apt and Blake Wood, would be the first of five victories at this now-iconic race (a record matched only by Kílian Jornet). His tally of 100 mile victories would continue, year after year, until he was able to claim yet another record: more 100 mile victories than anyone else in the sport.

As Meltzer's competitive profile continued to develop in the early 2000s, he was recruited to the Montrail-Patagonia team – which was by now getting rather large – and Meltzer began putting together a sponsorship portfolio that would support frequent racing. By 2006 – a year during which he completed eight 100 mile races (including six victories) – he was competing in a vest adorned with sponsors, including Red Bull, Montrail, Nathan, PowerBar and Petzl. As an early adopter of the athlete/coach combination, in 2007 Meltzer was just about making a livelihood within the sport – although, as he would explain, 'we're not going to get rich doing what we're doing'. As with Jurek, and many others who would soon follow, sponsorship was about finding the freedom to pursue personal passion in the mountains. Reflecting on this minimalist lifestyle – in a 2016 film, *Made to be Broken*, which documented his record-breaking run that year on the Appalachian Trail – Meltzer would remark: 'You could be a big businessman who wants to make billions of dollars. To me, I'm richer than all those guys because I get out. They can watch their bank account rollover, I don't care'.[29]

'Who the hell is the naked guy?', Karl Meltzer remarked as he descended from Hope Pass at the Leadville 100, 'He looks like he's going to totally blow up.'[30] In 2006, Leadville continued to be one of the most important and competitive 100 mile events in the United States. Founded in the former silver mining town of Leadville, in 1983, by Jim Butera (a Western States finisher), and two local residents, Merilee Maupin and Ken Chlouber, the race had become an important feature in the American ultrarunning calendar. This success was in part due to the charisma of Chlouber – a former miner, bull rider, mountaineer: every inch a grizzled, denim-wearing, red-blooded cowboy – but also due to a striking race route that followed the Colorado Trail, before ascending to the thin-aired heights of Hope Pass (3,850 metres), and then down to the abandoned mining town of Winfield, before doubling back to the finish.

The 'naked guy' – dressed only in shorts and shoes – was an unknown, 23-year-old, recent Colorado College graduate: Anton Krupicka. Arriving in Leadville the day before, Krupicka and his team of pacers – easily mistaken for a long-haired, check-shirted grunge band – had spent the night sleeping in a public bathroom. This was only Krupicka's second ultra-distance race, but he had spent a year training hard in the mountains around Leadville, including 200 mile training weeks, all with the ambition of beating the 15:42:59 course record set the previous year by local legend Matt Carpenter. Krupicka was in the middle of an obsession with mountain minimalism – hence the lack of clothing – which included a modified pair of shoes. Krupicka had removed the insole, and carved the heel from the outsole, making his already lightweight Slingshots even lighter and zero-drop for a more natural running form. Running hard, he established a growing lead early, but began to falter with glycogen depletion on the return, before an astonishing revival for the final fast fifteen miles.[31] It was not a course record – Carpenter's record would remain unbeaten until it was eclipsed by David Roche in 2024 – but in a time of 17:01:56, Krupicka was nearly two hours ahead of second place. From nowhere, Krupicka had blasted himself onto the American ultrarunning stage with both a tremendous result and a distinctively outrageous running style. More than a decade later, he was to reflect on this breakout success:

> I had no preconceived notions to limit myself. I had no indoctrination from the community about acceptable practices. So, I just did my usual thing – go running in the mountains, carry only what you need and nothing more. It turns out this was just a lot less than most people were comfortable with. A pair of shoes, a pair of shorts, a bottle, and a handful of gels were all it really took.[32]

Sponsorship from La Sportiva quickly followed. Krupicka was also entering the sport at a moment of digitally driven growth and expansion. Embracing this new world of self-publishing, Krupicka would become known as the sport's first 'social media star'.[33] This first involved Krupicka's blog – Riding the Wind – which he launched in 2007. The blog was a meticulous record of his training and racing – with detailed race and adventure reports (running, climbing, biking) – but it was also a space where he was able to write at length on everything from running and mountain sport culture, to philosophy, cinema and music. 'Why does one blog?' he asked in his very first post on 8 October:

> There is no reason to post one's life on the internet ... other than to feel as if you have some sort of agency as a human being. That is, that your actions – and posts – are meaningful to someone other than oneself and that they affect other humans in some way: to inflame, inspire, degrade, invoke joy, etc., etc. That is the only – yet incredibly crucial – difference between maintaining a meticulous Word document on one's hard drive and posting to a public blog of one's own creation. The internet allows others to see you – provides an audience – and this helps tremendously to validate one's existence.[34]

Thoughtful and articulate, Krupicka was not just adept at the written and spoken word, he also had visible presence: long-haired, bearded and with large double-stud earrings – hipsterish – he echoed the youthful glamour of Hian from a decade earlier. As Buzz Burrell, Krupicka's sponsorship manager at La Sportiva, would sum up: 'Tony has charisma like you can't believe.'[35] Working with friends at Colorado College, in 2007, Krupicka was filmed for a 36-minute biopic film – *Indulgence: 1000 Miles Under the Colorado* Sky – that detailed training and preparation for the defence of his Leadville title. Beautifully shot, the film depicts a shirtless Krupicka running in the mountains – backed by an indie-acoustic soundtrack – interspaced with interview segments where Krupicka recounts his personal story and life/running philosophy. The film was financially supported by La Sportiva and the Colorado Running Company, and it soon became a breakout Internet success: it was both subtle advertising and cultural content – an innovative advert/biopic film model, made possible by digital platforms, that in time would become de rigueur for athletes and brands within the sport.

As the trend of minimalist running began to explode – ignited in part by the success of *Born to Run* – Krupicka was to be a cultural icon within this new running movement. With New Balance looking to launch a range of minimalist running shoes in 2009 – the MT100 – Krupicka was lured by a small salary to help design and market the shoe. Along with Jurek and Meltzer, he was becoming a professional athlete – barely earning a living, yet drawing just enough to maintain a lifestyle dedicated to the outdoors.

Krupicka was joined on the New Balance team by two friends, the brothers Kyle and Erik Skaggs, who would similarly embody the ethos of stripped-back, minimalist mountain running. Kyle Skaggs had emerged in 2005 – winning almost every race that he entered – but then suddenly withdrew from the sport with overuse injuries after only three years of competition. '[Kyle] Skaggs was a supernova', Andy Jones-Wilkins reflects, 'a once-in-a-generation talent who blasted onto the scene, did extraordinary things, and promptly disappeared.'[36] His penultimate race, at Hardrock in 2008, is often described as one of the greatest ultrarunning performances of all time: it was the first sub-24-hour finish – six hours ahead of second place – with a near-perfect race execution that seemed to redefine possibilities within the sport.[37]

The retirement of Skaggs from the sport with overuse injury was sudden, but in hindsight not entirely surprising. Krupicka and the Skaggs were known for their excessive training – more than 30 hours of running over the course of a week – at a time when the physiological limits of ultrarunning were not well known. They were experimenting and pushing the boundaries. It was a style of running that was complemented by their burning commitment and rootsy connection to the wild. As Krupicka was to remark in 2007:

> A big reason why I run is the ability it allows me to tap into this more primitive, primal mode of existence that it seems like modern man has been divorced from over the last two hundred years. That's something I've found is essential for me to experience on a daily basis. I think people have this perception of me as being anti-technology, but it's really not the case, there are some technologies – the automobile is one of those – that are just wildly inappropriate for what they are used for.[38]

Krupicka's comments were a familiar but paradoxical lament. The notion that over-civilisation has brought with it loss – our connection to the land and to ourselves – but that new technologies and commercial applications are also capable of perhaps renewing those same connections. This ambivalence would extend to his own involvement in the outdoor industry:

> It frustrates me that there is an entire industry making the outdoor, mountain lifestyle this iconic, cool thing to be doing, when really it's all about selling products. I feel that I'm not compromising my values by representing a corporation when I'm racing or whatever, because we need to wear shoes, and I haven't quite figured out how to build my own yet.[39]

Through extensive blogging – and then later social media posting – Krupicka would become the face of ultrarunning at a time when it was becoming more than just a *participative* sport – it was also becoming a *spectator* sport.

The 2010 Western States would have been an historic year anyway. Hal Koerner is back to defend his title – after victory in 2007 and 2009 (the 2008 race was cancelled due to wildfires) – but he is facing a remarkable depth of competition. Anton Krupicka and Geoff Roes are the leading American challengers, joined by Kílian Jornet, a fresh-faced 23-year-old runner from Spain. Krupicka, Roes and Jornet are all racing Western States for the first time. They know that the course and the conditions require immense respect – and yet all are used to repeated victory. The race is guaranteed to be fiercely competitive, but will be elevated to legendary status by something else: scattered across the route are camera crews, working under the direction of a young film director, J. B. Benna. The resulting film – *Unbreakable: The Western States 100* – will explode in popularity and eventually become a cult classic for an emerging generation of runners.

The race begins – as it always does – in the pre-dawn darkness of Olympic Valley. A leading group of eight men reach the top of the escarpment together – black silhouettes framed by the growing haze of morning light – before heading down a rerouted section to avoid the late-season snow on Red Star Ridge. As they loop through Duncan Canyon and around to Robinson Flat, Krupicka, Roes and Jornet are together, stride for stride, with Koerner around 3 minutes back. Koerner is running well but losing time against this new and hungry generation of ultrarunning talent.

The fierce battle between the leading three continues. They hit every single aid station together – none is willing to concede the front position – but as they climb from Deadwood to Devil's Thumb, Roes falters beneath a scorching midday sun: 'I felt pretty bad', he remembered, 'The climb up Devil's Thumb hit me really hard … I was really struggling at that point.'[40] By the time they drop down to Eldorado Creek, Jornet and Krupicka have a 3-minute lead – increasing to 8 minutes by Michigan Bluff (55 miles) – and then 12 minutes by Foresthill (62 miles). Koerner is still racing – not far back in fourth – but this two-time champion is fading and will eventually make the surprising decision to drop at Green Gate.

As they leave Foresthill in the unrelenting afternoon sunshine, down the punishing descent towards the American River, Jornet and Krupicka soar onward like a pair of flaming comets. Both are focused, but intimately aware of one another and their a cappella melody of breath and rhythmic stride. Arriving at the Rucky Chucky crossing together – now more than 11 hours into the race – they run every step up the climb to Green Gate. The race is remarkably close, yet somehow it appears that Jornet has miscalculated the delicate balance of effort versus heat. As Krupicka replenishes his water, he glances over to see Jornet, dizzy and dehydrated, taking a seat in the shade. With only 20 miles to go – and comfortably under course record pace – Krupicka is seemingly destined for an historic victory. Of course, the race is not yet over.

Back at the river crossing, seemingly forgotten, Roes is finding a second wind: 'probably at that point, I was more predator hungry than I'd ever felt before in a race. I really got the competitive juices going. It was fun. It was exciting.' Moving quickly into second place – like an eager bloodhound detecting fresh scent – Roes begins to track down Krupicka. The gap narrows rapidly. Turning a corner, Roes can see Krupicka and his pacer, Jen Shelton, up ahead. Roes considers this moment of strategy: he needs to make a strong and decisive pass. Silently approaching, he then suddenly explodes past: 'I felt kind of bad about that, because Tony's a really great person and I like him, but it's a race and it's what you need to do to win.'[41] Momentarily dispirited, Krupicka tries to hold on, but Roes is determined to leverage this ever-so-slight advantage. He hammers it on the stretch between Highway 49 and No Hands Bridge – turning a 1-minute lead into a full 6 minutes – and then sustains this pace down from Robie Point to the finish. Roes crosses the line at Placer High School in a new course record of 15:07:04. He is followed by Krupicka – also under course record pace – in 15:13:53. Jornet finishes third in 16:04:49 – a time that in almost any other year would have been enough for victory. It was an incredible race – and J. B. Benna was there to capture it all on film.

Western States had been filmed several times before: in 1982 and 1983, with *Desperate Dreams I* and *II*; in 1985, with a segment on ABC's *Wide World of Sports*; and then in 2001, with a full-length PBS documentary, *Race for the Soul*. However, you either managed to catch these programmes on live television, or you tracked down a rare VHS recording – or you missed them entirely. Benna's film might have remained similarly obscure, but new digital distribution methods – pay-per-view online release and then eventually YouTube – ensured a larger and continually fresh audience.

The film itself is remarkable. Benna's intimate, roving camerawork tracks alongside the front-runners, over the snowy escarpment, into the shaded maze of canyons, through Foresthill, and then all the way down to the crowded finish line. It was unparalleled. For an audience that would eventually number in the millions, the film provided a glimpse into not just the character and landscape of Western States, but also the dynamics of a stunningly competitive race.

Remarkably, Benna's camerawork was not the only important media occurrence at the 2010 Western States; also on course that year were Bryon Powell and Meghan Hicks from iRunFar.

In 2005, Powell – at the time a recreational runner and young lawyer revising for the bar – had registered the domain name 'iRunFar.com' and started an enthusiastic blog about the sport:

> This was a thing back in the mid to late noughts, there were tens of thousands of them, it wasn't just Anton … but like me, the Joe-Schmoe runner would just get on Blogspot and post about my training, or a question I had about shoes, or whatever.[42]

The blog – which by 2007 was evolving into a more professional website – was slowly becoming an online hub for trail and ultra running content. It included race reports, shoe reviews and training advice. Gradually, Powell – first alone, and then through collaboration with his partner, Hicks – would transition iRunFar into a commercial media venture. The financial model would prove to be significant: advertising, gear reviews with commissioned click-through links, and a small coaching service. But as passionate advocates for the sport, Powell and Hicks were determined to use their growing platform to create content that would be of benefit for the wider community. This included long-form articles and training advice for prospective ultrarunners, along with a desire to somehow cover the sport more rapidly and with a greater range of content. Monthly magazines made for great reading – but races were usually done and mostly forgotten by the time the relevant issue landed on the doormat.

So it was, in December 2009, that Powell and Hicks hosted their first Twitter livecast, at a highly competitive race in San Francisco, the North Face 50 (TNF). While Powell had earlier that year trialled live coverage direct on their website, at the Massanutten 100 Mile, this would be the first time that a race would be covered on Twitter for an international audience. Powell and Hicks were both out on the course, Powell tweeting race updates in real time while Hicks captured photographs for post-race coverage. It was a significant moment. While there had been early attempts to broadcast ultra-distance racing on local radio – the earliest was the Laurel Highlands 70-miler in 1983 – iRunFar at the 2009 TNF was the first substantive and sustained effort to make ultrarunning a live and mediated spectator sport. Six months later, after their success at the 2009 TNF, Powell and Hicks decided to cover their second race: the 2010 Western States. With an evolving media format, they recorded pre-race and post-race YouTube interviews to accompany the Twitter livecast. This too was an evolution – it provided hype and punditry that would help to structure the race narrative.

Andy Jones-Wilkins – who would become a contributor to iRunFar with his regular AJW's Taproom column – recounted the sudden surge of interest for this type of digital spectating:

> [At first] it was a cell phone and very rudimentary coverage, just a couple of spots along the course. And then they realized, people are really into this ... They started doing it for Western States, they started doing it for Hardrock, they went out to UTMB and then did it for Transvulcania. So really in those first few years, race coverage was those five races. And then races started coming to them saying, 'Hey, we want you to cover our race', because they were realizing you get a ton of exposure from iRunFar tweets.[43]

Accompanied by photographs, videos and race commentary – all live and on course – iRunFar was suddenly enabling fans of the sport to follow iconic races from anywhere in the world. In a circular motion, this media coverage further cemented the status of these races, ensuring that they were viewed as being worthy of such attention.

The turning of this new decade was proving to be a critical juncture and a momentous convergence of digital media, sporting celebrities, commercial activity and raw numerical growth. A growing wave of future stars in the sport – many just beginning to cut their teeth – were at that very moment being carried forward and encultured by this incredible bust of energy: Dylan Bowman, Rob Krar, Timothy Olson, Kaci Lickteig, Jared Hazen, Dakota Jones, Clare Gallagher, Sage Canaday, David Laney, Magda Boulet and Rory Bosio (to name just a few). MUT running was rapidly becoming a true sport – mediated, spectated, competitive and semi-professional. The impact of this sporting phenomenon would soon ripple out across the Atlantic – American-style ultrarunning was about to go global.

James Elson, the founder of Centurion Running, speaks for an entire generation when reflecting on the electrifying impact of American ultrarunning on an otherwise quiescent British scene: 'In 2004, there was next to nothing going on in the UK, one or two events a month maximum. And so, as a tiny scene, there wasn't too much to get stuck into on home soil … just car boot stuff really.'[44] This was perhaps something of an understatement. In 2004, there were fewer than two dozen ultra-distance races in the UK. It was an eclectic mix of track, road and trail. Only two races covered the 100 mile distance – the West Highland Way (1985), through winding Scottish valleys, and the Grand Union Canal (1993), along a flat towpath from Birmingham to London. The Fellsman (1962), Old County Tops (1988) and the Howarth Hobble (2003) – all of which were part of the fell running scene – were the only ultra-distance races that traversed rougher mountain terrain. Entrants to these races rarely reached anything even approaching triple figures.

Elson entered this space in the early 2000s, fresh from university and reflecting on what the future might hold. Looking for post-college adventure, a television documentary inspired Elson to enter to the 2006 Marathon des Sables. He followed this with successful competition in three other events (in China, Argentina and Egypt), which, along with MDS, comprised a newly launched desert racing series: Racing the Planet. Elson was entranced with this new sport, but he found the racing scene in Britain lacklustre and looked across the Atlantic for inspiration:

> It was the rapid expansion of the U.S. scene that got me interested, more so than the European mountain scene ... mainly the likes of Kyle Skaggs, Anton Krupicka, and their generation, Hal Koerner, a little bit, Jen Shelton, who were out there doing long, self-supported runs in the mountains with huge amounts of training. It was captivating, especially Anton's blog.[45]

Elson began an annual pilgrimage to the United States, where he would successfully compete in classic American races, including Rocky Racoon, Old Dominion, Badwater, Western States and Leadville. It was satisfying, but expensive – and beyond the reach of most runners in Britain. Elson began to reflect on this gap in the market. 'I need to put something on in the UK', he remembers thinking at the time, 'I'm having to go to the U.S. to do the type of racing that I want to do, point-to-point, 100 mile races, on good trails.' So, in November 2010, he established Centurion Running – named with a reverential nod to the Surrey-based Centurion racewalkers – and, in 2011, the first Centurion event was launched: the North Downs Way.

Starting in the small market town of Farnham, the route followed the North Downs Way – a broken expanse of low-lying chalk hills and stream beds, running parallel and immediately to the south of Greater London – on an eastward trajectory to Knockholt Pound. Those in the 50 mile race finished there on the village green, while the 100 mile runners turned around to retrace their steps. Three runners dominated the 100 mile race from the start: Neil Bryant, Mark Collinson and Robbie Britton.

Bryant led for most of the race, gradually increasing his lead to 30 minutes, with Collinson in second and Britton trailing more than an hour behind. As darkness descended into a muggy summer night – and with 30 miles to go – the runners continued to move alone through the silent English countryside: wooded dells and grassy hills, overlooking neat-looking farmyards and cheerful thatched villages. Finding a late surge of energy, Britton began to push hard through the stillness of the night, catching Collinson soon after the final aid station, and then racing hard for the last few miles, past a startled Bryant, and down into Farnham for a stunning and victorious finish.[46] Britton, Bryant and Collinson were emblematic of a new wave of athlete that was just beginning to embrace ultrarunning in Britain. Each would compete on track, road and trail. Britton would find particular success, both as an athlete – placing third in the IAU World 24-hour championships in 2015, followed by a new British 24-hour record in 2023 – and also as a successful coach, including for elite athletes that would include the likes of Hayden Hawks (USA) and Daniel Jones (New Zealand).

The North Downs Way event had proved itself viable – and Centurion Running began to blossom. More races were added – up to around half a dozen recurring events – including what would become the flagship Centurion race, the South Downs Way 100 (in 2012). Elson established an online running store to provide specialist running gear and teamed up with Ian Sharman to create a coaching business for endurance athletes. Like Elson, Sharman had been dabbling in the small UK scene but found himself drawn to the ultrarunning boom taking place across the United States – and with tremendous success, including repeated victories at Leadville and an impressive nine top ten finishes at the more competitive Western States. The Centurion coaching business would grow quickly, adding Britton to the coaching team, followed by other Centurion alumni, including Bryant, and the competitive triathlete and endurance runner Edwina Sutton.

In 2005, there were eighteen ultra-distance events in the UK and only 1,500 participants (it was a tiny sport); by 2016 there would be as many as 300 different events and 20,000 participants.

Centurion Running would remain dominant in the south-east of England – with a focus on runnable and rolling routes – but other players were beginning to carve out their own regional principalities. The Hardmoors 110, launched in 2008, would traverse the rough coastline of the North York Moors. The Lakeland 50 and 100 – also from 2008 – would bring ultra-distance racing to the Lake District and grow to become Britain's premier mountain ultra (with almost 3,000 competitors across two races). The 268 mile Spine Race – established in 2012 – would carve a fantastical line through the heart of the country. The Dragon's Back Race would be recreated and relaunched – from 2012 – with a similar multi-day journey down the length of Wales. The 100 mile Arc of Attrition – from 2015 – invited runners to contend with the stormy Cornish headlands. The Cape Wrath Ultra – from 2016 – would transport participants to a multi-day attempt around the remote north-westerly coastline of Scotland. The 190 mile Northern Traverse – in 2016 – would trace Alfred Wainwright's coast-to-coast route over the Lake District, Yorkshire Dales and North York Moors.

This new wave of ultrarunning reflected not just the climate and geography of Britain, but also channelled a diverse heritage that combined fell running, challenge hiking and ultrarunning. There would be successful British athletes noted for their raw speed over long distances, such as Ian Sharman, Robbie Britton, Lizzy Hawker, Jez Bragg and Beth Pascall. Other athletes, such as Damian Hall, Jasmin Paris, Nicky Spinks and Sabrina Verjee, would display a particular strength with self-navigation, rugged terrain and poor weather conditions. Of course, most would combine elements of all of this – speed, endurance and mountain craft – continuing in the very best tradition of a sport that remains diverse and difficult to define.

American trail and ultra running was exported to Britain with tremendous success, but this Anglo-American relationship is only part of the story. Since the mid-2000s, global consumer markets and digital media have rapidly brought together a range of diverse running cultures and communities. There has always been an international component to ultra-distance running – even from the earliest days of Victorian pedestrianism – but the last two decades have created a cultural and competitive space that transcends locality and region. For recreational and elite runners, it is increasingly commonplace to line up against competitors from around the world. The best professional athletes – such as Kílian Jornet and Courtney Dauwalter – are regularly splashed across international running media. While the sport remains still mostly local and regional, there is nonetheless a sense in which the borders and boundaries between different off-road and endurance running cultures have become ever more blurred. There is one brand that has dominated this new global running scene: Ultra-Trail du Mont-Blanc.

The opening pages of this book began with an account of historic victories by Courtney Dauwalter and Jim Walmsley at the 2023 UTMB Mont-Blanc. By revisiting Chamonix and UTMB, it is possible now to draw together themes that have been woven throughout this long and eventual history – and, by doing so, to reflect on the evolving future of MUT running.

Epilogue

Closing the loop

In 2003, Europe is undergoing a heatwave and the most dangerous summer on record since the middle of the sixteenth century: crops were being devastated, roads melting, rail lines buckling, and in France alone there would be an estimated 15,000 heat-related deaths. The 700 runners signed up for the first edition of a new and experimental race in the French Alps are facing scorching and potentially hazardous conditions. And then, suddenly, the weather flips: a storm begins to sweep in on 29 August – only a day before the race – with howling wind, torrential rain, flash flooding and snow falling over higher ground. There is widespread uncertainty. Only a handful of people have ever raced around Mont Blanc in one sustained push – and now hundreds of runners are about to make the attempt, in biblical conditions, with participants hastily scrabbling around to buy or borrow cold weather clothing.

While France has a long tradition of ultra-distance running – including Victorian pedestrianism and post-war road ultramarathoning – trail racing was a relatively new concept that had been partially imported from the United States. In 1989, two French journalists, Gilles Bertrand and Odile Baudrier, had travelled to cover Leadville and Western States for *VO2 Magazine*. Inspired by American trail racing, they decided to recreate something similar in France. The result, La Grande Course des Templiers (first held in 1995), saw runners racing for 65 kilometres through the limestone plateaus and gorges of the Central Massif. It attracted 500 runners for the first edition and rapidly ballooned to more than 2,000 entrants by the early 2000s. Shorter distance Alpine mountain running was already well established in France – long adventure-style hiking/running races had become increasingly popular (including the French-origin Marathon des Sables in Morocco and the 'Grand Raid' on the island of Réunion) – and there had even been previous road relay races around Mont Blanc. Given this surge of enthusiasm for off-road endurance in France, the prospect of something longer and more ambitious in the heart of the Alps was perhaps inevitable.

It was within this context that two Chamonix residents, Catherine and Michel Poletti (himself a keen runner) – working with a small group of enthusiastic volunteers – began to make plans for a continuous 150 km race around Europe's highest mountain. A chance encounter with Karla Valladares from North Face provided a sponsoring brand and an important connection to American athletes. The race was given a name – Ultra-Trail International du Tour du Mont-Blanc (the race name would be shortened in future editions, while the race distance would be lengthened) – and the race was opened for entrants in December 2002. Exceeding all expectations, hundreds of applications flooded in from around the world. The immense logistics were rapidly finalised, including a route change due to the weather, and on the morning of 30 August there is only one thing left to do: 700 runners are going to have to run around Mont Blanc – in a storm.[1]

As crowds gather just before 4 a.m. in the dark streets of Chamonix – with rolling rain clouds unable to dampen the excitement and suspense – three young American runners are posing for a picture. Krissy Moehl and Brandon Sybrowsky are both athletes for the Montrail/Patagonia running team – and recently married to one another – and Topher Gaylord is here as a representative for North Face. Gaylord has already raced in Europe, but this will be a new venture for Moehl and Sybrowsky. In the early 2000s, international competition is undeveloped, and it is rare for American ultrarunners to compete abroad. With little fanfare, Catherine Poletti counts down through a microphone, and then everyone is off and away into the pre-dawn gloom.

Perhaps because of infamous endurance spectacles in France – from Les Mans (motorcar racing) to the Tour de France (cycling) – there is a vibrant spectating culture for this kind of event. Even at this first edition, during a storm, bedraggled groups of spectators can be found scattered across the massif, or emerging from chalet doorways to show their support. And yet, rather than a spectating phenomenon, the 2003 race will mostly be one of chaotic madness and shoestring survival. Catherine Poletti huddles alone in the HQ tent – singlehandedly managing volunteers through a shortwave radio and flip phone – while Michel Poletti competes in the race himself and urges embattled runners onward. Unusually, the race has an option in this first edition to withdraw at three different places, allowing runners to claim a shorter distance 'finish'. It is a tempting and deadly lure – especially as waves of rain and sleet begin to lash the mountainside – and only 63 runners will eventually make it to the end in Chamonix.

Running alone at the front is Dawa Sherpa – a Nepalese mountain guide based in Switzerland – who leaps ahead and does not see another runner for the entirety of the race. Running his lonely loop through the mountains, he arrives in Chamonix a little after midnight – having traversed the course in just over 20 hours – to find a small group of spectators crowded beneath umbrellas. A handful of schoolchildren run alongside him for the final stretch. Sherpa becomes the first ever UTMB Mont-Blanc finisher. As with many other first-time participants this year, he will be back for future editions.

With this exciting but rather damp victory over, the crowd disperses, leaving Catherine Poletti alone in the deserted and rain-slicked town centre. A little after 2 a.m., a pair of headlamps appear, bobbing up the street: Topher Gaylord and Brandon Sybrowsky cross the finish line together in joint second place. A smiling Poletti hands them hot tea and wraps them in foil blankets, before receiving a call from a volunteer in Trient: 'There's a girl here who's injured but she wants to keep going. She's the first woman. She's from the U.S. and her name is Krissy Moehl.'[2]

Moehl has been battling through the elements – working with another runner for most of the race – and they arrive together at the aid station in Trient's historic church, which is staffed by volunteers and kept warm by a handful of portable heaters. Wringing out her clothes to dry, Moehl is concerned about muscle inflammation and a strained flexor, which has caused her to repeatedly trip and fall. Her companion decides to wait out the night, but he offers Moehl his long trousers and encourages her to continue. Moving outside, she teams up with someone else for safety and companionship over the final stretch – by chance it happens to be Michel Poletti – who has himself been struggling with vomiting and exhaustion. Limping along, it takes Moehl another six hours – she eventually encourages Poletti to run on ahead without her – but she is determined to finish. 'As I came back into Chamonix, I was pretty much in my own head', she remembers, 'literally, because of the weather, that Houdini shell was cinched around my face. I remember it was pretty quiet.'[3] Crossing the finish line, on a sleepy Sunday morning, it has taken Moehl a little under 30 hours: she is the first woman – and the first American – to claim victory at a race that over the next two decades will become the inspirational (and sometimes controversial) pinnacle of a sport that is undergoing rapid change.

If you want to comprehend the impact of Ultra-Trail du Mont-Blanc, then just reflect on this for a moment: almost every athlete mentioned in the previous chapter – virtually without exception – has competed at UTMB Mont-Blanc. Over the last two decades, MUT running has become increasingly globalised and commercialised – and UTMB has been at the heart of these changes. Catherine and Michel Poletti could not possibly have known at the time, but UTMB Mont-Blanc was established at the very beginning of a transformational boom in ultra-distance running: the number of runners participating globally in ultra-distance events would rise from approximately 55,000 individual runners in 2003 to 388,000 by 2023 – an average year-on-year growth rate of around 10 per cent.[4]

Professional trail and ultra running barely existed in 2003 – it was still a grassroots sport and a relatively small consumer market

– but this exponential growth would continue to generate rising commercial and corporate interest. UTMB did not create this boom in trail and ultra running, but it caught the wave at just the right moment. It also provided something unique that was not easily replicable elsewhere: a location with Alpine terrain and infrastructure suitable for a large-scale mountain running event, along with a tremendous carnivalesque spectacle and festival buzz during race week.

Participant numbers at UTMB Mont-Blanc grew rapidly following that inaugural event. In 2006, an additional 100 km race was added (with over 1,000 entrants) – Courmayeur-Champex-Chamonix (CCC) – while the flagship UTMB Mont-Blanc race sold out within three weeks (prompting an additional 500 places to be made available through a lottery and taking the starting line to the current number of 2,500). Other races would be added: Les Traces du Duc de Savoie (TDS) (105 km) and La Petite Trotte à Léon (PTL) (250 km) in 2009 and OCC (55 km) in 2014. European interest in what was now a week-long trail running event was strong from the outset – athletes from Britain would find early success (including Lizzy Hawker's impressive string of five victories) – but gradually participants from around the world, including the United States, would begin to target these races as a pinnacle international event in the fast-growing sport of MUT running.

UTMB Mont-Blanc has become the crown jewel in a sport that – at an elite level – is now global and interconnected. Every August, Geneva airport finds itself festooned with enormous, banner-sized adverts for trail shoes and running apparel, as tens of thousands of competitors, spectators and industry professionals travel through to Chamonix. A logistically complicated, multi-language livestream broadcast – involving dozens of camera teams and remote drones scattered around the Mont Blanc massif – ensures that the event can be witnessed by millions of viewers worldwide. For elite athletes, it is the biggest stage in MUT running: success guarantees a sponsorship contract and professional career. For recreational athletes, it is a chance to experience the razzamatazz of a gigantic spectacle – and to rub shoulders, however fleetingly, with internationally renowned athletes. For corporate sponsors, UTMB Mont-Blanc is the most lucrative advertising opportunity in the calendar – Internet searches for leading athletes rise by as much as 3000 per cent during race week.[5]

This enormous success was perhaps inevitably – and controversially – going to lead to something more ambitious than a singular UTMB event. Just as Nike did not confine itself to a single product line of sneakers, neither would UTMB confine itself to only one event.

In 2021, the Ironman Group, a billion-dollar triathlon events company, owned by media conglomerate Advance Publications, acquired a 45 per cent stake in the UTMB Group (the Poletti family retains controlling interest). It was heralded on both sides as a partnership that would see the global Ironman Group work with UTMB to develop their brand and international event footprint. With a self-declared strategy of growth and consolidation, the new UTMB-Ironman juggernaut began to quickly expand beyond the original Chamonix race series, purchasing many of the largest and most established trail and ultra running events around the world. The aim was to construct a self-contained transcontinental racing calendar – the UTMB World Series – as an exclusive route through for qualification to what would now be known as the 'UTMB World Series Finals' in Chamonix. In the space of four years, the UTMB World Series would grow from one event (i.e., the original UTMB races in Chamonix) to more than fifty events on six different continents. If you want to race at any of the flagship UTMB races in Chamonix – and tens of thousands of runners continue to enter the lottery every year – then it is necessary to complete one of their 'by UTMB' events. The more of these events that you finish, the more points you accumulate (known as 'running stones') – and the greater your chance in the lottery for the UTMB finals in Chamonix.

There was widespread unease at this development. To some, the consolidation and expansion of UTMB felt like not just the supercharging of corporate commercialisation, but also a market dominance and potential monopolisation that would endanger the viability of independent events. Defenders would point out that UTMB events

– while seemingly extensive – were still only a tiny fraction of the wider sport.

These fears seemingly came to fruition in late 2023 when a beloved Canadian race – Whistler Alpine Meadows (WAM) – would be cancelled due to a permitting disagreement with the landowners Vail Resorts, only for UTMB then to be granted a permit for a near identical race on the same course. WAM's race director, Gary Robbins, would be careful not to directly accuse UTMB and Vail Resorts of collusion – which both have strongly denied – but the implication for some was that an independent race had been forced to close by corporate muscle. In his statement, Robbins captured a prevailing concern: 'I will never fault anyone for wanting to do the UTMB races, but their new structure and strategies are completely counter to the ethos of our sport.'[6] James Elson – himself a champion for independent race organisers – would similarly feel compelled to describe UTMB as a 'vortex' at the heart of the sport.[7]

These concerns were not just confined to independent race organisers. In 2024, a survey of more than 1,000 recreational runners found that only 10 per cent believed the Ironman/UTMB partnership to be 'good for the sport'.[8] Further questions were also being raised about the environmental sustainability of this new racing series – which seemed to promote frequent air travel – and the choice of a European car company as one of the title sponsors.[9]

These controversies are not straightforward. A professional framework of MUT running has been built up around the UTMB phenomenon. For many professional athletes, bonus structures and commitments relating to UTMB are written explicitly into their sponsorship contracts. Following the WAM controversy, a small number of athletes and industry professionals did call for a boycott of UTMB events – sometimes at personal cost to their own prospects and racing plans. Most sought a middle ground: not committing to a boycott, but critiquing a perceived failure in values and calling for a 'course correction'. In a letter to other professional athletes, Zach Miller and Kílian Jornet, two of the most celebrated athletes in the sport, captured this wider sense of ambivalence:

> Thanks to UTMB, we now have a world championship-esque event that draws many of the best runners in the sport as well as sponsors, media, and fans from all over the world. It has truly become the big event of the year and has really helped to put our sport on the map. Having an event like this has created a lot of opportunity for people like ourselves, as it drives a lot of money and attention to the sport. This, we feel, is a good thing. However, while it may be good for the sport to grow and develop in these ways, it is also important that the growth occurs in a positive, healthy manner. Unfortunately, the current direction that UTMB, UTMB Group, and Ironman have taken has given us cause for concern.[10]

This is a sport that has long prided itself on grassroots integrity, a spiritual connection to the natural world, and an oddball, countercultural idiosyncrasy. It is a sport that places the dirtbag runner on a pedestal – runners like Zach Miller, living in the back of a converted van, fuelled by burritos and a burning commitment to the transcendent majesty of the mountains, or Anton Krupicka, long-haired and shirtless, unfettered and free in the American wilderness, or the carefree and smiling exuberance of Courtney Dauwalter. Yet these same runners now find themselves wrestling with the ethics of a corporate merger and the pressures of commercial sponsorship.

UTMB would meet with Miller and Jornet – and representatives from the Pro Trail Runners Association (PTRA) – in an attempt to foster a dialogue that might address these concerns. There would be no mass boycott. Despite unease among recreational runners, entries to UTMB events have continued to grow. As a competitive space, UTMB remains just as important for professional athletes. And yet the fundamental question remains the same: what does the future of the sport look like?

As I write these closing words, it is possible to have an entirely paradoxical and conflicted view of the sport: to be simultaneously excited by growth and change – to be deeply engaged with the commercial and media buzz around the sport – while also romanticising the idea of a ragtag mountain sport community and the attraction of running alone through the stillness of a remote wilderness. Such is the human condition – or, as the great American poet Walt Whitman was to remark on the subject of internal contradictions: 'I am large, I contain multitudes.' MUT running has always contained a multitude; it has never really been a singular sport but a constellation of desires and traditions, circling the existential lure of self-reliant movement, mental resilience, and endurance in the natural world.

As Buzz Burrell likes to say, 'Run your own race'. There are those who enjoy the spectacle and glamour of high-profile international events such as Western States or UTMB Mont-Blanc, whether as participants or spectators. Others prefer low-key community races that have hardly changed in decades. Some seek exploration and exotic travel in the great mountain ranges of the world – from the Himalayas to Patagonia – while others enjoy the intimacy of every nook and hollow on home ground. A few seek to push the limits of personal endurance, while others simply want to enjoy a long day out. There are many runners who favour solitude, while others seek conviviality and companionship. The MUT running ecosphere accommodates all of this, and more.

Or perhaps this is too simplistic. At times there can certainly be a clash of values between old hands and new entrants to the sport. When interviewing athletes and industry insiders, I was struck by one event organiser who remarked that, while they are happy to see their event growing, they feel culturally alienated by a new cohort of runners that are obsessed with the commodified aspects of gear and clothing rather than the pure simplicity of running. This more pervasive concern – the idea of a culture shift – sits beneath the debate concerning monopolisation and commercialisation in the sport.

Similarly, a story that remains untold is growing internationalisation and diversification. Many of the values and practices of MUT running have been formed through a 200-year history of athletic and outdoor traditions in the Western world. We can draw a clear line from nineteenth-century scientific rationalism and romanticism – through the traditions of athletics, hiking and mountaineering – all the way to the contemporary sport. What challenges are posed by the emergence of alternative running cultures in the MUT running space? The success of Chinese athletes at high-profile races has been a recent and interesting storyline – China is now the tenth largest ultrarunning nation in the world. As athletes from non-Western countries become more prevalent – including the recent drift of East African athletes to shorter distance mountain running – will these athletes bring with them values and motivations that might change the sport? Or are we witnessing the global exportation of American and European mountain cultures?

The sport is also changing in other ways – including through the new expression of old values. Perhaps the most encouraging development has been the enormous success of the 'Backyard Ultra' racing format. Launched in 2011 by Gary Cantrell – the founder of the Barkley Marathons – participants must run a 4.167 mile loop (known as 'a yard') every hour. The race only ends, and a winner is only declared, when every other participant has dropped out. Backyard races possess a rootsy, homespun and often kooky vibe that can chime with traditional sentiments in the sport. They also channel something that has long defined the attraction of ultrarunning: mental struggle. Competitors do not know when the race will end, or how far they will need to run. The format has become something of a global phenomenon. In 2024, simultaneous backyard ultras took place in sixty-one countries, with the top competitors in each race qualifying to compete at the original backyard event, held every year at Cantrell's home (i.e., in his 'backyard'), in Bell Buckle, Tennessee. The male world record stands at 458 miles (110 yards), the female record at 362.5 miles (87 laps) – both were set in 2024.

Similarly, there are other high-profile race organisers who continue to promote a diverse counterculture within MUT running. The World Trail Majors, launched in 2023, brings together nine different races – all independently managed and owned – from Hong Kong and Japan, to North America, South Africa and Europe. The stated ethos: 'to understand the uniqueness of each race in this sport, escaping from uniformity and embracing the individuality as something enriching that enhances trail running as a sporting, cultural and social activity'.[11] Runners are invited to tick off each of these 'bucket list' races, thus sampling diverse running cultures, landscapes and traditions that each contribute to the sport.

And then there is the world of sub-ultra trail and mountain running – an area that is witnessing the most significant growth among casual recreational runners. The Golden Trail Series, a European-origin championship (first launched in 2018), has a changing circuit of races in the series every year (from Japan and China, to the United States and Europe) that are typically around the 20–30 km mark. Fast and highly competitive, the series is televised on Eurosport in seventy-one countries and in twenty-three languages,[12] and attracts those athletes who specialise in shorter-distance racing. It makes for incredible viewing – with athletes tearing down steep slopes and sprinting over the finish line – and there is intense speculation that this might prove to be a more spectator-friendly version of the sport. This would also perhaps provide the model for any future inclusion of trail running into the Olympics, which is itself a hotly contested topic: does MUT running want to align itself more closely with mainstream athletics?

The sport is changing, then – but also remaining the same. While the story of the last two decades has been around the formation of a shared global athletic culture – *the making of a sport* – perhaps the next two decades will witness the continued flourishing of distinct MUT running subcultures. Already, those who complete at UTMB are often different to those who compete at Backyard Ultras, who are different in turn to those who compete at track 24-hour racing, who are different again to those who compete at the Golden Trail Series … and so on. The sport is vast and complicated – there is no guarantee that it can hang together.

And yet the sport continues to tap into atavistic human desires that are rooted in mind and body, and our place in the natural world. It seems fitting to end with someone who is approaching fifty years at the heart of the sport. Gary Cantrell – or 'Lazarus Lake' as he is mysteriously known – was to reflect on the enduring attraction of the sport back in the early 1980s:

> Though we may not always want to admit it, we enjoy the slightly amazed response of family and friends to our running feats. That amazement, however, is no substitute for the understanding of others who have seen the sun rise, set, and rise again during a single run.[13]

These are words that continue to ring true. No matter how the sport grows and changes, it is likely that this peculiar mix of personal achievement and camaraderie will continue to define mountain, ultra and trail running for decades to come.

Notes

Introduction

1 Quoted in Tom Wilson, 'Chasing the world's top ultra-runners around Mont Blanc', *Financial Times*, 15 September 2021.
2 Bryon Powell, '"A Team Sport": A short film on Courtney Dauwalter's historic 2023 season', *iRunFar*, 10 July 2024.
3 Meghan Hicks, 'Jim Walmsley, 2023 UTMB champion, interview', *iRunFar*, 3 September 2023.
4 Sarah Barker, 'Do you think that's wise?', *Like the Wind*, 13 December 2023.
5 Interview with Nancy Hobbs, November 2023.
6 Interview with Damian Hall, December 2023.
7 'The casual champion', *Trail Runner*, 26 April 2017.
8 Ludwig Wittgenstein, *Philosophical Investigations* (Oxford: Basil Blackwell & Mott, 1953), p. 66.
9 Andy Jones-Wilkins, 'Ultra prize money doesn't change why they run', *iRunFar*, 1 December 2011.
10 Robert Rinehart, *Players All: Performances in Contemporary Sport* (Bloomington: Indiana University Press, 1998). Belinda Wheaton, 'Selling out? The globalization and commercialisation of lifestyle sports', in Lincoln Allison (ed.), *The Global Politics of Sport* (London: Routledge, 2004), pp. 127–146.
11 Pamela N. Danzinger, 'Why Amer Sports' IPO didn't meet expectations, despite its unique positioning', *Forbes*, 2 February 2024.
12 'Trail running shoes market size…', *Business Research Insights*, 14 October 2024.
13 Michael Crawley, *To the Limit: The Meaning of Endurance from Mexico to the Himalayas* (London: Bloomsbury Sport, 2024).
14 Freetrail, 'Eric Senseman on retirement & the realities of being a pro trail runner', *Freetrail* podcast, 9 November 2023.
15 Zoë Rom, 'He qualified for Team USA. Then came the bill', *Trail Runner*, 11 October 2023.
16 Interview with Buzz Burrell, December 2023.
17 Singletrack, 'The return of Anton Krupicka', *Singletrack* podcast, 24 September 2024.

18 Running for Real, 'Jasmin Paris: Do what you feel is right and what makes you happy', *Running for Real* podcast, 30 September 2022.
19 Carl Morris, *Trail Ultra Survey Report: 2022* (Preston: University of Central Lancashire, 2022). Available at https://www.trailultraproject.com/survey (accessed 14 May 2025).
20 Teal S. Eich and Janet Metcalfe, 'Effects of the stress of marathon running on implicit and explicit memory', *Psychonomic Bulletin & Review*, 16 (2009): 475–479.
21 Zbigniew Waśkiewicz *et al.*, 'Motivation in ultra-marathon runners', *Psychology Research and Behaviour Management*, 12 (2022): 31–37.
22 Jim Cherrington, Jack Black and Nicholas Tiller, 'Running away from the taskscape: Ultramarathon as 'dark ecology', in Ricardo Melo, Derek Van Rheenen and Sean Gammon (eds), *Nature Sports* (London: Routledge, 2023), pp. 241–261.
23 Michael Atkinson, 'Entering scapeland: Yoga, fell and post-sport physical cultures', *Sport in Society*, 13(7–8) (2010): 1249–1267, p. 1262.
24 Morris, *Trail Ultra Survey Report: 2022.*
25 J. Claude Evans, *With Respect for Nature: Living as Part of the Natural World* (Albany: SUNY Press, 2005).
26 Carl Cederström and Andre Spicer, *The Wellness Syndrome* (Cambridge: Polity Press, 2015), p. 12.
27 Shelley McKenzie, (*Getting Physical: The Rise of Fitness Culture in America* (Lawrence: University Press of Kansas, 2013), p. 8.
28 Stefan Lawrence, *Digital Wellness, Health and Fitness Influencers: Critical Perspectives on Digital Guru Media* (Abingdon: Taylor & Francis, 2022).
29 James Suzman, *Work: A Deep History, from the Stone Age to the Age of Robots* (London: Penguin, 2021).

Chapter 1

1 *The Evening Post*, New York, 8 June 1824, p.1.
2 Derek Martin, 'A forgotten sport: Pedestrianism in the West Midlands', *Midland History*, 46(2) (2021): 164–177.
3 'A celebrated pedestrian', *Luton Times and Advertiser*, 7 March 1879, p. 6.
4 *Ibid.*
5 'Foster Powell, the pedestrian', *Sheffield Daily Telegraph*, 14 January 1875, p. 8.
6 R. H. Westley, *A Short Sketch of the Life of Mr. Foster Powell, The Great Pedestrian* (London, 1793).
7 *Ibid.*
8 Aled Jones, *Powers of the Press: Newspapers, Power and the Public in Nineteenth-Century England* (Abingdon: Routledge, 1996).
9 *Leicester Journal and Midland Counties General Advertiser*, 11 December 1773, p. 2.
10 *The Derby Mercury*, Derbyshire, 24 December 1773, p. 1.

11 Linkboys were boys who were paid to carry flaming torches made from tow and cotton. Typically paid one farthing, they provided illumination on the streets of London before the introduction of gas lighting in the early nineteenth century.
12 *The Leeds Intelligencer and Yorkshire General Advertiser*, 22 April 1793, p. 3.
13 Martin, 'A forgotten sport'.
14 *Maryland Gazette*, 8 July 1790, p. 2.
15 Nancy Fix Anderson, *The Sporting Life: Victorian Sports and Games* (Santa Barbara, CA: Praeger, 2010).
16 Alan Guttmann, 'English sports spectators: The Restoration to the early nineteenth century', *Journal of Sport History*, 12(2) (1985): 103–125.
17 Mike Huggins, *The Victorians and Sport* (London: A&C Black, 2004).
18 Samantha-Jayne Oldfield, *Narratives of Manchester Pedestrianism: Using Biographical Methods to Explore the Development of Athletics During the Nineteenth Century* (Manchester: Manchester Metropolitan University, 2014), p. 2.
19 William J. Baker, 'The leisure revolution in Victorian England: A review of recent literature', *Journal of Sport History*, 6(3) (1979): 76–87.
20 *The Observer*, London, 30 October 1808, p. 2.
21 Walter Thom, *Pedestrianism; or, An Account of the Performance of Celebrated Pedestrians During the Last and Present Century; with a Full Narrative of Captain Barclay's Public and Private Matches; and An Essay on Training* (Aberdeen: A. Brown and F. Frost, 1813).
22 Alan Tomlinson, 'Speculations on the body and sporting spaces: The cultural significance of sport performance', *American Behavioral Scientist*, 46(11) (2003): 1577–1587.
23 *Caledonian Mercury*, Edinburgh, 30 September 1815, p. 2.
24 Jessie Aitken Wilson, *Memoir of George Wilson* (Norderstedt: Books on Demand, 2022).
25 Steve Ward, *Beneath the Big Top: A Social History of the Circus in Britain* (Barnsley: Pen & Sword Books, 2014).
26 Nicholas Mason, '"The sovereign people are in a beastly state": The Beer Act of 1830 and Victorian discourse on working-class drunkenness', *Victorian Literature and Culture*, 29(1) (2001):109–127.
27 Peter Swain, 'Pedestrianism, the public house and gambling in nineteenth-century south-east Lancashire', *Sport in History*, 32(3) (2012): 382–404.
28 Stephen Hardy, 'Sport in urbanizing America: A historical review', *Journal of Urban History*, 23(6) (1997): 675–708.
29 Samantha-Jayne Oldfield, 'Running pedestrianism in Victorian Manchester', *Sport in History*, 34(2) (2014): 223–248.
30 *Ibid.*
31 Thomas C. Crochunis, 'Captain Barclay's performance: Decoding pedestrianism in early nineteenth-century Britain', in Alexander Dick and Angela Esterhammer (eds), *Spheres of Action: Speech and Performance in Romantic Culture* (Toronto: University of Toronto Press, 2009).
32 Anderson, *The Sporting Life*.

33 Dahn Shaulis, 'Pedestriennes: Newsworthy but controversial women in sporting entertainment', *Journal of Sport History*, 26(1) (1999): 29–50.
34 *Liverpool Mercury*, 21 September 1864, p. 3.
35 'A thousand miles in a thousand hours', *The Daily Post*, 2 November 1864.
36 *Freeman's Journal and Daily Commercial Advertiser*, 22 September 1864, p. 4.
37 *Bury Times*, 18 August 1866, p. 2.
38 *Era*, 8 January 1843; *Sheffield and Rotherham Independent*, 28 September 1850, p. 8.
39 Peter Lovesey, *The Official Centenary History of the Amateur Athletic Association* (London: Guinness Superlatives Ltd, 1979).
40 Steven W. Pope, 'Amateurism and American sports culture: The invention of an athletic tradition in the United States, 1870–1900', *The International Journal of the History of Sport*, 13(3) (1996): 290–309, p. 306.
41 Peter Borsay, *A History of Leisure* (Basingstoke: Palgrave Macmillan, 2006).
42 *New York American*, 26 October 1830, p. 2.
43 Andy Milroy, *North American Ultrarunning: A History* (Mansfield: JMD Media Ltd, 2012).
44 John Helyar, *The Lords of the Realm: The Real History of Baseball* (Norderstedt: Books on Demand, 1995).
45 Nick Harris, Helen Harris and Paul Marshall, *A Man in a Hurry: The Extraordinary Life and Times of Edward Payson Weston, the World's Greatest Walker* (Liverpool: De Coubertin Books, 2012).
46 Matthew Alego, *Pedestrianism: When Watching People Walk Was America's Favorite Spectator Sport* (Chicago Review Press, 2014), p. 13.
47 P. S. Marshall, *King of the Peds* (Bloomington, IN: AuthorHouse, 2008).
48 *Ibid.*
49 Alego, *Pedestrianism*, p. 199.
50 Joss Marsh, 'The rise of celebrity culture', in Sally Ledger and Holly Furneaux (eds), *Charles Dickens in Context* (Cambridge: Cambridge University Press, 2011), pp. 98–99.
51 Ryan Murtha and Thomas M. Hunt, 'Daniel O'Leary and the sporting experiences of Irish immigrants in the United States', *Immigrants & Minorities*, 39(1) (2021): 10–31.
52 John E. Tansey, *Biographical Sketch of Daniel O'Leary, Champion Pedestrian of the World* (1878).
53 Marshall, *King of the Peds*, p. 59.
54 Jim Reisler, *Walk of Ages: Edward Payson Weston's Extraordinary 1909 Trek Across America* (Lincoln: University of Nebraska Press, 2015).
55 Ralph Wilcox, 'Irish Americans in sports: The nineteenth century' in J. J. Lee and M. Casey (eds), *Making the Irish American: History and Heritage of the Irish in the United States* (New York: NYU Press, 2007), pp. 443–456.
56 Cited in P. S. Marshall, *Weston, Weston, Rah-Rah-Rah! Edward Payson Weston: The Original Sporting Superstar* (AuthorHouseUK, 2012) p. 105.
57 Alego, *Pedestrianism*.

58 John A. Lucas, 'Pedestrianism and the struggle for the Sir John Astley belt, 1878–1879', *Research Quarterly*, American Association for Health, Physical Education and Recreation, 39(3) (1968): 587–594.
59 A. Easterling, 'Challenge to English pedestrians', *Illustrated Sporting and Dramatic News*, 11 December 1875, p. 23.
60 'Edward Payson Weston, the American Pedestrian', *The Australian Town and Country Journal*, 29 April 1876, p. 28.
61 'English vs. American pedestrianism', *Illustrated Sporting and Dramatic News*, 25 March 1876, p. 6.
62 *Sporting Life*, 13 May 1876, p. 3.
63 'Great Walking Match for £1000', *Reynolds's Newspaper*, 8 April 1877, p. 5.
64 'Miscellaneous', *St. Louis Post-Dispatch*, 9 February 1878, p. 3.
65 Edward Plummer, *The American Championship Record and a History of Mixing Races* (New York: Snowden and Beaudine, 1881).
66 Lucas, 'Pedestrianism and the struggle for the Sir John Astley belt, 1878–1879'.
67 Alego, *Pedestrianism*, p. 134.
68 W. E. B. DuBois, *WEB DuBois on Sociology and the Black Community* (Chicago, IL: University of Chicago Press, 2013).
69 'The Astley belt walk', *St. Louis Post-Dispatch*, 27 September 1879, p. 7.
70 'Fifth contest for the Astley belt', *Frank Leslie's Illustrated Newspaper*, 4 October 1879, p. 5.
71 Cited in Alego, *Pedestrianism*, p. 183.
72 Neil Tranter, *Sport, Economy and Society in Britain* (Cambridge: Cambridge University Press, 2010).
73 Alan Guttmann, *From Ritual to Record: The Nature of Modern Sports* (New York: Columbia University Press, 1978).

Chapter 2

1 Dan Bailey, 'All-in, to the end', *UK Climbing*, 23 May 2023.
2 *Ibid.*
3 *Ibid.*
4 Jane Eblen, *Adirondack Wilderness: A Story of Man and Nature* (Syracuse, NY: Syracuse University Press, 1980), p. 17.
5 John Urry, 'The making of the Lake District', in David Pepper, George Revill and Frank Webster (eds), *Environmentalism: Critical Concepts in the Environment* (Abingdon: Routledge, 2002), pp. 151–170 (p. 151).
6 Ghazali Musa, James Higham and Anna Thompson-Carr (eds), *Mountaineering Tourism* (Abingdon: Routledge, 2015).
7 Stephen Prickett (ed.), *The Romantics* (Abingdon: Routledge, 2017).
8 Peter Gay, *Why the Romantics Matter* (New Haven, CT: Yale University Press, 2015).
9 Barbara L. Packer, *The Transcendentalists* (Athens: University of Georgia Press, 2007).

10 U. C. Knoepflmacher and G. B. Tennyson (eds), *Nature and the Victorian Imagination* (Berkeley: University of California Press, 1977).

11 Irshad Ahmed Shaheen, 'Romanticism: A study in retrospect', *University of South Asia Journal*, 4(1) (2018): 11–19.

12 Saeko Yoshikawa, *William Wordsworth and the Invention of Tourism, 1820–1900* (Abingdon: Routledge, 2014).

13 Jarkko Saarinen, 'Tourism and touristic representations of nature', in Alan A. Lew, C. Michael Hall and Allan M. Williams (eds), *A Companion to Tourism* (London: Blackwell, 2004), pp. 438–449.

14 Klaus Meyer-Arendt, 'Tourism and the natural environment', in Alan A. Lew, C. Michael Hall and Allan M. Williams (eds), *A Companion to Tourism* (London: Blackwell, 2004), pp. 423–427.

15 John Sears, *Sacred places: American Tourist Attractions in the Nineteenth Century* (Amherst: University of Massachusetts Press, 1998).

16 Isaiah Berlin, *The Roots of Romanticism, 2nd edn* (Princeton, NJ: Princeton University Press, 2013), p. 2.

17 Charles Taylor, *The Ethics of Authenticity* (Cambridge, MA: Harvard University Press, 1991), p. 26.

18 Keith Hanley, 'The imaginative visitor: Wordsworth and the Romantic construction of literary tourism in the Lake District', in Jason Wood and John K. Walton (eds), *The Making of a Cultural Landscape* (London: Routledge, 2016), pp. 113–131.

19 *Kendal Mercury*, 18 September 1869.

20 Mike Huggins, 'Sport helps make us what we are: The shaping of regional and local sporting identities in Cumbria c. 1800–1960', *Transactions of the Cumberland and Westmorland Antiquarian and Archaeological Society*, 11 (2011): 81–96, p. 83.

21 *Soulby's Ulverston Advertiser and General Intelligencer*, 24 August 1876; *Maryport Advertiser*, 20 August 1898.

22 Katherine Morse, 'The Grasmere Sports', *The Sewanee Review*, 35(2) (1927): 137–142.

23 Arthur Lynon Bowley, *Wages in the United Kingdom in the 19th Century* (Cambridge: Cambridge University Press, 1900).

24 *Richard Askwith, Feet in the Clouds: A Tale of Fell-Running and Obsession (London: Aurum Press, 2004).*

25 Daniel E. Lieberman *et al.*, 'Running in Tarahumara (Rarámuri) culture: Persistence hunting, footracing, dancing, work, and the fallacy of the athletic savage', *Current Anthropology*, 61(3) (2020): 356–379.

26 *Ibid.*

27 Peter Nabokov, *Indian Running: Native American History and Tradition* (Santa Barbara, CA: Capra, 1981).

28 *The Oregon Daily Journal*, 11 November 1906.

29 *Freeport Evening Standard*, 7 July 1906.

30 Tara Keegan, 'Runners of a Different Race: North American Indigenous Athletes and National Identities in the Early Twentieth Century', MA thesis, University of Oregon, 2016. https://scholarsbank.uoregon.edu/server/api/core/bitstreams/f3fac0ad-d23c-4fc1-aef5-c38437e145ea/content

31 Darcy C. Plymire, 'The legend of the Tarahumara: Tourism, overcivilization and the white man's Indian', *The International Journal of the History of Sport*, 23(2) (2007): 154–166.
32 *The Hamilton Spectator*, 'Indians who run', 23 April 1928, p. 16.
33 Plymire, 'The legend of the Tarahumara'.
34 Lieberman *et al*, 'Running in Tarahumara (Rarámuri) culture'.
35 Bruno Balke and Clyde Snow, 'Anthropological and physiological observations on Tarahumara endurance runners', *American Journal of Physical Anthropology*, 23 (1965): 293–301.
36 Michael Crawley, *To the Limit: The Meaning of Endurance from Mexico to the Himalayas* (London: Bloomsbury Sport, 2024).
37 Peter L. Bayers, *Imperial Ascent: Mountaineering, Masculinity, and Empire* (Denver: University Press of Colorado, 2003).
38 Caroline Schaumann, *Peak Pursuits* (New Haven, CT: Yale University Press, 2020), p. 86.
39 William Martin Conway, *The Alps from End to End* (London: Archibald Constable & Co., 1900).
40 W. T. Palmer, *In Lakeland Dells and Fells* (London: Chatto & Windus, 1903), pp. 65–66.
41 Steve Chilton, *The Round: In Bob Graham's Footsteps* (Saltcoats: Sandstone Press, 2015).
42 Jonathan Westaway, '"Men who can last": Mountaineering endurance, the Lake District fell records and the campaign for Everest, 1919–1924', *Sport in History*, 33(3) (2013): 303–332, p 314.
43 Paddy Buckley, Roger Smith and A. Harry Griffin, *42 Peaks, The Story of a Bob Graham Round* (Hayloft Publishing, 2007).
44 Westaway, '"Men who can last"', p. 314.
45 Derek Walker, 'The evolution of climbing clubs in Britain', *Alpine Club Journal*, 2004: 187–195.
46 Steve Dean, 'Eustace Thomas: Manchester mountaineer', *Climbers Club Journal*, 2002–2003.
47 Westaway, '"Men who can last"'.
48 James P. Ronda, 'Exploring the explorers: Great Plains peoples and the Lewis and Clark expedition', *Great Plains Quarterly*, 13(2) (1993): 81–90.
49 Quoted in Maurice Isserman, *Continental Divide: A History of American Mountaineerin* (New York: W. W. Norton, 2017), p. 106.
50 Ralph Waldo Emerson, *The Complete Works of Ralph Waldo Emerson*, vol. 1 (Wm. H. Wise, 1903), p. 65.
51 Samantha C. Harvey, *Transatlantic Transcendentalism: Coleridge, Emerson and Nature* (Edinburgh: Edinburgh University Press, 2013).
52 Lawrence Buell, *The Environmental Imagination: Thoreau, Nature Writing, and the Formation of American Culture* (Cambridge, MA: Harvard University Press, 1995).
53 Barbara Cutter, '"A feminine utopia": Mountain climbing, gender, and women's rights in nineteenth-century America', *Journal of Women's History*, 33(2) (2021): 6-184.
54 Musa *et al.*, *Mountaineering Tourism.*

55 William Lowell Putnam *et al.*, *A Century of American Alpinism* (Flagstaff, AZ: Light Technology Publishing, 2002).
56 Chic Scott, *Pushing the Limits: The Story of Canadian Mountaineering* (Victoria, BC: Rocky Mountain Books Ltd, 2000).
57 Mel Scott, *The San Francisco Bay Area: A Metropolis in Perspective* (Berkeley: University of California Press, 1985).
58 Erik Lawrence Weiselberg, *Ascendancy of the Mazamas: Environment, Identity and Mountain Climbing in Oregon, 1870 to 1930* (Eugene: University of Oregon, 1999).
59 Frederick Turner, *John Muir: From Scotland to the Sierra – A Biography* (Edinburgh: Canongate, 2014).

Chapter 3

1 Nick J. Watson, 'Muscular Christianity in the modern age', in J. Parry *et al.* (eds), *Sport and Spirituality: An Introduction* (London: Routledge, 2007), pp. 80–94 (p. 80).
2 Richard Holt, 'The amateur body and the middle-class man: Work, health and style in Victorian Britain', in Dilwyn Porter and Stephen Wagg (eds), *Amateurism in British Sport* (London: Routledge, 2007), pp. 18–35 (p. 18).
3 Charles Kingsley, quoted in Bruce Haley, *The Healthy Body and Victorian Culture* (Cambridge, MA: Harvard University Press, 1978), p. 18.
4 Andrew Boyd Hutchinson, *The Complete History of Cross-Country Running: From the Nineteenth Century to the Present Day* (New York: Simon & Schuster, 2018).
5 Harvey Taylor, 'Play up, but don't play the game: English amateur athletic elitism, 1863–1910', *Sports Historian*, 22(2) (2002): 75–97.
6 Richard Wettan and Joe Willis, 'Effect of New York's elite athletic clubs on American amateur athletic governance – 1870–1915', *Research Quarterly. American Alliance for Health, Physical Education and Recreation*, 47(3) (1976): 499–505.
7 Steven W. Pope, 'Amateurism and American sports culture: The invention of an athletic tradition in the United States, 1870–1900', *The International Journal of the History of Sport*, 13(3) (1996): 290–309, p. 291.
8 *Spirit of the Times*, 2 October 1869.
9 Joseph M. Turrini, *The End of Amateurism in American Track and Field* (Champaign: University of Illinois Press, 2010), p. 13.
10 John A. Lucas, 'The modern Olympic games: Fanfare and philosophy, 1896–1972', *Quest*, 22(1) (1974): 6–18, p. 6.
11 Joe Willis and Richard Wettan, 'Social stratification in New York City athletic clubs, 1865–1915', in Neil L. Shumsky (ed.), *Social Structure and Social Mobility* (London: Routledge, 2020), pp. 135–153.
12 Kevin McCarthy, *Gold, Silver and Green: The Irish Olympic Journey, 1896–1924* (Cork: Cork University Press, 2010).

13 Pamela Cooper, 'Community, ethnicity, status: The origins of the marathon in the United States', *The International Journal of the History of Sport*, 9(1) (1992): 50–62, pp. 55–56.
14 Roberta J. Park, 'British sports and pastimes in San Francisco, 1848–1900', *The International Journal of the History of Sport*, 1(3) (1984): 300–317.
15 Barry Spitz, *Dipsea: The Greatest Race* (San Anselmo, CA: Potrero Meadow Publishing, 2010).
16 *San Francisco Chronicle*, 20 November 1905.
17 'Gritty schoolboy wins handicap prize', *San Francisco Chronicle*, 20 November 1905, p. 8.
18 Spitz, *Dipsea: The Greatest Race.*
19 George James, quoted in Rita M. Liberti, 'Trailblazing in Marin: Women's Dipsea hikes, 1918–1922', *California History*, 81(1) (2002): 54–65, p. 54.
20 *San Francisco Examiner*, 8 March 1921.
21 Spitz, *Dipsea: The Greatest Race.*
22 Liberti, 'Trailblazing in Marin'.
23 'Runners in training for Indian Race', *San Francisco Call and Post*, 1 September 1912, p. 23.
24 *Los Angeles Times*, 29 March 1908.
25 'Climbs mount in fast time', *Los Angeles Herald*, 30 April 1908, p. 9.
26 *Los Angeles Evening Express*, 15 April 1909.
27 'Challenges Estoppey for return race to San Diego', *Los Angeles Herald*, 15 November 1909, p. 6.
28 *Hay Springs Enterprise*, 2 July 1909.
29 Rich Mole, *Rebel Women of the Gold Rush: Extraordinary Achievements and Daring Adventures* (Manningtree, Essex: Heritage House Publishing, 2010).
30 *Willmar Tribune*, 4 December 1907.
31 *Marshall Messenger*, 28 September 1926.
32 *Brooklyn Citizen*, 2 May 1927.
33 Available at https://results.pikespeakmarathon.org/archive/1936.htm (accessed 8 February 2023).
34 'Sport: Vertical milers', *TIME* Magazine, 18 July 1938.
35 Millie Spezialy, *Mount Marathon: Alaska's Great Footrace* (Portland: Alaska Northwest Books, 2013), p. 1.
36 *Ibid.*
37 David Duff, *Queen Victoria's Highland Journals* (Devon: Webb & Bower, 1980).
38 *Inverness Courier*, 4 October 1895.
39 Hugh Dan MacLennan, 'The Ben race: The supreme test of athletic fitness', *Sports Historian*, 18(2) (1998): 131–147.
40 'The Ben Nevis record', *Glasgow Daily Mail*, 5 June 1898, p. 4.
41 MacLennan, 'The Ben race'.
42 *Otago Witness*, 31 December 1902, p. 27.
43 Hugh Dan MacLennan, 'Kathleen Connochie – a star in a golden age', *Discover* (Winter 2017): 14–15.

Chapter 4

1 *Evening Standard*, London, 1 May 1903, p. 5.
2 *Manchester Courier and Lancashire General Advertiser*, 2 May 1903, p. 8.
3 *Manchester Courier and Lancashire General Advertiser*, 22 June 1903, p. 8.
4 Alex Wilson, *Len Hurst Champion Belter: The Story of Len Hurst, Britain's First Marathon Champion* (Witney: DB Publishing, 2019).
5 Anthony Bijkerk, 'The professional amateur', *Journal of Olympic History*, 8(2) (2000): 55.
6 Harvey Taylor, 'Play up, but don't play the game: English amateur athletic elitism, 1863–1910', *Sports Historian*, 22(2) (2002): 75–97.
7 Pathé Newsreels, 'Tom Payne Wins London–Brighton Walk', 30 September 1920.
8 Raymond Fielding, *The American Newsreel: A Complete History, 1911–1967* (Jefferson, NC: McFarland, 2011).
9 Mike Huggins, 'Projecting the visual: British newsreels, soccer and popular culture 1918–39', *The International Journal of the History of Sport*, 24(1) (2007): 80–102, p. 81.
10 Michael Crawley, *To the Limit: The Meaning of Endurance from Mexico to the Himalayas* (London: Bloomsbury Sport, 2024).
11 Pathé Newsreels, 'USA: Athletics – Coast-to-Coast Marathon Walkers Crossing the Mojave Desert', 1 January 1928.
12 'Tom Payne: The World-Famous Musician-Athlete'. Phosferine advertising brochure, 1920. Available at http://www.vrwc.org.au/tim-archive/articles/Tom%20Payne%20-%20the%20world-famous%20musician-athlete.pdf (accessed 24 April 2025).
13 T. Lloyd Johnson, 'An Echo from the Past', 1934. Available at http://www.vrwc.org.au/tim-archive/articles/wo-tom-payne.pdf (accessed 13 March 2023).
14 'Thirty Years of Walking: Tom Payne', South Shields Harriers and Walking Club, June 1936. Available at http://www.vrwc.org.au/tim-archive/articles/Tom%20Payne%20-%2030%20years%20of%20Walking.pdf (accessed 12 March 2023).
15 Peter Marlow, 'A brief history of race walking', *New Studies in Athletics*, 5(3) (1990): 21–24.
16 Jürgen Schiffer, 'Race walking', *New Studies in Athletics*, 23(4) (2008): 7–15.
17 Tim Erickson, 'Tom Payne – Walker and Musician Extraordinaire', 2018. Available at http://www.vrwc.org.au/tim-archive/articles/wo-tom-payne.pdf (accessed 12 March 2023).
18 Harry Hendrick, *Images of Youth* (Oxford: Clarendon Press, 1990), p. 137.
19 J. A. Mangan, *'Manufactured' Masculinity: Making Imperial Manliness, Morality and Militarism* (Abingdon: Routledge, 2014).
20 Matt Cook, 'Twentieth-century masculinities', *Journal of Contemporary History*, 43(1) (2008): 127–135.

21 Timothy P. O'Hanlon, 'School sports as social training: The case of athletics and the crisis of World War I', *Journal of Sport History*, 9(1) (1982): 5–29.
22 'Tom Payne: The World-Famous Musician-Athlete'.
23 Emmett Dedmon, *Fabulous Chicago: A Great City's History and People* (New Orleans, LA: Garrett County Press, 2012).
24 Jennifer Jensen Wallach, *How America Eats: A Social History of US Food and Culture* (Lanham, MD: Rowman & Littlefield, 2013).
25 Clément Genty, *Albert Corey (1878–1926) – La France aux Jeux Olympiques de 1904* (Paris: L'Harmattan, 2021).
26 *The Boston Globe*, 12 August 1904, p. 2.
27 Meghan McCarthy, *The Wildest Race Ever: The Story of the 1904 Olympic Marathon* (New York: Simon & Schuster, 2016).
28 *The Lancaster Examiner*, Pennsylvania, 9 December 1905, p. 2.
29 *The Chicago Inter-Ocean*, 8 December 1905, p. 4.
30 *The Journal Times*, Racine, 4 September 1906, p. 7.
31 *The Boston Globe*, 25 October 1907, p. 8.
32 *Chicago Tribune*, 19 July 1909, p. 11.
33 *Chicago Tribune*, 25 July 1909, p. 19.
34 *The Daily News*, Jersey City, 18 October 1916, p. 3.
35 Susan Currell, *American Culture in the 1920s* (Edinburgh: Edinburgh University Press, 2009), p. 19.
36 Jim Reisler, *Cash and Carry: The Spectacular Rise and Hard Fall of CC Pyle, America's First Sports Agent* (Jefferson, NC: McFarland, 2009), p. 6.
37 *Ibid.*
38 *The Los Angeles Times*, 28 April 1927, p. 42.
39 *The Los Angeles Times*, 10 February 1928, p. 39.
40 Geoff Williams, *CC Pyle's Amazing Foot Race* (Tantor eBooks, 2013).
41 *TIME* Magazine, quoted in Mark Whitaker, *Running for Their Lives: The Extraordinary Story of Britain's Greatest Distance Runners* (London: Random House, 2012), pp. 106–7.
42 *Somerset Standard*, 25 June 1926, p. 2.
43 Whitaker, *Running for Their Lives.*
44 Charles B. Kastner, *Race Across America: Eddie Gardner and the Great Bunion Derbies* (Syracuse, NY: Syracuse University Press, 2020).
45 *Ibid.*
46 *The Los Angeles Times*, 14 February 1928, p. 37.
47 *The Los Angeles Times*, 20 March 1928, p. 23.
48 *Ibid.*
49 Kastner, *Race Across America*, p. 77.
50 Quoted in Reisler, *Cash and Carry*, p. 5.
51 Charles B. Kastner, *The 1929 Bunion Derby: Johnny Salo and the Great Footrace Across America* (Syracuse, NY: Syracuse University Press, 2014).
52 Whitaker, *Running for Their Lives.*
53 *The Billings Gazette*, Montana, 18 June 1929, p. 7.
54 Whitaker, *Running for Their Lives.*

Chapter 5

1 BBC Breakfast Interview, 17 January 2019.
2 Talk Ultra, 'Jasmin Paris', 2019.
3 Florian Obkircher, 'How Jasmin Paris became the first woman to win the 430km Spine Race', *Red Bull*, 2020.
4 *Ibid.*
5 Helen Walker, 'The popularisation of the outdoor movement, 1900–1940', *The International Journal of the History of Sport*, 2(2) (1985): 140–153.
6 Ann Holt, 'Hikers and ramblers: Surviving a thirties' fashion', *The International Journal of the History of Sport*, 4(1) (1987): 56–67.
7 *Manchester Guardian*, 5 May 1933.
8 Lewis Paton, 'Over the hills', *Journal of the Holiday Fellowship*, no. 54, Spring 1937.
9 Alfred Wainwright, *A Pennine Journey: The Story of a Long Walk in 1938* (London: Frances Lincoln, 2004), p. 4.
10 Sinclair McKay, *Ramble On* (London: Fourth Estate, 2012).
11 Holt, 'Hikers and ramblers'.
12 Geoffrey Glasby, *Mass Trespass on Kinder Scout in 1932: And the Founding of Our National Parks* (Xlibris Corporation, 2012).
13 Quoted in Silas Chamberlin, *On the Trail* (New Haven, CT: Yale University Press, 2016), p. 47.
14 Chamberlin, *On the Trail*, p. 137.
15 *The Bellingham Herald*, 9 December 1908, p. 3.
16 *The Bellingham Herald*, 21 May 1911, p. 12.
17 *The Tacoma Daily Ledger*, 30 June 1911, p. 12.
18 *The Bellingham Herald*, 2 July 1911, p. 13.
19 *The Bellingham Herald*, 1 September 1911, p. 1.
20 *The Bellingham Herald*, 10 August 1911, p. 6.
21 *The Bellingham Herald*, 10 August 1911, p. 1.
22 *The Bellingham Herald*, 11 August 1911, p. 1.
23 *The Bellingham Herald*, 10 August 1911, p. 6.
24 Barry Spitz, *Dipsea: The Greatest Race* (San Anselmo, CA: Potrero Meadow Publishing, 1993).
25 *Buffalo Morning Express*, 2 August 1912, p. 13.
26 *The Fresno Morning Republican*, 16 August 1913, p. 11.
27 *The Bellingham Herald*, 16 June 1914, p. 5.
28 *The Bennington Evening Banner*, 14 July 1926, p. 1.
29 *Ibid.*
30 Quoted in Chamberlin, *On the Trail*, p. 137.
31 *Rutland Daily Herald*, 20 August 1926, p. 7.
32 *Ibid.*
33 *The Burlington Free Press*, 26 August 1926, p. 2.
34 *The North Adams Transcript*, 1 September 1926, p. 3.
35 *News and Advertiser*, 12 July 1927, p. 7.
36 *The Barre Daily Times*, 15 July 1927, p. 9.

37 *The Barre Daily Times*, 21 July 1928, p. 7.
38 Chamberlin, *On the Trail*, p. 138.
39 *Ibid*, p. 157.
40 Kristi M. Fondren, *Walking on the Wild Side: Long-Distance Hiking on the Appalachian Trail* (New Brunswick, NJ: Rutgers University Press, 2015).
41 *The York Dispatch*, 9 October 1948, p. 1.
42 *Glenn Scherer and Don Hopey, Exploring the Appalachian Trail: Hikes in the Mid-Atlantic States (Harrisburg, PA: Stackpole, 2013), p. 87.*
43 *Morning Sentinel*, 6 August 1948, p. 11.
44 *Kennebec Journal*, 29 July 1948, p. 1.
45 *The Baltimore Sun*, 6 August 1948, p. 14.
46 Chamberlin, *On the Trail*, p. 134.
47 *Stockton Evening and Sunday Record*, 15 September 1937, p. 4.
48 *The Burlington Free Press*, 17 September 1937, p. 13.
49 Ben Montgomery, *Grandma Gatewood's Walk* (Chicago, IL: Chicago Review Press, 2014).
50 *Janesville Daily Gazette*, 8 July 1955, p. 5.
51 *The North Adams Transcript*, 17 September 1955, p. 4.
52 *Huddersfield Daily Examiner*, 20 September 1965, p. 6; *Manchester Evening News*, 14 May 1965, p. 14.
53 *The Observer*, 23 June 1974, p. 23.
54 *Evening Chronicle*, 13 June 1932, p. 7.
55 Dudley Hoys, *English Lake Country* (London: HarperCollins, 1969).
56 Des Oliver, 'The Lakeland 24 Hour Fell Record', *Fellrunner*, Autumn 1972), p. 11.
57 Brian Moynahan, *Jungle Soldier: The True Story of Freddy Spencer Chapman* (London: Quercus Publishing, 2009).
58 *Liverpool Daily Post*, 23 May 1932, p. 9.
59 *The Guardian*, 21 May 1932, p. 15.

Chapter 6

1 Laura Frances Chase, *Beyond Boston and Kathrine Switzer* (London: Routledge, 2015).
2 Andy Frye, 'Kathrine Switzer talks Boston marathon, 1967 and now', *Forbes*, 2 April 2019).
3 Annemarie Jutel, '"Thou dost run as in flotation": Femininity, reassurance and the emergence of the women's marathon', *The International Journal of the History of Sport*, 20(3) (2003): 17–36.
4 *Elaine Romanelli, 'Women in sports and games', in Lois Decker O'Neill (ed.), The Women's Book of World Records and Achievements (Harlow: Anchor Press, 1979), p. 576.*
5 Pamela Cooper, 'Marathon women and the corporation', *Journal of Women's History*, 7(4) (1995): 62–81.

6 Becky Nicolaides and Andrew Wiese, 'Suburbanization in the United States after 1945', *Oxford Research Encyclopaedia of American History*, 26 April 2017.
7 Mark Clapson and Ray Hutchison, 'Introduction: Suburbanization in global society', *Suburbanization in Global Society* (Bingley: Emerald Group Publishing, 2010), pp. 1–14.
8 Shelly McKenzie, *Getting Physical: The Rise of Fitness Culture in America* (Lawrence: University Press of Kansas, 2013), p. 3.
9 John F. Coghlan and Ida Webb, *Sport and British Politics Since 1960* (London: Routledge, 2003).
10 McKenzie, *Getting Physical*, p. 15.
11 Kenneth C. Land, *et al.*, 'Organizing the boys of summer: The evolution of US minor-league baseball, 1883–1990', *American Journal of Sociology*, 100(3) (1994): 781–813.
12 Barrie Houlihan, *The Government and Politics of Sport* (London: Routledge, 2014).
13 Martin Polley, *Moving the Goalposts: A History of Sport and Society Since 1945* (London: Routledge, 1998).
14 Kevin Jefferys, *Sport and Politics in Modern Britain: The Road to 2012* (London: Bloomsbury, 2012).
15 Quoted in Andrew Glass, 'JFK calls on Americans become physically fit, Dec. 5, 1961', *Politico*, 12 May 2017.
16 Jennifer Smith Maguire, *Fit for Consumption: Sociology and the Business of Fitness* (London: Routledge, 2007).
17 Fred M. Leventhal, '"A tonic to the nation": The Festival of Britain, 1951', *Albion*, 27(3) (1995): 445–453.
18 Becky Elizabeth Conekin, 'The Autobiography of a Nation: The 1951 Festival of Britain, Representing Britain in the Postwar Era', MA thesis, University of Michigan, 1998.
19 *Sunday Pictorial*, 12 August 1951, p. 14.
20 Road Runners Club, 'Ernest Neville', *Roadrunner: The Journal of the Road Runners Club*, (228) (Autumn 2022): 19–21.
21 Road Runners Club, *Road Runners Newsletter*, no. 3, May 1953.
22 Road Runners Club, *Road Runners Newsletter*, no. 8, January 1954.
23 John Chodes, *Corbitt: The Story of Ted Corbitt, Long Distance Runner* (Tafness Press, 1974).
24 Arthur Remillard, 'Ted Corbitt: The once-forgotten and now-remembered pioneer of American distance running', in Jeffrey Scholes and Randall Balmer (eds), *Religion and Sport in North America* (London: Routledge, 2022), pp. 201–215.
25 John Hanc, 'Ted and Jackie: Separated at birth?', *New York Running News*, June/July 1997, pp. 77–79.
26 Pamela Cooper, *The American Marathon* (Syracuse, NY: Syracuse University Press, 1998).
27 *Abilene Reporter*, 12 April 1927, p. 2.
28 *Evening Standard*, 29 September 1962, p. 15.
29 *Kitsap*, 5 July 1956, p. 4.

30 David M. Burns *et al.*, 'Cigarette smoking behaviour in the United States', *Smoking and Tobacco Control Monograph*, 8 (2020): 13–112.
31 *The Shreveport Journal*, 20 June 1956, p. 30.
32 An American mountaineering term for a mountain peak with an elevation of at least 14,000 feet.
33 *Poplar Bluff Republican*, 16 August 1956, p. 4.
34 *Fort Worth Star-Telegram*, 14 January 1959, p. 9.
35 *New Castle News*, 8 August 1958, p. 18.
36 Karen Given, 'Arlene Pieper: The marathon pioneer almost forgotten by history', *WBUR*, 21 April 2017.
37 6 *Colorado Springs Gazette Telegraph*, 7 August 1959.
38 *The San Francisco Examiner*, 21 July 1968, p. 19.
39 *The Guardian*, 27 June 1960, p. 1.
40 Youth Hostel Association, 'The history of YHA: The Journey: 90th Anniversary', 18 November 2020. Available at https://www.yha.org.uk/sites/default/files/media/document/The-Journey-90th-editions.pdf (accessed 28 April 2025).
41 *Western Morning News*, 22 September 1952, p. 1.
42 *Liverpool Daily Post*, 22 September 1952, p. 5.
43 Hugh Dan MacLennan, 'Kathleen Connochie – a star in a golden era', *Discover*, Winter 2017, pp. 14–15.
44 *Daily Record*, 5 September 1955, p. 14.
45 MacLennan, 'Kathleen Connochie'.
46 *Daily Mail*, 28 April 1970, p. 7.
47 John F. Kennedy, 'The *soft American*', *Sports Illustrated*, 25 December 1960.
48 *Oakland Tribune*, 12 February 1963, p. 1.

Chapter 7

1 *The Napa Valley Register*, 27 June 1978, p .6.
2 Known as 'Squaw Valley' since 1949, the used of the term 'squaw' had long been criticised by the Washoe people as an ethnic and sexist slur against Native American women. It was renamed as 'Olympic Valley' in 2021. This term will be used throughout, with the exception of contemporaneous references in historical sources.
3 Pamela L. Cooper, 'The "visible hand" on the footrace: Fred Lebow and the marketing of the marathon', *Journal of Sport History*, 19(3) (1992): 244–256.
4 Ian O'Riordan, 'Shufflin' Mac – an aristocrat of the running spirit', *The Irish Times*, 27 September 2008.
5 *The Sacramento Bee*, 10 January 1967, p. 44.
6 *The Sacramento Bee*, 19 February 1968, p. 25.
7 Quoted in Gary Corbitt, '50th Anniversary National 50 Mile Championship – Rocklin CA: Perhaps the greatest ultramarathon race ever in the United States (October 18, 1970)', 3 December 2020.

8 Bruce Anderson, 'Running for his life', *Anderson Valley Advertiser*, 19 November 2020.
9 *The Sacramento Bee*, 19 October 1970, p. 18.
10 Corbitt, '50th Anniversary National 50 Mile Championship'.
11 *The Baltimore Sun*, 22 September 1972, p. 28.
12 *Hartford Courant*, 14 May 1974, p. 27.
13 Nick Marshall, 'In it for the long haul', *UltraRunning Magazine*, 1 February 2021.
14 *The Sacramento Bee*, 8 July 1976, p. 60.
15 *Auburn Journal*, 3 August 1972, p. 3 6.
16 Luke Francis Ponnet, 'Endurance Running in the United States: A History of the 20th and Early 21st Century', BA thesis, Portland: Concordia University, 2016, p. 32.
17 *Ibid.*
18 *Auburn Journal*, 4 June 1977, p. 6.
19 Charles Levinson, 'Western States Endurance Run held Saturday: Legendary cowman returns to Tahoe', *Sun News Service*, 19 December 2001.
20 Quoted in Davy Crockett, 'The 100-miler: Part 18 (1977) Western States 100', *Ultrarunning History*, 22 January 2021.
21 Quoted in *Freetrail*, 'The amazing history of the Western States 100', *Freetrail* podcast, 25 June 2024.
22 Ruth Anderson, 'Women endurance runners excel at Western States', *UltraRunning Magazine*, September 1981, p. 5.
23 Keith Warman, 'LDWA: The story so far: 1972–2019', *LDWA*, Easingwold, 15 March 2020.
24 Long Distance Walkers Association, 'The Downsman Hundred: Results & Report of the Inaugural Event', 1973.
25 *The Surrey Advertiser*, 1 June 1973, p. 35.
26 Anita Verschoth, 'A hurried peek at Pikes', *Sports Illustrated*, 18 August 1975.
27 Joss Naylor, 'Pike's Peak marathon', *Fellrunner Magazine*, Autumn 1975, pp. 46–49.
28 Verschoth, 'A hurried peek at Pikes'.
29 Interview with Buzz Burrell, December 2023.
30 Peter Knott, 'Editorial', *Fellrunner Magazine*, Autumn 1975, pp. 1–2.
31 Verschoth, 'A hurried peek at Pikes'.
32 *Bennington Banner*, 25 July 1978, p. 7.
33 Tony Rehagen, 'Warren Doyle and the life-changing magic of the Appalachian Trail', *Atlanta*, 28 April 2023.
34 *Red Deer Advocate*, 10 November 1977, p. 24.
35 Alex Mold, 'Fun, running and the jogging boom in Britain, 1970s–1980s', *Sport in History*, 44(4) (2024): 1–24.
36 *The Albuquerque Tribune*, 14 October 1971, p. 44.
37 *Leicester Mercury*, 8 July 1969, p. 16.
38 *The Miami News*, 7 July 1976, p. 2.
39 *Red Deer Advocate*, 10 November 1977, p. 24.
40 *Edmonton Journal*, 20 July 1977, p. 84.

Chapter 8

1 Gary Cantrell, 'Choi–Krolewicz duel highlights Weston six-day race', *UltraRunning Magazine*, September 1983, pp. 5–7.
2 S. Robert Lathan, 'A history of jogging and running – the boom of the 1970s', *Baylor University Medical Center Proceedings*, vol. 36. no. 6 (Taylor & Francis, 2023).
3 Hal Higdon, 'Proud to be a jogger', *Runner's World*, May 1976, pp. 29–31.
4 Walter Thompson and Noel Nequin, 'Ultrarunners – Who are they?' *UltraRunning Magazine*, October 1983, pp. 22–23.
5 DUV Ultra Database: https://statistik.d-u-v.org (accessed 28 May 2024).
6 'Charles', quoted in Shelly Mckenzie, *Getting Physical: The Rise of Fitness Culture in America* (Lawrence: University of Kansas Press, 2013), p. 148.
7 Jürgen Martschukat, *The Age of Fitness* (London: Polity Press, 2021), pp. 121–122.
8 Thompson and Nequin, 'Ultrarunners – Who are they?'.
9 Raúl Sánchez García, 'Informalisation and sport: The case of jogging/running in the USA (1960–2000)', in Cas Wouters and Michael Dunning (eds), *Civilisation and Informalisation: Connecting Long-term Social and Psychic Processes* (Basingstoke: Palgrave Macmillan, 2019), pp. 247–266. Aaron Haberman, 'Escape and pursuit: Contrasting visions of the 1970s long-distance running boom in American popular culture', *Sport History Review*, 48(1) (2017).
10 Michael Atkinson, 'Fell running and voluptuous panic: On Caillois and post-sport physical culture', *American Journal of Play*, 4(1) (2011): 100–120.
11 'Bureaucrats bear down', *UltraRunning Magazine*, September 1984, p. 5.
12 'New faces on Western States victory stand', *UltraRunning Magazine*, September 1986, p. 6.
13 Dan Brennan, '1983: A year to remember at Western States', *UltraRunning Magazine*, September 1983, p. 8.
14 Grand Slam of Ultrarunning: https://grandslamofultrarunning.net/ (accessed 2 May 2024).
15 Dan Brennan, 'Spinnler, Carole Williams set records in 20th JFK', *UltraRunning Magazine*, January/February 1983, p. 6.
16 *The Tennessean*, 4 May 1979, p. 47.
17 Davy Crockett, 'Passing of ultrarunning legend Ken Young', *Ultrarunning History*, 6 February 2018.
18 Ross Zimmerman, '40 Years on foot: The first 40 years of the Tucson Trail runs', *Tucson Trail Runners*, 2018.
19 Mark Dorion, 'Where are they now?: High altitude mountain goat John Cappis', *UltraRunning Magazine*, March 1999, p. 40.
20 John Cappis, *Mountain Runner Newsletter*, quoted in Dorion, 'Where are they now?: High altitude mountain goat John Cappis'.
21 Davy Crockett, 'Bernd Heinrich – Naturalist ultrarunner', *Ultrarunning History*, 1 October 2024.
22 'TAC take charge of records … Rejects Heinrich's 24 hour mark', *UltraRunning Magazine*, March 1984, p. 8.

23 Bernd Heinrich, 'Letter', *UltraRunning Magazine*, June 1984, pp. 26–27.
24 Selwyn Wright, *F.R.A. News*, May 1986, p. 1.
25 Selwyn Wright, *F.R.A. News*, October 1986, p. 1.
26 Quoted in Richard Askwith, *Feet in the Clouds* (London: Aurum Press, 2004), p. 76.
27 *F.R.A. News*, May 1986, p. 4.
28 Hugh Symonds, 'Editorial' in The *Fellrunner*, Summer 1985, p. 3.
29 Peter Riegel, 'Course measurement', *UltraRunning Magazine*, June 1983, p. 12.
30 Kathy Clark, 'Austrheim-Smith on Western States prize money', *UltraRunning Magazine*, June 1984, p. 19.
31 Dan Brannen, 'TAC/USA Convention '86: More attention to ultras', *UltraRunning Magazine*, January/February 1986, p. 35.
32 Gary Cantrell, 'Letter to the Editor', *UltraRunning Magazine*, October 1984, pp. 28–29.
33 Dan Brennan, 'International Association of Ultrarunners (IAU) formed', *UltraRunning Magazine*, June 1984, p. 5.
34 Paul Blackman, 'Letter', *UltraRunning Magazine*, July/August 1984, p. 31.
35 Dan Brennan, 'IAU update', *UltraRunning Magazine*, July/August 1984, p. 30.
36 Cantrell, 'Letter'.
37 Jane E. Hunt, 'Opportunities and obstacles for women in Australian triathlon governance: Lessons from a feminist history', *Sporting Traditions*, 40(1) (2023): 1–18.
38 Sally Edwards, 'Ultramarathoning – A dying sport?', *UltraRunning Magazine*, September 1983, p. 14.
39 Andrey S. Adelfinsky, 'Of Iron Men and the beer: Democratization and commercialization in the triathlon history', *The International Journal of the History of Sport*, 40(12) (2023): 1120–1139.
40 Edwards, 'Ultramarathoning – A dying sport?'.
41 Curt Sproul, 'Western States – The Race Director's view', *UltraRunning Magazine*, November 1983, p. 10.
42 Gary Cantrell, 'From the South', *UltraRunning Magazine*, November 1983, p. 23.
43 Jeff Connor, 'Letter', *The Fellrunner*, Summer 1985, pp. 63–64.
44 *Ibid.*
45 Ewen Rennie, 'Cowboys on the fells', *The Fellrunner*, Summer 1986, p. 76.
46 Selwyn Wright, quoted in Askwith, *Feet in the Clouds*, p. 75.

Chapter 9

1 Rune Larsson, 'The Dragon's Back: Race report', 1992, available at www.dragonsbackrace.com (accessed 7 September 2024).
2 Adrian Crane, 'Five days (and 220 miles) along the backbone of Wales', *UltraRunning Magazine*, December 1992, p. 36.

3 Quoted in Kyle Kusz, 'Extreme America: The cultural politics of extreme sports in 1990s America', in Belinda Wheaton (ed.), *Understanding Lifestyle Sport: Consumption, Identity and Difference* (London: Routledge, 2004).
4 Belinda Wheaton, *The Cultural Politics of Lifestyle Sports* (London: Routledge, 2013).
5 Belinda Wheaton, 'Introduction', in Wheaton, *Understanding Lifestyle Sport.*
6 Rosemary Ricciardelli *et al.*, 'Investigating hegemonic masculinity: Portrayals of masculinity in men's lifestyle magazines', *Sex Roles* 63 (2010): 64–78.
7 Daniel Turner and Sandro Carnicelli (eds), *Lifestyle Sports and Public Policy* (London: Routledge, 2017).
8 Ryan J. Gagnon *et al.*, 'Competition climbing: From leisure pursuit to lifestyle sport', *Journal of Unconventional Parks, Tourism & Recreation Research* 6(1) (2016).
9 Yvon Chouinard and Vincent Stanley, *The Responsible Company: What We've Learned from Patagonia's First 40 Years* (Patagonia, 2013).
10 Gordon Hardman, 'Hardrock 100 – The most difficult 100, but 18 finish', *UltraRunning Magazine*, September 1992, pp. 12–13.
11 Analysis of race results.
12 Gary Cantrell, 'Little Big Horn, Gettysburg, Barkley. Just another massacre', *UltraRunning Magazine*, June 1994, p. 14.
13 David Biddle, 'The Barkley Marathons', 5 December 1996, available at https://www.lehigh.edu/~dmd1/dave.html (accessed 8 December 2023).
14 Gary Cantrell, 'Barkley 1993 – A mountain goat beats the thoroughbreds', *UltraRunning Magazine*, June 1993, p. 8.
15 Cantrell, 'Little Big Horn, Gettysburg, Barkley. Just Another Massacre'.
16 Gary Cantrell, 'Mark Williams first ever to finish Barkley 100 Mile'. *UltraRunning Magazine*, June 1994, p. 6.
17 Biddle, 'The Barkley Marathons'.
18 Brad Plumer, 'The evolution of airfares in one chart', *The Washington Post*, 13 October 2012.
19 Dirk Glaesser *et al.* 'Global travel patterns: An overview', *Journal of Travel Medicine*, 24(4) (2017).
20 Eric Clifton, 'An Arctic adventure (or, What I did on my winter vacation)', *UltraRunning Magazine*, May 1994, pp. 28–32.
21 Paul Cuno-Booth, 'The Nolan's project', *Trail Runner*, 22 July 2021.
22 Fred Vance, 'The Story Behind Nolan's 14', (2000), available at https://mattmahoney.net (accessed 12 November 2023).
23 Fred Vance, 'Nolan's 14 record set', *UltraRunning Magazine*, October 2000, p. 56.
24 Cuno-Booth, 'The Nolan's project'.
25 'The origins of the FKT', *Trail Runner*, 10 October 2017.
26 Annemarie Jutel, '"Thou dost run as in flotation": Femininity, reassurance and the emergence of the women's marathon', *The International Journal of the History of Sport*, 20(3) (2003): 17–36.
27 Alison Wade, 'Starting line 1928: Bjorg Austrheim-Smith', *Fast Women*, 7 October 2021.

28 Ben Redfern, 'Brava! Brava!', *The Fellrunner*, Spring 1977 p. 38.
29 Gary Cantrell, 'From the South', *UltraRunning Magazine*, November 1984, p. 12.
30 Martin Stone, 'Long distance news: Awards', *The Fellrunner*, January 1990, p. 37.
31 Sarah Lavender Smith, 'Ultrawoman', *Berkeley Monthly*, 1996.
32 Norman Klein, 'Twietmeyer, Trason shine at memorable Western States', September 1995, pp. 8–14.
33 Email correspondence with Helene Whitaker, August 2024.

Chapter 10

1 Graham Meikle, *Social Media: Communication, Sharing and Visibility* (London: Routledge, 2016).
2 Muqaddas Jan *et al.*, 'Impact of social media on self-esteem', *European Scientific Journal*, 13(23) (2017): 329–341; Cecilie Schou Andreassen *et al.*, 'The relationship between addictive use of social media, narcissism, and self-esteem: Findings from a large national survey', *Addictive Behaviors*, 64 (2017): 287–293.
3 Kevin Moore, *Wellbeing and Aspirational Culture* (New York: Springer, 2019); B. Joseph Pine and James H. Gilmore, 'The experience economy: Past, present and future', in Jon Sundbo and Flemming Sørensen (eds), *Handbook on the Experience Economy* (Cheltenham: Edward Elgar, 2013), pp. 21–44.
4 Freetrail, Courtney Dauwalter: Hardrock 100 post-race interview', *Freetrail*, 14 July 2024.
5 The Outdoor Foundation, 'Outdoor Participation Report: 2016', September 2016, available at https://outdoorindustry.org/wp-content/uploads/2016/09/2016-Outdoor-Recreation-Participation-Report_FINAL.pdf (accessed 30 April 2025).
6 Jens Jakob Andersen, 'The state of running 2019', *Run Repeat*, 25 March 2024.
7 Frank Fleetham, 'Cle Elum 50km', *UltraRunning Magazine*, November 1997, pp. 18–19.
8 Brian Metzler, 'The evolution of trail running shoes', *Run*, 24 January 2024.
9 Singletrack, 'Scott McCoubrey: 90s trail running teams, Scott Jurek stories, Seattle trail scene', *Singletrack* podcast, 22 September 2023.
10 Martin Dugard, 'Running: Never mind the skull tattoos', *Outside Magazine*, May 1995.
11 Singletrack, 'Scott McCoubrey: 90s Trail Running Teams, Scott Jurek Stories, Seattle Trail Scene'.
12 Dugard, 'Running: Never mind the skull tattoos'.
13 Steve Friedman, 'It's gonna suck to be you', *Outside Magazine*, 1 July 2001.
14 Dean Karnazes, *Ultramarathon Man: Confessions of an All-Night Runner* (New York: Jeremy P. Tarcher, 2006), pp. 38–39.

15 Pam Reed, *The Extra Mile: One Woman's Personal Journey to Ultrarunning Greatness* (Emmaus, PA: Rodale Books, 2007) p. 123.
16 Henry Miller, (1935) *Tropic of Cancer* (Paris: Obelisk Press, 1935), p. 105.
17 Edward Abbey, *Beyond the Wall: Essays from the Outside* (New York: Holt Paperbacks, 1971), p. xv.
18 Kim Humphery, *Excess: Anti-consumerism in the West* (Cambridge: Polity Press, 2010).
19 Florence Williams, 'Desperate housewife stalks male supermodel in sports death march', *Outside Magazine*, 1 October 2005.
20 Richard Askwith, *Feet in the Clouds* (London: Aurum Press, 2004), p. 324.
21 Christopher McDougall, *Born to Run* (London: Profile Books, 2010), pp. 14–17.
22 Endurance Planet, 'The best of Endurance Planet 2007', *Endurance Planet* podcast, 27 December 2007.
23 Williams, 'Desperate housewife stalks male supermodel'.
24 Interview with Andy Jones-Wilkins.
25 Interview with Buzz Burrell.
26 Doug Mayer, '"You can't run that": Trail running hits the White Mountains', *Appalachia*, 65(2) (2014): 7–27.
27 Singletrack, 'Scott McCoubrey: 90s trail running teams, Scott Jurek stories, Seattle trail scene', *Singletrack* podcast, 22 September 2023.
28 'The casual champion', *Trail Runner*, 26 April 2017.
29 Red Bull, *Karl Meltzer: Made to Be Broken*, Interpret Studios, available at https://www.redbull.com/gb-en/films/karl-meltzer-made-to-be-broken (accessed 30 April 2025).
30 Andy Jones-Wilkins, 'Karl Meltzer's 2006 ultrarunning season', *iRunFar*, 25 January 2019.
31 Andy Jones-Wilkins, 'Anton Krupicka and the 2006 Leadville Trail 100', *iRunFar*, 1 June 2018.
32 Anton Krupicka, 'Looking back at Leadville 2006', *La Sportiva*, online blog, 21 June 2018.
33 Nicholas Triolo, 'Anton Krupicka: Running will always be my first love', *Trail Runner*, 23 February 2024.
34 Anton Krupicka, 'Now', *Riding the Wind* blog, 8 October 2007.
35 Interview with Buzz Burell.
36 Andy Jones-Wilkins, 'Unforgettable moments in ultrarunning: Kyle Skaggs and the 2008 Hardrock 100', *iRunFar*, 8 July 2022.
37 Robbie Britton, 'What was the greatest running race of all time?', *The Guardian*, 12 June 2014.
38 Quoted in Brennan Galloway and Alex Nichols, *Indulgence: 1000 Miles Under the Colorado Sky*, Negative Split Pictures, 21 November 2007.
39 *Ibid.*
40 John Trent, 'Western States 100: Showdown', *UltraRunning Magazine*, September 2010, p. 16.
41 *Ibid.*, p. 18.
42 Freetrail, Bryon Powell: The present & future of iRunFar', *Freetrail* podcast, 4 August 2021.

43 Interview with Andy Jones-Wilkins.
44 Interview with James Elson.
45 *Ibid.*
46 James Elson, 'North Downs Way', *UltraRunning Magazine*, April 2012, p. 52.

Epilogue

1 Doug Mayer, *The Race That Changed Running: The Inside Story of UTMB* (Lausanne: Helvetiq, 2023).
2 *Ibid.*
3 Doug Mayer, 'Krissy Moehl and the story of the first Ultra-Trail du Mont-Blanc', *Run the Alps*, 22 August 2021.
4 DUV Ultra Marathon Statistics. Available at https://statistik.d-u-v.org/ (accessed 10 September 2024).
5 Based on an analysis of Google Analytics' search terms for UTMB winners in 2023.
6 Gary Robbins, 'What really went down in Whistler', 26 October 2023, available at https://garyrobbinsrun.com (accessed 30 April 2025).
7 Bad Boy Running, 'The devastating impact of UTMB "The Vortex" on all UK races – James Elson', *Bad Boy Running* podcast, 4 August 2024.
8 Carl Morris, *Trail Ultra Survey Report: 2024* (Preston: University of Central Lancashire, 2024), available at https://www.trailultraproject.com/news/trail-ultra-survey-now-published (accessed 30 April 2025).
9 The Green Runners, 'Sportswashing: What's next for UTMB and Dacia?', *The Green Runners*, 4 May 2024.
10 Jessy Carveth, 'Kilian Jornet and Zach Miller call on world's top trail runners to boycott UTMB in leaked email', 18 January 2024, available at https://marathonhandbook.com/kilian-jornet-and-zach-miller-leaked-email/ (accessed 30 April 2025).
11 Quoted at https://worldtrailmajors.com/about-us/ (accessed 28 October 2024).
12 Andy Cochrane, 'American women are driving the boom in sub-ultra trail running', *Run*, 3 September 2024.
13 Gary Cantrell, 'From the South', *UltraRunning Magazine*, November 1983, p. 23.

Plates

11 Helene Diamantides and Martin Stone at the Dragon's Back Race finish, 1992. Courtesy of Rob Howard Media.

12 Scott Jurek at the Badwater finish, 2006. Courtesy Chris Kostman/AdventureCORPS.

13 Kyle Skaggs at the Hardrock 100, 2008, as featured on the cover of *UltraRunning Magazine*. Courtesy of *UltraRunning Magazine*.

14 Anton Krupicka during his Sagebrush & Summits run/bike/climb tour, 2021. Courtesy of Anton Krupicka/La Sportiva.

15 Jasmin Paris and daughter at the Montane Spine Race finish, 2019. Courtesy of Yann Besrest-Butler.

16 Courtney Dauwalter at the UTMB Mont-Blanc finish, 2023. Courtesy of Agence Zoom.

Acknowledgements

Running often provides a series of metaphors for the various challenges and experiences of life. Writing this book was no different – it truly was a feat of endurance – and like all good adventures, it would not have been possible without the help and assistance of those who provided their time, support and encouragement.

I would like to particularly thank Boff Whalley and Buzz Burrell. Not only did they take time to read through early versions of the manuscript, but their encouragement and enthusiasm was both generous and heartfelt. As writers and athletes, Boff and Buzz have long provided many of us with inspiration – it was a profound privilege to have their support.

There are too many others to mention by name, but at the risk of missing someone, and in no particular order, I would like to thank the following. Damian Hall, for his cheerful generosity and the time he took to put me in touch with others. Meghan Hicks and Byron Powell for the early support that iRunFar provided, and their feedback and help towards the end. Andy Jones-Wilkins, for sharing his wisdom and knowledge of the sport. Gary and Sandra Cantrell for their correspondence and photographs from their family collection. John Trent for his historical work on Western States and taking the time to review everything related to WSER in the manuscript. Gary Corbitt for reviewing several chapters and his ongoing work to preserve ultrarunning history. Peter Todhunter for facilitating access to Joss Naylor's personal archive and some fantastic (and often very funny) stories from fell running history. Chris Kostman for reviewing several chapters and for his enthusiastic support and encouragement. James Elson for taking time from his many different roles and responsibilities at the heart of British ultrarunning. And my thanks to those who kindly read relevant sections, provided photographs and context, and offered important feedback: Dale Garland, Nancy Hobbs, Helene Whitaker, Kathy Hubel, Martin Stone, Chris Knez, Jasmin Paris, Shane Ohly, Anton Krupicka and Karl Meltzer.

Thank you to everyone who participated in one of the almost a hundred interviews that I conducted for the book. While the tight word limit meant that it was simply not possible to refer to every specific interview, everyone that I spoke with provided insight and information that contributed to the book in some way.

At Manchester University Press, I am grateful to the whole team, but especially Alun Richards and Tom Dark for their professionalism and expertise. Their support helped me to realise the full potential of the final manuscript. I would also like to thank the anonymous reviewers for giving me the confidence to draw out the storytelling and to water down what would otherwise have been overly academic theorising.

Finally, thanks to mum and dad for driving me around when my legs have failed, and for always waiting patiently on remote mountainsides. To Lisa, for love and partnership. And to Rowan and Freya, who don't yet fully understand the central role they have in everything I do.

Abbreviations

AAA Amateur Athletics Association
AAC Amateur Athletic Club (UK)
AAU Amateur Athletic Union (USA)
AMC Appalachian Mountaineering Club
ATC Appalachian Trail Conference
ATRA American Trail Running Association

BAF British Athletics Federation
BGR Bob Graham Round
BOFRA British Open Fell Runners' Association
BWSF British Workers Sports Federation

CAC California Alpine Club
CCC Courmayeur-Champex-Chamonix

DNF did not finish

FKT fastest known time
FRA Fell Runners Association
FRCC Fell and Rock Climbing Club

GMC Green Mountain Club

IAAF International Amateur Athletic Federation
IAU International Association of Ultrarunners

LAC	London Athletics Club
LDMT	Lake District Mountain Trial
LDWA	Long Distance Walkers Association
MARRC	Middle Atlantic Road Runners Club
MDS	Marathon des Sables
MLAC	Mincing Lane Athletic Club
MUT	mountain, ultra and trail
NCAA	National Collegiate Athletic Association
NCRF	National Council of Ramblers' Federations
NRDC	National Running Data Center
NSPA	Northern Sports Promoters Association
NYAC	New York Athletic Club
NYPC	New York Pioneer Club
NYRRC	New York Road Runners Club
OAC	Oregon Alpine Club
PCT	Pacific Crest Trail
PTL	La Petite Trotte à Léon
PTRA	Pro Trail Runners Association
RRC	Road Runners Club
RRCA	Road Runners Club of America
SAAA	Scottish Amateur Athletic Association
TAC	The Athletics Congress
TDS	Les Traces du Duc de Savoie
TGR	The Green Runners
TNF	North Face 50
TTR	Tucson Trail Runs
UROY	Ultrarunner of the Year
USATF	USA Track and Field
UTMB	Ultra-Trail du Mont-Blanc

WAM	Whistler Alpine Meadows
WERA	Western Endurance Racers Association
WSER	Western States Endurance Run
YHA	Youth Hostels Association
YMCA	Young Men's Christian Association

Index

Index